PRAISE FOR *DAUGHTERS OF DIVORCE*

"Rarely have I read a book that is as honest, courageous, and optimistic as Terry Gaspard's *Daughters of Divorce*. Ms. Gaspard has skillfully crafted a book that combines authenticity, warmth, and clinical expertise—a rare combination in the self-help genre. This gem of a book is chock filled with intriguing personal reflection, vignettes, tasks, and assignments. It is a virtual handbook for daughters seeking to stop this transgenerational pattern dead in its tracks. Bravo, Ms. Gaspard!"

—Ross Rosenberg, MEd, LCPC, CADC, CSAT, psychotherapist, international trainer, and author of *The Human Magnet Syndrome: Why We Love People Who Hurt Us*

"Finally! A book about divorce that is specifically focused on women. This thoughtful, insightful, and uplifting book acknowledges the unique impact of divorce on its daughters while offering concrete steps and practical solutions."

—Elisabeth J. LaMotte, LICSW, author of *Overcoming Your Parents' Divorce*

"*Daughters of Divorce* is an original and timely treatment of a very important topic. Bravely told from the perspective of the authors, a divorced mother and her daughter, *Daughters of Divorce* provides empathy, guidance, and wisdom for those who are struggling to understand the impact of divorce on their lives and choices. Highly recommended!"

—Joshua Coleman, PhD, psychologist and author of *When Parents Hurt: Compassionate Strategies When You and Your Grown Child Don't Get Along*

"If you're in a family of divorce as a daughter or parent, this book is for you. Gaspard and Clifford are a mother and daughter who have gone through it themselves. From self-esteem to the impact on your relationships, this book gives you practical doable action steps to help you learn how to change your story or narrative and see divorce through adult eyes. It can be very helpful for adult children of divorce and for mothers and fathers who are looking for insights and ideas to help their daughters."

—Jeff Zimmerman, PhD, ABPP clinical psychologist and coauthor of *Adult Children of Divorce* and *The Co-Parenting Survival Guide*

daughters
of divorce

OVERCOME THE LEGACY OF YOUR PARENTS' BREAKUP AND ENJOY A HAPPY, LONG-LASTING RELATIONSHIP

Terry Gaspard, MSW, LICSW

Tracy Clifford

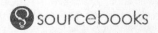 sourcebooks

Published by Sourcebooks, Inc.
P.O. Box 4410, Naperville, Illinois 60567-4410
(630) 961-3900
Fax: (630) 961-2168
www.sourcebooks.com

Library of Congress Cataloging-in-Publication Data

Gaspard, Terry.
Daughters of divorce : overcome the legacy of your parents' breakup and enjoy a
happy, long-lasting relationship / Terry Gaspard, Tracy Clifford.
     pages cm
Includes bibliographical references and index.
(trade paper : alk. paper) 1. Adult children of divorced parents. 2. Divorce—
Psychological aspects. 3. Women—Psychology. 4. Interpersonal relations—
Psychological aspects. 5. Man-woman relationships—Psychological aspects. I.
Clifford, Tracy. II. Title.
HQ777.5.G37 2016
306.89—dc23

                              2015009866

To the late Dr. Judith S. Wallerstein, distinguished researcher and author of The Unexpected Legacy of Divorce: The 25-Year Landmark Study *and numerous other publications.*

Contents

Author's Note

My interest in the lives of women who grew up in divorced families began with my own experience. Not only were my parents divorced, but divorce goes back five generations in my family. My passion for this topic grew along with my personal experiences of divorce: I and two of my sisters experienced divorce, and my clinical practice included many daughters of divorce. After watching my female patients struggle with distinct emotional challenges from their parents' divorce—and after experiencing it myself—I knew it was time to create a guide that helps daughters of any age overcome the unique legacy of divorce, so they can establish healthy, happy, and long-lasting relationships.

When I decided to write this book, I supplemented my clinical and personal experience by interviewing a large, diverse group of women raised in divorced families. My initial research study included 198 women and was published in 1995. One year later, I examined a larger sample of 325 men and women to explore gender differences. This study was published in 1996. Both of these publications were coauthored with my mentor, Roger Clark, PhD, professor of sociology at Rhode Island College. Over the last five years, my daughter Tracy and I interviewed more than three hundred daughters of divorce between the ages of eighteen and fifty-nine, with the average age of participants being twenty-four. These interviews provided the basis for my recent study of daughters of divorce (2009–2014).

The women quoted in the following pages were participants in that study, and the stories told here are profiles and composites based on real people. However, names and details have been changed to protect their confidentiality and identities. Details about the location of the interviews were altered in some cases as well for the participants' protection. Please note this book isn't meant to replace therapy with a licensed mental health professional. Rather, it is intended to offer an in-depth chronicle of the impact of parental divorce upon women and to provide concrete ways they can improve their relationships. In the end, divorce does not have to define us. We are all capable of creating and enjoying successful partnerships, and this book will help you achieve that.

—*Terry Gaspard, MSW, LICSW*

Preface

Though we often prize it as the ultimate goal, love is a rare happening among human beings and by far the most intimate experience any of us will ever go through. This is why when love is lost, it's also one of the most crushing experiences you can endure, even if you are just witnessing those you love going through a breakup. When a woman is raised by divorced parents, her view of marriage is necessarily shaped by her parents' divorce. Witnessing their breakup has the potential to wound deeply, but it can also transform a woman's life in ways she couldn't possibly foresee.

For children of divorce, a breakup can set in motion an unending chain of consequences they will continue to experience as adults. As a young woman venturing forth into the world, trying to establish intimate, loving relationships, you may find yourself held back, paralyzed with anxiety or a fear of breaking up. Or you may find yourself committed to partners who are totally wrong for you. You might be in awe of people who stay together, because you're constantly plagued by the fear that people can change their minds at any time. More than anything, you want love. You crave commitment, devotion, and security. But living through divorce taught you never to expect it. In fact, you feel terrified of attaining it and losing it. After all, your parents' divorce taught you early on to be skeptical of relationships and leery of love.

Young women who have experienced parental divorce suffer from a unique set of challenges, especially low self-esteem. It's not that these "daughters of divorce" can't be outwardly successful. Many go to good colleges, enjoy thriving careers, and have plenty of friends. Many appear to have it all. But inside, a nagging feeling persists: *I am not good enough.*

Like many children of divorce, you may have been told over and over again that your parents' breakup was not your fault. But no matter how competently or incompetently their split was handled, for many girls pain is unavoidable. No matter how good you were, you were not good enough to keep your family together. And you probably didn't grow up with a healthy template for how couples achieve intimacy and resolve conflict. And so skepticism of long-lasting love colors your actions, making you mistrust your own judgment or others' intentions. Your family, the core support that was supposed to prepare you for going out into the world, has been shattered. If you can't rely on that, then what *can* you rely on?

As a woman taking your first tentative steps in adulthood, your parents' divorce indelibly shapes your feelings about yourself and relationships. Even if your parents' divorce is years behind you, you may lack confidence in your ability to create lasting romantic relationships of your own. Fear of loss, fear of reencountering the dreaded fate you endured as a child, stays with you. This is the focus of our work and of this book.

The inspiration for our study was sparked when it became clear to us in our own lives that we suffer from unique challenges that most women raised in intact homes just don't face. Much research has been done about the fallout of parental divorce on children. But very little is devoted to young women who are particularly vulnerable, since being a daughter of divorce more than doubles your risk of getting a divorce, compared to counterparts from intact homes. So we sought to answer these questions: How does the experience of parental divorce impact us now that we are adults trying to create relationships of our own? And how can we help ourselves and other women overcome the problems of the past and forge a brighter future?

My mother, Terry Gaspard, and I set out to write this book together because we are both daughters of divorce. We know firsthand how broken promises and fractured families have forever changed us. But instead of resigning ourselves to feeling pessimistic about lasting love, we have embarked on a process of healing. We have set out not only to identify the many challenges faced by daughters of divorce, but also to provide ways to overcome these challenges. We interviewed hundreds of women and incorporated both their and our own experiences into these pages. The stories and advice that follow are for all of us, the daughters of divorce. Within them, we hope you will recognize yourself and find the strategies and encouragement you need to restore your faith in love. Although there is undoubtedly pain and loss in any divorce experience, there can also be strength and hope, and our goal is to help you find that. We may be daughters of divorce, but the uncharted path ahead is ours to create.

—*Tracy Clifford*

Introduction

BREAKING UP IS HARD TO DO—EVEN IF YOU'RE JUST A BYSTANDER!

TERRY'S STORY

No one goes through a breakup or divorce for fun. It's messy, it's complicated, it can be scary, and it is incredibly painful. And for those of us who have witnessed our parents' divorce—whether after five years or twenty-five years of marriage—that pain can have a far greater impact than we could ever imagine on our own relationships down the line.

But daughters who have endured their parents' breakup face more serious emotional challenges when it comes to forming successful relationships than sons do (for reasons we'll explore later on). What's worse is that often many of these problems don't surface until well into the teenage years or adulthood. If you're reading this book, you've likely recognized that your parents' divorce is hindering you from creating and/or maintaining successful, healthy relationships. We're here to help.

Before we get further into the purpose of this book and what you can expect to gain from it, I first want to share my own personal experience with divorce, as it illustrates many of the unique emotional difficulties that daughters of divorce face. They're common ones—you may recognize some (or all) of these in yourself as well. But they can be very tricky to identify, let alone overcome. That's what this book is for.

My parents divorced when I was seven years old, precipitated by my mother leaving our family abruptly during the first week of school. By all accounts, I was a shy, easygoing child who went through my second grade year without speaking much—let alone telling anyone about my parents' breakup. When my mother returned seven months later and was determined to gain custody of me and my older sister, my father decided not to put up much of a fight. After all, he had been struggling to raise four daughters on his own—quite unusual in the early 1960s before the divorce epidemic hit the United States. One day I was living in a lovely home in an affluent seaside community, and the next day I was swept away to a two-bedroom apartment in a Los Angeles suburb. For the most part, I lost contact with my friends and had to start from scratch in a new school with unfamiliar faces.

A gradual realization came over the next several years that contact with my dad would be limited due to his subsequent remarriage and lasting tension between my parents. In those days, joint custody was rarely considered a viable option. So over time, my relationship with my dad went from a reality to a fantasy. Always a "daddy's girl," I developed an intense craving for the love and affection of my father, as our interactions became fewer and farther between. As I struggled to deal with the aftermath of essentially losing my father, I never talked about my feelings of loss to anyone. I was afraid others would just brush it off as me being needy, saying something like "You'll get over it," or worse, reassure me of what I no longer knew to be true: "Your daddy still loves you."

Due to our ever changing custody arrangement, my three sisters and I never shared the same residence for more than a year after our parents divorced. I didn't dare tell my classmates or teacher that I was thrust into such a chaotic lifestyle, or that I was dealing with a succession of my mother's boyfriends, her second husband, and multiple moves—never living in the same dwelling for more than one entire school year.

My father's lifestyle was unpredictable as well. An artist who made his living traveling to various art shows, he helped my stepmother—whom he married when I was eight—pursue her own art career and catering business. While they enjoyed a successful long-term marriage—lasting thirty-five years until my father died—their beachfront home wasn't my permanent residence while growing up. For a period of five years after my parents' divorce, my visits with my father were sporadic mostly due to his schedule and continual conflict between my mother and stepmother. The absence of my father in my life on a regular basis caused a breach of trust between us. I felt left behind and unloved. Worse, since I couldn't make sense of it, I assumed my dad's lack of contact was because of a flaw within myself.

Although I wasn't aware of it at that time, my experience of feeling betrayed by my father, coupled with my mother's persistent bad-mouthing of him, created a major fear of abandonment in me as well. Truth be told, I lacked a sense of control in my life but had no way to understand or translate it. Like many daughters of divorce, I lived between my parents' two desperate worlds for many years and learned to adapt fairly well—at least on the outside. Although I didn't attribute it at the time to the absence of my father, I did experience an intrinsic mistrust of men, and oddly enough a strong craving for their attention and approval at the same time.

As I entered high school, my parents decided to give me a say in where I lived, and I chose to live with my father and stepmother.

It was during these years that I developed more confidence in myself as a student and made solid friendships. With the onslaught of new people and transitions, I figured out that school was a place where I could shine. I finally found the predictability I craved, and my hard work paid off.

For the first time, my life felt fairly secure because my father stopped traveling and opened a restaurant. During my adolescence, my dad and I strengthened our bond, my self-esteem improved, and I formed a positive relationship with my stepmother and stepbrother. But while I didn't miss living in Los Angeles, living apart from my mother and my three older sisters was a significant loss that caused a strain in our relationships later on.

The absence of my three sisters from my daily life was perhaps the worst fallout of my parents' divorce. My sisters and I don't have much in common, and interestingly, we have vastly differ-ent takes on our parents' split. Perhaps this is because of our dissimilar alliances to our parents and loyalty conflicts. Parental divorce often puts children in a position of feeling they must choose between their parents and take sides. This feeling that we needed to choose sides was amplified by the way that our mother's and father's lifestyles became so different after the divorce that it was akin to being raised in two different families. Additionally, we were subjected to intense rivalries between our mother and stepmother—intensifying our experience of divided loyalties. However, the one thing we do share is the legacy of divorce—we have all seen our own marriages end in divorce.

While my parents' divorce was certainly not the worst, it was the most defining experience of my life. Throughout my child-hood, I recall thinking that I wanted to avoid my own divorce at all costs. I never imagined passing on the legacy of divorce to two of my children (who are now adults) and truly believe that I wasn't prepared for the inevitable ups and downs of marriage. Looking for security, I married young and didn't realize how clueless I was about all the challenges that come with commitment. I rushed into marriage because I was fearful of being alone. As my marriage progressed, I walked on eggshells to avoid confrontations with my former husband. In *The Love They Lost: Living with the Legacy of Our Parents' Divorce*, author Stephanie Staal identifies several relationship patterns among adult children of divorce, one of which is the "nester." This type exemplifies adult children of divorce (ACODs as we refer to them) who eagerly enter into a committed relationship with high hopes of finding the security they didn't receive as a child. This profile certainly describes me. But what I didn't understand is that in order to have a successful, secure relationship, I had to find that security in myself first!

Like many daughters of divorce, I was also faithful to an idealized image of my father due to a loss of daily access to him, and this led to unrealistic expectations of men in my life. I naively entered marriage with an idealized mind-set of what it would be, never stopping to consider what I deserved and needed from a partner. At the time, I lacked the insight to realize that I was reenacting the painful pattern of my parents' marriage by selecting a spouse who I wasn't compatible with—just like my parents did. After dating for only a year, I leaped headlong into my first marriage without considering that our backgrounds, values, personalities, interests, and needs for intimacy were drastically different.

Another lesson I learned growing up was to be skeptical of relationships and not to put my trust in a romantic partner. After all, being able to trust others is based on experiences of counting on people in our past, particularly our mom and dad. And even though I had overcome many challenges prior to marrying my former husband, being married brought me face-to-face with how many more there were left to conquer.

For better or worse, most couples follow the marriage example set by their parents. In my family, I learned early on that when people have difficulties resolving conflicts, it leads to the demise of a relationship. As a result, I gave up easily on love and perhaps considered divorce an option too quickly when love in my marriage morphed into mutual unhappiness and ongoing conflicts after sixteen years. In hindsight, I've come to realize the importance of taking time to pick a partner with whom you are compatible.

In whatever form it exists, your parents' relationship creates a template about love and relating. It is your first and greatest teacher about love. However, your parents' divorce doesn't have to determine the outcome of your relationships. Instead of repeating the past, you can create a new story for your life and build partnerships based on love, trust, and intimacy.

WHY WE WROTE THIS BOOK

My daughter Tracy and I wrote this book for all of the women raised in divorced homes who continuously feel that there is something wrong with them, something missing, and who are eager to build healthy, long-lasting relationships but struggle to do so. As children, they may have done their best to be "good girls" and play well the hand that divorce dealt them. But as young women, many daughters of divorce have trouble with trust and intimacy. When they fall in love, it reawakens long-hidden emotions they buried in childhood, such as the fear that no matter what they do to ensure a successful relationship, they'll be left anyway. This fear of abandonment can translate into fear of commitment to romantic partners. They long for love and lasting partnerships but feel utterly powerless to sustain a relationship. In addition, many daughters of divorce have also endured damage in their relationships with their fathers, which can leave a lasting imprint. Studies show that a girl stands a better chance of becoming a self-confident woman if she has a close bond with her father.

As a therapist, college instructor, and nonfiction writer, I have specialized in studying divorce and helping people impacted by it. Although my work includes all individuals affected by divorce, I'm especially interested in helping adult children of divorce address their challenges because they often suffer silently and needlessly. I began researching the long-term impact of parental divorce in the mid-1990s because I was going through my own breakup and wanted to avoid passing the legacy of divorce on to my children.

After publishing two studies on adult children of divorce in 1995 and 1996, I remarried and settled into a blended family life (with three children) and my clinical practice. Then in 2009, my daughter Tracy, now a young woman, stunned me by expressing a keen interest in processing her experience of my divorce years ago. Though her father and I had worked so hard to protect her, it was clear she still suffered wounds from our breakup regardless, and I wanted to do everything to help her mend those. Astounded by the lack of information available to help daughters of divorce heal from their parents' breakup, I decided to pursue a third research study. This time, with Tracy's assistance, I began to address how we could help other daughters of divorce resolve and integrate issues related to their parents' split in concrete ways, and the idea for this book began to emerge. We supplemented our personal experience with research from experts as well as interviews of more than three hundred women who had been raised in divorced families.

Research studies show that adult children of divorce have double the risk of getting divorced themselves compared to their counterparts from intact homes. So it's time to discover the root of the divorce "bug" and figure out how to shake it.

We learned that childhood experiences, including our parents' divorce, create the framework for how we experience love as adults. In my case, my parents split when I was a young child, and I longed to recapture the love they lost, even though it was a fantasy. But since I didn't grow up with a healthy template for how couples achieve intimacy and resolve conflicts, I was more prone to reenact unhealthy relationship patterns. Although I desperately wanted to build a rewarding, long-lasting, intimate relationship, I didn't know how to go about it.

As we began to interview women who volunteered for our study on daughters of divorce, similar themes emerged over and over again. When the volunteers spoke about the impact of their parents' split on their romantic relationships, we realized that we view love and commitment with a similar lens—one which was colored by fear of loss and a reluctance to commit. One respondent, Abby, age thirty-eight, reflects: "I've built up walls and rarely let anyone in. It's like I'm testing them, trying to force guys into proving their love. I'm always wondering when it's going to end. The worst part of it is that I'm waiting for the rug to be pulled out from underneath me—so I can't relax and just be me."

While parental divorce can certainly be problematic for all children, it appears to pose unique challenges for girls. As adults these women may feel pessimistic about love, mistrust their romantic partners, and live with constant fear that their relationships will fail. Or if they pick a partner who might be a good fit for them, they might engage in self-sabotaging behaviors because they are accustomed to living with chaos and uncertainty.

Why is the father-daughter relationship so vulnerable to disruption after parental divorce? In *A Generation at Risk*, Paul Amato, PhD, and Alan Booth, PhD, conclude that the disruptive effects of parental divorce persist for daughters into adulthood and are associated with lowered feelings of closeness with their fathers. They noted fathers generally give more attention to sons than daughters post-divorce—a tendency that grows more pronounced as children get older. In *Between Fathers and Daughters*, Linda Nielsen, EdD, a nationally recognized expert on father-daughter relationships, observes that daughters often compete with stepmothers after divorce and that mothers don't always encourage a close bond between their daughters and their former spouse. She writes, "Sadly, divorce usually damages a daughter's relationship with her father more than a son's." Her research findings indicate that the father-daughter relationship is the one that changes the most post-divorce and that only 10 to 15 percent of dads and daughters enjoy the benefits of shared custody. Since many daughters perceive limited contact with their fathers as a personal rejection, this can lead to lowered self-esteem and trouble trusting romantic partners during adolescence and adulthood.

WHY STUDY ONLY DAUGHTERS OF DIVORCE?

The leading researchers in the field of divorce who inspired our research are E. Mavis Hetherington, PhD, Paul Amato, PhD, and the late Judith Wallerstein, PhD. They all agree that parental divorce has a lifelong impact upon children and that the legacy of divorce is often passed down in families. These scholars concur that the effect of parental divorce upon ACODs deserves special examination. However, only Wallerstein studied women separately from men. She concluded that females raised in divided homes are particularly vulnerable to self-doubt and fears about commitment because they identify with their mothers after divorce and view her to have failed at love and marriage. This vulnerability makes sense because girls are socialized to be nurturers and caregivers from an early age and tend to be more focused on relationships than men are.

In "Daughters of Divorce: Report From a Ten-Year Follow-Up," Wallerstein discovered that daughters of divorce show a distinct "pathway" that includes a delayed emergence of the powerful effects of parental divorce. She coined the term "Sleeper Effect" to describe how daughters often experience fear of conflict with their partners and shaken faith in love when they venture out on their own and make decisions about love and commitment. Over a decade later, in *The Unexpected Legacy of Divorce*, Wallerstein detailed the struggle that ACODs face in adulthood because they worry about following in their parents' footsteps. A unique aspect of Wallerstein's research is that she conducted a longitudinal study—interviewing the same families over a period of twenty-five years—at different stages in their development. But even she wasn't expecting to find that the greatest effects of divorce on children don't emerge until adulthood.

In her highly acclaimed book, *For Better or For Worse: Divorce Reconsidered*, Hetherington describes her findings from a sample of fourteen hundred families whom she interviewed over the course of thirty years at the University of Virginia. She reveals that although divorce presents children with many challenges, which make them more at risk to have problems, the vast majority (or 75 percent) have adjusted reasonably well six years after their parents' breakup. Several protective factors that foster resilience in children emerged from her research, such as low parental conflict after divorce and having competent parents with a warm, authoritative style. Like Wallerstein, Hetherington posits that daughters are more likely to have vulnerabilities that emerge during adulthood in intimate relationships when compared to sons, primarily due to their altered relationship with their fathers after divorce.

Building on the work of Hetherington and Wallerstein, we sought to examine the impact of parental divorce on women specifically. We conducted 326 in-depth interviews, over a period of five years, in which we asked respondents to describe their experiences growing up in a divided home and to identify their most prominent memories—such as their belief about why their parents divorced and whose fault it was. They were also asked to answer questions such as: what is the most difficult part of a romantic relationship for you?

From these interviews and other research, we were able to identify key emotional challenges faced by daughters of divorce that are nearly universal, such as trouble trusting romantic partners, reluctance to commit, damaged self-esteem, intimacy issues, extreme self-reliance to an almost harmful degree, and mistrust in the permanence of relationships. Most of the women we interviewed also experienced a damaged father-daughter connection due to spending less time with their fathers after their parents' breakups. In chapter 5, we offer steps to deal with a broken father-daughter relationship since it was the most common theme that was explored during our interviews.

A NEW STUDY OF DAUGHTERS OF DIVORCE

Today, about 40 percent of all children in the United States will experience a parental divorce prior to the age of eighteen. For years, researchers have identified the damage divorce inflicts on the lives of children. In recent decades, many studies have examined the negative impact of parental divorce on children into adulthood. However, few have offered concrete strategies for overcoming these difficulties, and none have shed light on the unique challenges faced by women as daughters of divorce.

My original research study in 1995, which sought to describe why women raised in divorced homes have unique challenges, was designed to be a follow-up study of Wallerstein's ground-breaking findings about the specific vulnerabilities daughters of divorce face. My results supported her theory that adult daughters of divorce have lower self-esteem than adult females raised in intact homes. In my study of 198 women, I discovered that the loss of regular access to parents and the exposure to intense conflict during and after parental divorce were associated with diminished self-esteem in the adult daughters of divorce in my sample—even when family climate variables such as abuse were controlled.

One year later, I studied a larger sample of 325 men and women raised in divorced homes in order to describe and explain gender differences in the psychological well-being of ACODs. This study examined a version of Paul Amato's resources and stressors model for children of divorce. In "Towards a Resources and Stressors

Model: The Psychological Adjustment of Adult Children of Divorce," I discovered that parental conflict, financial hardship, and a parenting plan that limits access to both parents (as resources) are risk factors impacting a daughter's more so than a son's vulnerability to parental divorce in terms of their self-esteem and ability to sustain healthy interpersonal relationships. In chapter 1 you will learn more about my findings and why my daughter Tracy and I choose to focus on daughters of divorce in this book.

Our current study on adult daughters of divorce, published for the first time in this book, explores the specific factors that make them more sensitive to the risks for marital dissatisfaction and breakup, along with ways to reduce their greater tendency toward divorce.

The goal of our book has been to better understand the challenges daughters of divorce face so that we can help women to rise above them. One of the women we interviewed put it like this: "When will I stop waiting for the other shoe to drop?" We sought to answer her question and give her tools to help her overcome her difficulties with love, trust, and intimacy. Every woman we met with, over a period of many years, contributed to our understanding of how parental divorce can impact daughters. They enlightened us, surprised us, and inspired us.

THE RESEARCH SAYS IT ALL

Why is it that adult children of divorce are at such a high risk of seeing their own marriages end in divorce? Leading divorce researcher Nicolas Wolfinger posits that the legacy of divorce is passed on in families because adult children of divorce often don't have positive role models for long-lasting partnerships and they tend to marry companions from similar backgrounds. For instance, people from divorced families often marry other adult children of divorce with whom they share common ground. But this greatly increases their risk of divorce. In fact, when a wife alone comes from a divorced home, she's 59 percent more likely to divorce than her counterparts from an intact home. Even more alarming, if both partners experienced parental divorce, their marriage is three times more likely to dissolve when compared to couples who grew up in intact homes.

Why is this the case? Many family scholars, such as Amato and Hetherington, believe that ACODs learn that marriages are impermanent from their parents, putting them at increased risk for divorce. Hetherington's study demonstrates that the root of marital instability is that adult children of divorce are more likely to see divorce as an option to marital problems or even sporadic periods of unhappiness than other people are. Amato and Booth's research shows that individuals raised in divorced homes are at a slightly higher risk for marital difficulties—especially if they endured multiple parental divorces. These studies report that once married, ACODs exhibit behaviors that make it difficult to sustain a lasting relationship.

Further, Amato's extensive study, "Parental Divorce and Adult Well-Being: A Meta-Analysis," summarizes the results of thirty-seven studies and concludes that daughters raised in divorced families are more likely to have their own marriages end in divorce than sons of divorce are. While the reasons for this are complex, Amato found that one main reason is noncustodial fathers are more likely to maintain contact with their sons than with their daughters—making it difficult for daughters to trust men and to learn how to resolve conflicts in adult relationships. It's no wonder that daughters of divorce would be reluctant to commit to a romantic partner and pessimistic about lasting love.

In their landmark study, "Parental Divorce and Premarital Couples: Commitment and other Relationship Characteristics," researchers Susan E. Jacquet and Catherine A. Surra interviewed 464 couples and discovered that daughters of divorce experience more uncertainty about romantic relationships and more problems associated with intimacy compared to women raised in intact homes. One of the unique aspects of this study is that it examined the premarital relationships of young adults. Interestingly, they found the strongest effects of parental divorce upon young women who were dating. These daughters of divorce expressed higher levels of mistrust with partners, less relationship satisfaction, and more ambivalence about getting involved in a committed relationship compared to counterparts raised in intact homes or sons of divorce.

Ambivalence about commitment can persist even after daughters of divorce get engaged. A recent study by Sarah Whitton of Boston University queried 265 engaged couples just before they took a relationship education class. Whitton found that daughters of divorce were more ambivalent about remaining committed to their partners and had less confidence in their ability to keep their marriage together compared to counterparts from intact homes— even after they accepted a proposal to wed.

Given these facts, it is unsurprising that many daughters of divorce are skeptical about the future of matrimony. As everyone knows, marriage is a risky proposition. The divorce rate, though down from its peak in the early 1980s, remains considerable today. Approximately 40 percent of first marriages end in divorce. In addition, we have seen a dramatic rise in children being born outside of marriage, and most of them to women who cohabit with partners, rather than marrying them. According to a 2014 Pew Research report, about 24 percent of never-married adults (ages twenty-five to thirty-four) are living with a partner. Based on these facts, it appears that a generation of children that grew up with divorce is becoming an adult generation that is questioning commitment and marriage.

A Pew Research report titled *Barely Half of U.S. Adults Are Married—A Record Low* shows that the number of adults currently married is down 5 percent from 2009 to 2010. In fact, the rate of single women getting married dropped by 22.8 percent from 2010 to 2011, according to the Heritage Foundation's *2014 Index of Culture and Opportunity*. The U.S. marriage rate (the number of women's marriages per one thousand unmarried women fifteen years and older) is the lowest it has been in over a century at thirty-one marriages per one thousand unmarried women.

WHAT DO WOMEN WANT FROM LOVE AND MARRIAGE?

In spite of a declining marriage rate, demographers predict that most Americans will marry at some point in their lives. Currently, about 72 percent of U.S. citizens will marry by the age of thirty-five. A recent Pew Research report found that 61 percent of never-married adults in the United States said they would like to marry someday. Therefore, it's important to consider: What *do* women want from love and marriage?

In the 1950s and '60s the gold standard of marital success was a "companionate marriage." The essential feature of this type of union is teamwork and achieving life goals—like running a home and raising a family. In *Marriage, A History*, author Stephanie Coontz concludes that today "people expect marriage to satisfy more of their psychological and social needs than ever before." Today, people (and especially women) want a partner to share a deep love, communication, and to have great sexual and emotional intimacy, rather than just working toward common goals. Adults nowadays desire a relationship that promotes their personal growth and are more likely to consider divorce if they believe their partner is holding them back in any way.

In fact, wives are more likely to file for divorce than husbands. According to a report titled "'These Boots Are Made For Walking': Why Most Divorce Filers Are Women," women file for more than two-thirds of divorces in the United States. Another recent report, *Marriage: More Than a Century of Change*, found that 15 percent of women in the United States are divorced or separated today, compared with less than 1 percent in 1920.

While marriage is one of the most defining acts of our lives, and the stakes are pretty high, many twentysomethings focus more on their career than on their marriage. However, choosing a partner may be the most important decision of our lives, in terms of the high cost of divorce. After all, it's a lot easier to change jobs than to disengage from a spouse financially and emotionally. Most women are painfully aware of the significance of marriage, according to psychologist Meg Jay, PhD, and see a successful marriage as a victory. So while we hear a lot about young women wanting to delay marriage, many want to commit and hope to be luckier in love than their parents were.

In *The Defining Decade*, Jay writes, "Half of all women have been left in the wake of divorce, and all know someone who has." She explains that while it was tempting to minimize the impact of parental divorce in the twentieth century, the "unexpected legacy of divorce" described by Wallerstein in her landmark study was undeniable.

Consequently, one of the most common questions asked by the women we met with was: How can I overcome the loss I experienced in childhood and create a loving relationship that will last? Most daughters of divorce are aware they need to develop a healthy respect for commitment and don't want to repeat their parents' mistakes. As one respondent, Kayla, put it: "I don't want to be disrespectful to my parents but I want my marriage to succeed where theirs didn't." Fortunately, by keeping her eyes wide open and making intentional efforts, Kayla can learn to build relationships on a firm foundation instead of shaky ground.

The voices of the women we interviewed form the heart of this book, and their stories are testimonies to these women's strength and hope. The stories of these women reveal their innermost fears about ending up alone and losing out on love. These daughters of divorce share their struggles with dating and fear of commitment—yet also their eagerness to find the lasting love that eluded their parents. For many daughters of divorce, pain is what they know. Dealing with turmoil and conflict is in their wheelhouse. A partner who wants nothing more than to be with them and make them a top priority is a foreign concept they don't know how to translate.

When a girl grows up in a fractured home, she may feel deep in her heart that because her family is broken, she is broken. If her parents aren't together, she may feel something is wrong with her. There's not, and that's exactly what we address in this book. We posit that this girl, who is now a woman, has the ability to craft a new story for her life. There isn't anything missing, nothing imperfect or incomplete within her. She has all the tools she needs to build a healthy relationship, and we're here to help her (and you!) discover those skills and use them to create strong, happy, healthy, and long-lasting relationships.

We also hope that reading this book will encourage you to give yourself permission to look back at your history. Even as an adult, there is great value in taking an inventory of your life. It's understandable if you feel hesitant about doing this. However, it is possible to heal, and the first step is allowing yourself to be vulnerable and recognizing how your parents' divorce affected you. The next step is letting go and not being paralyzed by fear and shame. In doing so, you will begin to trust yourself and others, and increase your sense of worthiness and authenticity.

This book is about how you, a daughter of divorce, can learn to overcome the legacy of divorce and move forward to enjoy rewarding relationships built on love, trust, and intimacy. Each chapter describes a central theme and skill that are essential to achieving this and includes practical steps to go about it. At the end of each chapter, we include perspectives from both of us—mother and daughter—on our own experiences with divorce and lessons we've learned.

A note on how to approach this book: while you could go directly to the chapters that seem most relevant to you, we strongly recommend reading this book in its entirety. Though each chapter focuses on a particular challenge faced by daughters of divorce, the chapters are interrelated and you might miss crucial information if you read only some of the steps. You may also find that a step you don't think applies to you actually does help in ways you might not have realized if you had not taken the time to read about it. In short, reading each chapter will help you understand the full impact of your parents' divorce on your relationships and emotional well being, which will help you fully heal.

Although it may be hard for you to trust your own judgment when it comes to making a commitment, we support you on your journey and encourage you to take your time to develop a successful relationship. Over time, you can learn to trust your instincts and gain self-confidence. Rather than hold you back, your divorce experience can be the catalyst to make you stronger, more realistic, and better prepared for the requirements of love. It's time to take a chance on love and life!

1

Looking for Love We Can Be Sure Of

"I would fall right into a relationship and lose myself. The good in me died when I fell for a guy, because I gave too much."

—Caitlin, age 26

If you are worried about the future of your intimate relationships, you aren't alone. Since the divorce epidemic hit America in the 1960s and peaked in the late 1970s, couples have adopted more liberal attitudes toward divorce. As a result, Pamela Paul, author of *The Starter Marriage and the Future of Matrimony*, noted the divorce epidemic has left many people feeling that marriage is disposable or impermanent. In particular, women raised in disrupted homes learn the hard way that marriage isn't a sure thing and that fear often sticks. They wonder if it's even possible for them to get out from under the shadow of their parents' mistakes and forge healthy relationships.

Since many divorced parents model poor communication, problem solving, and conflict resolution skills, ACODs don't grow up with the expectation they can work through the inevitable ups and downs of married life with a partner. In his book, *Adult Children of Divorce*, Jeffrey Zimmerman, PhD, writes, "You haven't had the best of role models, and maybe you don't have much faith in the concept of long-term commitment. If all you saw (and maybe continue to see) is conflict and hostility, you may decide that romantic, long-term relationships are just not worth it."

By now you've probably gathered that your parents' divorce may have bestowed on you a distinctive view of marriage—one that predisposes you to think of divorce as a viable solution to unhappiness in your wedded state. In spite of this, you can conquer your fears and go on to have successful romantic relationships by looking at your history, taking an inventory, and examining your thoughts, attitudes, and beliefs about love and commitment. The pages that follow are a guide to helping you examine your divorce experience from an adult viewpoint and change self-defeating patterns in relationships. These patterns can prevent you from achieving the love and happiness you deserve. Instead, you can learn to recognize the forces that shape you and make conscious choices about what you want out of love and life!

Truth be told, whether your parents are divorced or not, there aren't any Band-Aid solutions to relationship problems, and there's no surefire way to ensure a successful, long-lasting partnership or marriage. But you can learn productive habits and strategies, which we'll teach you here, that can reduce your likelihood of divorce if you choose to marry. Of course, we're not suggesting that all divorces are preventable or that couples should stay together in an abusive or high-conflict marriage.

By reading this book, you will learn how unresolved issues from the past can be an obstacle to making your intimate relationships work. These include trouble trusting romantic partners, reluctance to commit, damaged self-esteem, extreme self-reliance, mistrust in the permanence of relationships, and a damaged father-daughter relationship. You will also find that if you don't deal with these issues, you could be more prone to divorce because these issues translate into weak relationship skills and difficulty getting close to people (or letting them get close to you). In fact, ghosts from the past may make you more guarded—only allowing you to give part of yourself to your partner. It's natural to fear being intimate and vulnerable with a romantic partner if you believe that your relationships are doomed to fail like your parents' marriage did.

But don't worry: you will soon realize you aren't alone or crazy! Your reaction to your parents' breakup is normal and shared by many women. For instance, many of the women we spoke with seemed controlled by the "approval trap." This term, coined by Harold Bloomfield, MD, in *Making Peace with Your Parents* describes people who bend over backward seeking approval from others due to unresolved issues with their parents.

BREAKING FREE OF THE PAST

Penny, age thirty-six, is a bright and articulate human service professional who has been stuck in the "approval trap" for most of her life. "After my dad left for another woman, when I was barely three years old, I worked very hard to get my mother's approval—at the expense of my own happiness," she says. Penny suffers from "daddy deprivation" and has a broken relationship with her absent father, who was an adulterer and married three times. In the past, she was unassertive and allowed her ex-husband Steven to manipulate and control her. At times, this meant giving up her own dreams and desires; she even moved to another country with Steven, knowing that in doing so, she'd have difficulty completing college and be miserable because of missing her sister and close friends.

Unfortunately, Penny married Steven at age twenty-one, before she had the insight to understand her own needs or develop self-confidence. Consequently, she allowed him dominate and control her due to her low self-esteem, an unhealthy pattern of relating to partners she'd learned from her mother and other female relatives. But after a few years of psychotherapy, Penny made a decision to end her marriage and has transformed her life. She is finally outspoken and comfortable with expressing her feelings and needs. A graceful conversationalist, Penny speaks with honesty and clarity as she describes her new outlook: "I have reclaimed my life and I'm starting to speak up for what I need." She's come to a place where she realizes she doesn't have to prove her self-worth to anyone.

Like many of the women we interviewed, Penny also suffered from extreme self-reliance and had difficulty asking for support from her partners. For many years, she didn't feel comfortable asking for what she needed even in small ways—such as carrying in groceries or cooking dinner after a long day at work. Competent at a cost to herself, Penny bought into the misconception that she could attain self-worth by pleasing others; she was also afraid of rejection. Currently, she strives to know and care about herself. Penny is working on finding self-worth that doesn't depend on others' view of her. You will learn how to do this in chapter 6, "Step Four: Building Self-Esteem: Let Go of Your Childhood Hang-ups."

Penny's story illustrates how unresolved issues from the past contributed to her tendency to be a people pleaser—causing her to walk on eggshells with partners. Operating from a basis of pessimism, mistrust, and fear of relationship failure, Penny avoided asserting herself and had difficulty being vulnerable and intimate with partners—preventing her from finding lasting love and self-worth.

Like Penny, you possess unique characteristics and strengths. For the most part, you are resilient, self-reliant, flexible, and competent in many areas of your life—even if you don't believe it! However, you may be fearful that if you allow yourself to be vulnerable and open about your needs, your partner will reject you. This pessimism about love may even cause you to avoid commitment altogether—as a way to protect yourself from disappointment, loss, and pain. But remember there are no guarantees in any relationship. Some work out and some don't, but approaching relationships with fear or doubt almost guarantees a negative outcome.

DAUGHTERS OF DIVORCE AND LOW SELF-ESTEEM

When children grow up feeling valued and cared for in a healthy way, they'll typically grow into adulthood with a sense of self-worth. Ideally, children will hold on to this sense of worthiness into adulthood, developing a positive identity and healthy self-esteem.

Self-esteem comes from recognizing that you have inherent value—based on your uniqueness as an individual. It means believing in yourself and trusting that you are worthy, even if others ignore you or just don't understand. Self-esteem is based on your belief system—which is a mixture of the way you feel about yourself and the way you believe others see you.

Most of the women we interviewed felt their self-esteem was impacted once they were no longer part of an intact family. This means their sense of identity as a competent or lovable person changed. Since girls have a tendency to define their identity through relationships and by caring about others, a rupture in the family unit may cause a grief reaction that is delayed and ignored. This feeling of being disconnected may help to explain why adult daughters of divorce are less likely to achieve high self-esteem than other young women.

Consequently, if a girl isn't encouraged to express her grief over her parents' divorce, her self-worth may plummet as she struggles to make sense of this loss. In other words, girls tend to blame themselves when they feel there is discord or a fracture in their family or when they don't feel connected to their parents.

Divorce is a major life transition and is anything but easy for children and adolescents—even with a "good" divorce. So it should come as no surprise that girls who experience negative emotions—such as anger and resentment—need to process and resolve these feelings so that they can be integrated into their life experience. Addressing the divorce experience encompasses reflecting upon it, appraising it, and challenging any distorted thought processes or beliefs (such as "My father doesn't love me"). Only by addressing her emotions can a girl heal from the past, resolve her feelings of loss, and move forward. However, if this doesn't happen, a daughter may suffer from low self-esteem into adulthood—causing her to lose confidence in her ability to make appropriate choices and achieve rewarding relationships.

Divorce experts concur that a girl's picture-perfect image of her family changes after her family dissolves. When this happens, girls often enter adulthood with low self-esteem and a strong need for approval. But they don't always realize this right away. Instead they may experience shame. Author Brené Brown, PhD, writes, "Shame is the intensely painful feeling or experience of believing we are flawed and therefore unworthy of acceptance and belonging." Often daughters of divorce who haven't worked through their feelings about their parents' divorce experience embarrassment or disgrace, which can result in low self-esteem, the feeling that they're just not good enough or worth it. Then they either pick men who are wrong for them or avoid intimacy—and don't understand why they never seem to be lucky in love.

During our interviews, we listened as women shared their struggles with identity and self-worth. It seems that the dicey waters of divorce may make some daughters even more vulnerable to feelings of self-blame, causing them to lose faith in themselves. In her book, *In a Different Voice*, Carol Gilligan, PhD, a renowned expert on women's psychology, notes that females may hide negative feelings for fear of fracturing relationships, striving instead to please others and seek connectedness through that. It's natural for daughters to want their relationship with both parents to run smoothly after divorce and to worry about taking sides in an argument or creating conflict. When faced with divided loyalties, some girls even become too eager to please others; they might bury their negative feelings as a way to resolve the conflict they experience. As children they may have done their best to be "good girls" and adapted to their situation by becoming people pleasers. However, as adults this tendency can cause them to be guarded—making intimacy with a romantic partner a challenge since vulnerability is the basis for true intimacy.

It's time to recognize that, in spite of your challenges and circumstances, you are a unique person who has a lot to offer others. You can learn self-acceptance and give yourself the same compassion, tolerance, and support you give others. In chapter 6, we will show you how to shed the old patterns of your childhood and build greater self-esteem.

THE SLEEPER EFFECT

As discussed earlier, females of all ages thrive on feeling emotionally connected to others to form their identity and feelings of self-worth. In her landmark study, Wallerstein found that most girls prefer that their family stay together even when there is intense conflict in their parents' marriage. A seasoned therapist and researcher, Wallerstein explains that parental divorce can be especially challenging for young females. She describes a "sleeper effect"—a tendency that young girls have to repress intense anxiety related to their parents' split—only to have a delayed emergence of powerful effects later on. The stories in this book will illustrate that when their family crumbles, daughters may initially feel crushed, blame themselves, and doubt their own ability to find love and happiness in the future. If you grew up in a divided home, it's normal for you to fear commitment and feel like you are always waiting for the "other shoe to drop," even if you find someone who appears to be a good match for you.

Emily, an upbeat and personable preschool teacher in her early thirties, illustrates the powerful impact of the sleeper effect. Her parents divorced when she was six years old, and she has struggled with both the approval trap and low self-esteem since childhood. After her parents' breakup, she became a model student and caretaker to her younger brother, while her mother worked hard to support the family as a single parent. Spending time in both of her parents' homes was challenging for Emily as an adolescent because each parent had radically different rules and perspectives on life. She also observed them arguing about child support payments, which she hated to see. As an adult, Emily now feels she had a delayed reaction to her parents' breakup because she wasn't given permission to grieve her parents' split and because she suffered from severe loyalty conflicts.

This sleeper effect has manifested itself in a number of ways. Emily has a tendency to pick men who are wrong for her due to her low self-esteem and fear of abandonment. In her case, her parents' high-conflict divorce left her with a fear of being alone or being left behind. Emily reflects on a ten-year relationship that she knew was doomed to fail from the start because her partner Justin began cheating on her early in their relationship. She says: "I tried so hard because I didn't want to be alone. God forbid I had to tell anyone that he was unfaithful and lied to me for many years." After a year of psychotherapy, Emily began coming to terms with her feelings, saying, "I felt ashamed and I was even willing to share him with someone else, rather than to admit that I had failed."

Like many daughters of divorce, Emily questioned what was wrong with her rather than holding Justin accountable or ending the relationship. Even though her need for love and security wasn't being met, her feelings of insecurity and low self-worth had to be examined and dealt with before she could assert herself and end an unhealthy relationship. She says the therapy she received was invaluable: "My therapist asked me, why is it that you are still paying the insurance on a truck that you own, when he's driving around in it without a license?" As Emily began to worry less about being nice and appearing selfish, she learned to take better care of herself and her self-esteem improved. For the first time, she began paying attention to what she was getting out of the relationship, rather than focusing on how she could meet her partner's needs. She finally cut the ties with her ex-boyfriend a few months before our interview.

Many women need special encouragement to let go of self-blame and reclaim their identity and self-worth. In their ground-breaking book *Meeting at the Crossroads*, Lyn Mikel Brown and Carol Gilligan highlight the fact that girls may have difficulty grieving losses, such as the dissolution of a family, during adolescence because it can be a time of turmoil. They write, "Adolescence is a time of disconnection, sometimes of dissociation or repression in women's lives, so that women often don't remember—tend to forget or cover over—what as girls they have experienced and known." In their study of nearly one hundred women, Brown and Gilligan discovered a link between women's desire for authentic connection and the experience of disconnection during adolescence.

In fact, this tendency to be focused on the welfare of others and to distrust themselves or their own experiences may be costly because it can jeopardize a woman's sense of self in relationships. If this goes untreated, women may experience dangerously low self-esteem and a complete lack of confidence in their ability to find and keep loving partnerships.

> Keep in mind that emotional intimacy isn't emotional dependency. If your relationship causes you to feel anxious or causes you to question your sense of self, it may not be the best relationship for you. Ask yourself this question if you are in a relationship: Is there something about the way

my partner treats me that makes me a better person? If the answer is no, you may be settling for less than you deserve due to fear of abandonment or of being alone. These are the two most common reasons women stay in relationships that aren't meeting their needs.

HOW DAD CAN MAKE A DIFFERENCE

The world of fathers and daughters after divorce is another central theme of this book because the real value of a father in a girl's life is far-reaching. A girl's relationship with her father is key to her femininity, sexuality, and identity as a woman. It influences the future she makes for herself. After all, a father is the first man in a girl's life and often her earliest role model for how she should be treated by a man. Author Deidre Laiken writes that many women continue to search for their dads in all of the men they meet. She explains that most daughters yearn for their fathers' approval and recognition, and after divorce, girls need their fathers more than ever. Fathers serve as a crucial buffer because girls naturally tend to distance themselves from their mothers during adolescence. Unfortunately, girls who don't have this buffer may seek approval from boys and young men who are unavailable or wrong for them. Likewise, some daughters of divorce may try too hard to save unhealthy relationships or retreat from commitment due to fear of rejection or anxiety about whether love will last.

Given these facts, it makes sense that a girl growing up in a divorced family can especially benefit from plenty of reassurance about her father's love and his consistent presence in her life. Without that, a girl may not always be able to interpret her father's absence or disinterest as his fault; instead she's left to feel his behavior is due to some flaw within herself. Problems between a daughter and her father—whether he is absent, distant, or unavailable—can propel a girl into young adulthood with a sense of apprehension about the future in general. Psychologists universally agree that all children need to feel loved and able to trust their caregivers to feel secure, good about themselves, and comfortable in relationships.

Hetherington explains that for girls, the loss of connection with their fathers is more common and profound than for boys, as most girls have limited contact with their fathers after divorce compared to boys. Hetherington writes, "Qualities like stability and competency have to be nurtured carefully and patiently by an active, engaged father." When a father isn't there to reinforce this after a divorce, the results can be devastating for daughters. Clearly, a daughter who feels close to her dad and valued by him is more secure in her abilities.

Caitlin, a college student in her midtwenties, comes across as cheerful and outgoing. She remembers feeling distant from her father after her parents split when she was thirteen. "I could always rely on him materialistically, but he never showed me much affection. Children don't only need food and a roof over their heads, they also need love, and things were never joyous when I was with my dad," she says. "This led me to have very low self-esteem for a long time and prohibited me from seeing who I really was."

As Caitlin began venturing into dating relationships during adolescence, she experienced a lot of turmoil. She describes herself as a nurturer and a people pleaser. "I would fall right into a relationship and lose myself. The good in me died when I fell for a guy, because I gave too much," she says. Caitlin acknowledges that she went through a very rebellious period during adolescence when her need for male approval was strong. Like so many daughters from disrupted homes, she found herself choosing men who were like her father, emotionally distant and controlling. Caitlin didn't realize until years later that she was repeating relationship patterns from her past. With the help of a therapist on campus, she finally learned to end relationships that weren't working for her, even though she was afraid of being alone. She adds with a wry smile, "I realized that I didn't need someone else to make me happy because I made myself happy for once."

Truly a resilient young woman, Caitlin worked hard to get past her feelings of not being good enough, and she made a decision not to let events in her childhood determine her future. Caitlin's story provides a good example of how a daughter of divorce can examine her relationship with her father from an adult perspective and create a new story for her life.

If the father-daughter wound isn't repaired, young women may grow into adulthood without a solid sense of how to relate well to men. Younger girls especially tend to create "fantasy fathers," according to author Suzanne Fields, which could go something like this: if her dad can't be there in real life, a girl makes him up. She may even look for her dad in other relationships when she is an adolescent or young adult. Sandra, age twenty-six, reflects: "I've had several partners who were like my father. I guess I thought that the way my dad treated my mom was the way I deserved to be treated." Intimate relationships may suffer if a young woman holds on to unrealistic images of "fantasy dad"—fearing rejection and yet tentative about committing to a partner because they don't live up to an ideal standard.

DARING TO TRUST OTHERS

Over a cup of coffee, Kelly, a thirtysomething happily married teacher, speaks candidly about her dad leaving her mom for another woman when Kelly was fourteen. "When triggers come up with my husband, like he takes longer to get home from work, I always question him—give him the third degree. But I'm learning not to overreact. He's aware that I have trust issues, and he's learning to answer my questions without getting mad or defensive," she says. When Kelly reacts with fear at the slightest imperfection in her husband's story, she knows she has a tendency to blow things out of proportion. She has learned to recognize that she might be reenacting painful memories of her parents' arguments in her childhood home. It's important for her to resist the temptation to interact with her husband, Mark, from a place of fear and mistrust.

So how does she do this? Kelly must examine her thought processes. Is her self-doubt and mistrust grounded in reality or a fragment of her past? She must be willing to let go of self-defeating patterns, trust, and surrender—to free herself from the blueprints her parents left her. Like many daughters raised in a divided home, Kelly feels that intimate relationships reawaken childhood fears as she grapples with issues of love, trust, and commitment. According to Fields, it's because our lives with our fathers can be viewed as a dress rehearsal for love and marriage. Once Kelly was able to work through her root issue of trust, she was able to rebuild a healthy relationship with Mark, who deserved her trust and has been faithful throughout their thirteen-year marriage.

Learning to trust is one of the biggest challenges daughters of divorce face. At the very root of mistrust is the fear that when a partner truly knows you, he'll leave you. When these mistrustful thoughts persist, it may become difficult to be vulnerable and intimate with your partner. The uncertainty of intimate relationships can be scary. The breakdown of your childhood home may have left you hesitant to trust, even if your partner is reliable, honest, and faithful. Trust is an act of courage that can be achieved through honestly facing your fears. By doing so, you'll open yourself up to the opportunity for the real love and intimacy you deserve.

Repeating the past can be problematic, especially if a child was exposed to unhealthy relationships and divorce. But psychologist Martin E. P. Seligman notes, "Contrary to popular belief, we don't have to be prisoners of our past." The failure of a girl's parents' marriage does not mean that hers is doomed. With insight and self-awareness, daughters of divorce can reject the faulty models they grew up with and create loving long-term partnerships. Coming to grips with fears and unhealthy patterns of relating will take time, but it is the first step in changing one's outlook on love and commitment.

SELF-RELIANCE: AN ASSET OR A LIABILITY?

Rachel's story is a powerful illustration of another issue daughters of divorce experience and one that we'll explore in more depth later on. Often self-reliant, daughters of divorce may use their independence as an armor to avoid getting close to others or relying on them and potentially getting hurt. A well-spoken woman in her late twenties, Rachel learned to be self-reliant early on. Her father deserted her family when she was an infant, and her mother and stepfather uprooted her to the Southwest from the East Coast when she was an adolescent. They then got a divorce shortly afterward due to her stepfather's infidelity.

Rachel says, "I still have to take care of me. I feel like I never want to depend on anyone because that's what my mom did, and look what happened to her." Her comments are natural: they reflect her determination to succeed as well as her strong desire to protect herself from heartbreak. Rachel expects and has become accustomed to losing out on love and security. But the root of her extreme self-reliance is fear of abandonment. She believes that showing vulnerability to a partner is a weakness and fears that if she reveals her true thoughts, wishes, and desires, that partner will abandon her.

Many women raised in divorced homes—especially those who have endured multiple parental divorces—feel they must do everything for themselves because they can't depend on others or don't believe they deserve nurturance and support. Some daughters of divorce take self-reliance to the extreme, which leaves them unable to trust their partners for even small things such as help with household chores or basic emotional support. They fear the people they love will leave them so they keep them at arm's length just in case. When they do feel they're getting too close to their partners, they may distance themselves by stonewalling or shutting down emotionally, or they may have an urge to flee or threaten to leave.

Indeed, most women from disrupted homes take pride in being able to take care of themselves no matter what challenges come their way. Growing up in a divorced home causes children to face life's realities far younger than many of their peers. To be clear, this self-reliance isn't always a bad thing: in fact, it can arm a daughter of divorce with great strength. Most of the women we interviewed were hardworking and trustworthy—and prided themselves on these traits. The problem is, self-reliance is a double-edged sword. While it has many virtues, if taken to the extreme, it can rob women of true intimacy and the type of relationship they deserve by not allowing their partners to get close to them.

In *Daring Greatly*, Brown defines vulnerability as uncertainty, risk, and emotional exposure. Given this definition, the act of loving someone and allowing them to love you may be the ultimate risk. Love is uncertain; there are no guarantees. Your partner could leave you without a moment's notice, or betray you, or stop loving you. In fact, exposing your true feelings may mean that you are at greater risk for being criticized or hurt. Some women might be freezing out the opportunity to love because they are so afraid to share their innermost thoughts, feelings, and wishes. However, enjoying the pleasure of real love and intimacy can make you feel complete and uplifted—and be a source of comfort and predictability in an uncertain world. A strong relationship encourages and challenges you to be the best person you can be. It also can be the support you need to achieve your goals outside your relationship.

In fact, as you'll learn throughout this book, vulnerability is often the glue that holds a relationship together. It helps couples navigate day-to-day life and allows them to feel comfortable letting their hair down and being themselves at the end of the day. Being vulnerable will allow a woman to communicate openly and feel closer to her partner. In contrast, it may be the lack of emotional attunement that comes from not showing vulnerability that can lead many couples down the path to divorce. If a woman is afraid of showing weakness or exposing herself to a partner, she might not be aware that her fear is preventing her (and thus her partner as well) from being totally engaged in the relationship.

RELUCTANCE TO COMMIT

We've already touched on this earlier, and it's an issue that underlies many of the other problems faced by daughters of divorce. Many are reluctant to commit to romantic partners. They just can't see a relationship working out, though they desperately want one. Diana is a successful, educated young woman, but relationships have been her Achilles' heel. Although she says she doesn't believe in men, Diana wants one who will be a true match for her. "I think I can have a happy marriage, but I fluctuate," she says. "If it's the right guy, if we're both faithful, I'll be optimistic. If it's true love, I'll be optimistic. But it's going to take a lot to prove it to me because I want it to be foolproof." Her craving for a fail-safe relationship will always be unsatisfied because such relationships don't exist. The truth is that intimacy is a mix of vulnerability and reciprocity that can only be achieved if a person has a willingness to trust another human being.

During our interviews with numerous daughters of divorce, we discovered that many of them were conflicted about their ability to find lasting love and intimacy, and their fear of intimacy and commitment displayed itself in unusual ways—such as hanging on to a dysfunctional relationship or trying to rescue an unsuitable partner. Many of the women we spoke with understood there was likely a connection between their parents' breakup and their own fear of relationship failure and sought advice about how to change their self-defeating patterns.

Diana is currently in a relationship with a wonderful young man who treats her well. But fear plagues her. "I've wanted to walk away many times, wanted to run, because deep down I know it's real. But I'm not used to real—it's like a self-fulfilling prophecy. I'll create the demise of the relationship because I don't trust him," she says.

"I'm very pessimistic," Diana reflects. "I'm looking for the worst in men, and they have to prove me wrong." Her fear of loss is so strong, she seems to always be on guard—testing her partners to see if they'll pass or fail as so many others have done. That is the paradox that daughters of divorce face. What Diana so desperately wants—love, commitment, and the comfort of a permanent relationship—is what she most fears.

There are many ways that a daughter of divorce might test her relationship. For instance, some women fall into a pattern of questioning a partner's intentions and seeking constant affirmation of their love. For some women, this translates into unrealistic expectations of frequent phone calls and text messages from their partners, or the expectation that their partners will buy gifts for them to demonstrate love and affection. In other cases, women may pick arguments with their partners or become overly critical—blowing small things out of proportion in an effort to get validation of their partners' devotion and commitment.

THE PERSONALITY STYLES OF DIVORCE

As you read this book and begin to practice addressing the issues we've covered so far, it's important to understand that daughters of divorce are likely to take on certain personality styles as a result of their upbringing. Hetherington posits that there are four primary personality types that daughters of divorce develop: competent-at-a-cost, competent-caring, competent-opportunist, and "good enough." Recognizing your own personality style can help you overcome any emotional issues successfully and completely.

According to Hetherington, many women develop a "competent-at-a-cost" personality style, a terminology she developed after studying fourteen hundred families for nearly three decades. In her book *For Better or For Worse*, Hetherington describes daughters who grow into successful, well-adjusted adults—for the most part—but with damaged relationships and lowered self-esteem due to becoming their parents' emotional caretakers. As we've mentioned previously, some women experience unresolved issues related to "parentification"—the burden of providing emotional support, advice, and solace to a needy parent while growing up.

Brooke is an example of a young woman who felt burdened as a child and is competent-at-a-cost as a young adult. A highly motivated honor student in her early twenties, Brooke plans to become a nurse-practitioner after graduation. Her father moved out when she was an infant, and their relationship has been distant. Due to her father's absence and her mother's difficulty coping, she often felt burdened as a child—as if the roles were reversed between herself and her mother. "Of course I hope for happiness and believe I'm capable, but my parents' divorce has made me much more cautious about partners. It has made me fear the future and marriage, as much as I am excited about it." She stopped for a moment and continued: "I fear that people I love will leave me and I won't see them again. I prepare myself for the worst."

Another personality type identified and illustrated by Hetherington is competent-caring. These women are socially skilled, self-sufficient, and flexible. Their confidence appears to have been enhanced by coping with the challenges in their families, and they often pursue careers in social service professions. Maura, a speech pathologist in her late thirties, has been happily married for thirteen years and is the mother of three young children. She is a competent professional, a wonderful mother, and active in her community. During our interview Maura appeared self-assured and comfortable discussing her parents' divorce and her own marriage.

Maura, who married her college sweetheart, said, "It was hard to deal with my parents' divorce growing up, but I knew that both of my parents would do anything for me. They tried hard not to put me in the middle." She has worked through a lot of her resentments toward her dad, who left when she was three years old, saying, "I guess my parents weren't meant to be together; their divorce motivates me to make my marriage a priority."

When Maura spoke about her marriage, she talked about taking her time to pick a partner who is a good match for her. "We took five years to get to know each other before we married and another five years before we had our first child," she says. She also selected a partner who believes in clearing the air when tensions arise rather than avoiding dealing with issues. She is hopeful about the future of her marriage, acknowledging that marriage is hard work and that she didn't have successful role models. While being competent-caring is mostly positive, the downside is that some women are too focused on others and get stuck in the "approval trap" that we discussed in the introduction.

The third personality style identified by Hetherington is competent-opportunist. Children with this style have a unique ability to perceive and respond to the needs and feelings of others and often use this skill to their advantage. Natural charmers, competent-opportunist children are oriented toward people in power such as teachers, coaches, or peers with a higher status. Due to their charisma, humor, and excellent social skills, they are often adept at winning people over and tend to be successful adults. As adults, they tend to be leaders in fields such as business, sales, law, or politics. Competent-opportunist women are often encouraged by their mothers to be autonomous and self-reliant as children.

Rachel, a college student, uses self-reliance as a way to protect herself from being abandoned. Raised by a single mother, she endured poverty, her father's absence, and the desertion of her stepfather, who was unfaithful to her mother. Rachel's story shines with optimism and speaks to her competent-opportunist personality style. Pursuing a business degree while working full-time at a Fortune 500 company, she hasn't allowed the challenges of her past to prevent her from seeking opportunities or taking a chance on life. With a surprisingly self-assured tone, Rachel says, "Certain situations in life are unforeseen and uncontrollable. They can either take you down a path of darkness or lead you out of a storm as a stronger person." Clearly, Rachel's ability to access resources is an advantage that has helped her to succeed in life so far. However, if she doesn't deal with her fear of being left, it will surely surface in her relationships since intimate partnerships tend to present us with reminders of our past. Later, we will discuss how Rachel overcame adversity due to her competent-opportunist personality.

We observed the competent-caring, the competent-at-a-cost, and the competent-opportunist styles in most of the women we interviewed and will refer to them in the book. The fourth personality style designated by Hetherington is "good enough," which describes a woman in the middle of the spectrum in terms of factors such as academic performance, peer relations, and psychological functioning. In other words, her emotional and psychological functioning is on par with women raised in non-divorced families. Although we only noted this style in a small number of participants (after all, if most daughters of divorce fell into this category, we wouldn't have to write this book!), it is important in our study because many women are adjusting fine overall.

Growing up in a divorced family can impact a woman's personality style, choice in partners, and attitudes toward love, marriage, and commitment. Fortunately, it is never too late to change the blueprint she inherited. Despite caution and fear, a woman raised in a divorced home can make peace with her parents' divorce, develop a sense of herself independent from her family, and build fulfilling relationships that endure the test of time.

LOOKING AHEAD TO A BRIGHT FUTURE

Laura, age twenty-five, is a warm and engaging young woman who is eager to talk about her past. Her parents divorced when she was eight years old and mutually agreed that shared custody would be in the best interests of their two daughters. Although Laura felt it was more difficult to schedule sleepovers and time with friends in middle school, she has positive memories of the time she spent with her father. "When Molly and I saw our dad, it was quality time and we would focus on each other," says Laura. "We'd play games and ask him to make up scary stories because we loved them." Today, Laura is a licensed occupational therapist who fits nicely into the competent-caring category. She is cautious about making the same mistake as her parents, but determined to break their pattern. Laura offers an example of a confident woman who seems to have worked through much of the pain related to her parents' divorce. She has been able to forge a successful life for herself based on self-worth and feeling loved and empowered by both of her parents. Laura spontaneously shared these insights: "I don't doubt that I'll have a great relationship one day as long as I'm smart in who I choose to invest my time in. My parents' divorce made me realize that having a good relationship is much more about lifestyle preferences and similar values than just being in love. I know what I'm looking for in a relationship, and if I don't see potential, then I won't waste my time. Call it unromantic, but it's practical and I know that I'll be happier in the long run."

Today more and more daughters of divorce are delaying marriage until they are ready, being smart about love, and striving to have healthier relationships than their parents. They understand that one of the most important ingredients for true intimacy is mutual understanding, which involves respect, trust, and learning to resolve conflicts successfully. In her book *We're Still Family*, author Constance Ahrons, PhD, explains that parental divorce doesn't have to define women. Rather than pointing a finger at divorce, she recommends focusing on post-divorce relationships and posits that healthy families come in all types. Divorce experts all agree that daughters of divorce are more likely to fear commitment and are more prone to divorce, but they also have a great opportunity to overcome the legacy their parents handed them.

Megan, in her midtwenties, is a successful artist who radiates positive energy. She was six years old when her parents split and they shared custody of her. When we asked Megan for details about her life after her parents' divorce, she told her story matter-of-factly: "I was about six, and they both told me about the divorce one night after dinner. We sat on the sofa and all cried together." A competent-opportunist, Megan exudes self-confidence and maturity as she reflects upon her parents' breakup: "My parents were very young when they married and very different. Looking back, I can understand why the divorce happened."

Megan has learned some valuable lessons from her parents' marriage. She has a healthy understanding of her divorce experience and has taken the time to examine her thoughts, attitudes, and beliefs about herself and relationships. "Know your partner inside and out before you marry. Know yourself before you commit to someone. Be sure that you make each other strive for the best, bring out the positive qualities in each other, and be certain that you can grow together," she says cheerfully. Megan acknowledges that being raised in a divorced family has presented her with many challenges and has caused her to be cautious about commitment. However, she is choosing to see it as an opportunity to break through family patterns and to forge successful intimate relationships. Megan is determined not to let her parents' divorce crush her chances of achieving happiness.

Storytelling has long been a powerful way to communicate and give listeners a sense of connection to others. Of the more than three hundred women we interviewed, most of them were eager to discuss their parents' breakup and readily reflected upon their relationships with their parents and intimate partners. Some of them volunteered poems and letters. Marisa, who recently resolved issues with her father before his death, even offered to help name this book *Father Loss* because she was profoundly impacted by her father's absence. Jenna became engaged shortly after she shared her story with us. Several months prior to the publication of this book, Elizabeth forwarded her wedding photos to us via email— beaming with pride and filled with optimism about her future.

We hope the stories that follow will allow you to gain insight into and enable you to make peace with your parents' divorce. Our journey, which began as a dialogue between mother and daughter over a cup of tea, was guided by listening to the voices of the women who met with us over many years. We were inspired by these women, who took time to talk to us in spite of the obstacles that could have interfered. Surprisingly, most of them aren't cynical or bitter but long to create loving relationships in their lives. Their resilience shines through in their stories.

We will explore ways of resolving issues from the past as well as accepting and forgiving, so that we may repair our ability to find lasting love and self-worth. Our work has always been about helping women of all ages defy the statistics that say we are doomed to repeat the patterns of the past because, contrary to popular opinion, history does not have to be repeated.

2

Restoring Your Faith in Love

THE SEVEN STEPS TO A SUCCESSFUL RELATIONSHIP

"My marriage is quite the opposite of my parents' marriage. My husband treats me with respect, trust, and consideration—and loves me for me. We have a bond just like I wanted for myself."

—*Catherine, age 39*

As a daughter of divorce, the single most important task ahead is restoring your faith in love. You might desperately want love and a lifelong commitment, but fear losing it. It's only natural to dread reencountering the same fate as your parents. As an adult, you may have come to the sudden realization that the relationship patterns you experience in your life mirror those of your parents. In the realm of romantic relationships, there is a lot to learn. The problem is that when parents divorce, they don't provide their children with healthy relationship templates to follow. But with courage and persistence, you can reject the models you were raised with and create a happy intimate relationship that endures the test of time.

Studies show that, as a daughter of divorce, you likely have a strong desire to succeed in your romantic relationships, even though the odds are stacked against you. All these statistics don't mean you're doomed to fail, but developing a mindset that makes self-awareness, insight, and learning interpersonal skills a priority is a crucial step to achieving lasting intimate relationships.

Various forms of self-defeating or dysfunctional relationship patterns might prevent you from achieving the happiness you deserve. That's why visualizing the type of relationship you want, becoming more self-aware, and discovering and adjusting ingrained beliefs and expectations are key to rebuilding your life. You can create a new story for your life, and that's exactly what we're going to show you to do in the rest of the book.

First you must admit that your attitudes toward commitment and marriage were forever changed by your parents' divorce. Then you need to learn it's OK to show weakness and allow others to nurture you. After all, the best relationships are ones born out of trust and vulnerability. The process of moving through unfinished business from the past takes courage and may cause some discomfort. But when you come to a place of healing and overcome your fear of intimate relationships failing, lasting love and commitment are yours for the taking.

SEVEN STEPS TO A SUCCESSFUL RELATIONSHIP

How can you learn to trust others and restore your faith in love when intimacy just reawakens your childhood fears? You don't have to repeat the mistakes of your parents. You have it within your ability to make healthier choices, and we'll show you exactly how to do that with our Seven Steps to a Successful

Relationship. Each of the steps was chosen as result of our interviews with over three hundred daughters of divorce and Terry's previous research studies. To show you how the book is structured and what you'll gain from each section, we'll give a quick preview now of each chapter and some of its action steps, as well as brief stories from some of the women featured in these chapters.

Step 1: Revisit your parents' divorce as an adult.

In chapter 3, we'll help you realize you don't have to define yourself by your parents' marriage or breakup. We'll also show you the many lessons you can learn from their divorce. For instance, you can break the cycle of destructive romantic relationships by picking a partner who is a good match for you or achieving a happy relationship with your current partner. We'll also give you actions steps you can start doing today that will help you assess your situation realistically and prepare for a strong future.

Victoria, a bright and engaging woman in her early fifties, is an example of someone who by all accounts was at great risk of repeating the legacy of divorce. She was on the verge of adolescence when her father had an affair and subsequently deserted her mother—staying in the same town but keeping his three daughters at arm's length. In her case, the only intact marriage she observed was her paternal grandparents'. She describes it as "a long-term, stable relationship that weathered the storms of raising three sons successfully and in which both grandparents were committed, mature, happy, and productive throughout their adult lives." Victoria's grandparents helped her visualize the type of marriage she wanted. As Victoria reflects on her own marriage, it's evident that it's quite different from her parents' and more closely resembles her grandparents' marriage: "I've always been internally motivated, went on to get a master's degree in education while raising two children. My mother was bitter after my dad left, but I didn't let that stop me (from finding love). Instead, I picked a partner who supported me and had the same family values I have. Even though we've had some tough times, we have a strong emotional tie to each other and our children. We're even looking forward to grandchildren and retirement years."

In spite of her parents' divorce and the turmoil and pain it caused, Victoria, an accomplished teacher, has been happily married for almost thirty years. She learned many valuable lessons from her parents' marriage and subsequent divorce. Victoria's risk factors for divorce were reduced by the way her grandparents modeled a stable and successful marriage and the fact that her husband was raised in an intact home. Most of all, Victoria is a resilient woman. Resiliency is the capacity to face stressors without a significant disruption in functioning. However, this doesn't imply that Victoria's marriage was smooth sailing. In fact, it has been challenged many times by her husband's serious illness, financial losses, and stressors related to Victoria's fractured relationship with her father.

On the whole, fierce determination and hard work have helped Victoria avoid the pitfalls that contribute to divorce. Victoria expressed these values when we shared a cup of coffee at a cozy café: "Compassion, mutual respect, honest communication, and a capacity for forgiveness are essential to a happy, long-term marriage."

Competent-caring Victoria pursued a rewarding career as a teacher and devoted herself to her husband and two children. While in college, she was fortunate to find a therapist and women's support group on campus where she could examine her parents' divorce. In a safe atmosphere, she was able to sort out the reasons for her parents' divorce and understand it wasn't her fault. Victoria also examined her thoughts, beliefs, and expectations about marriage—comprehending how her mother's issues with depression contributed to the problems in her parents' marriage. Before her mother's death, Victoria made peace with both of her parents. She eventually forgave her father for his limitations and has been able to maintain close ties with him.

Most importantly, Victoria never lost faith in love and marriage, and she hasn't let her parents' divorce define who she is. After dating many young men who were emotionally unavailable like her father, Victoria picked a partner who is trustworthy and with whom she can be vulnerable—asking for love and support through two decades of marriage. Her husband Rob was willing to sacrifice his own needs when she returned to graduate school in her late thirties and took on more responsibility for their children. Victoria understands that a healthy relationship doesn't drain you; instead it nourishes you and contributes to your personal growth.

Step 2: Attempt to forgive others and move on from the past by developing a forgiving mind-set.

In chapter 4, we'll show you that though you can't change the past, you can make better choices today. Through understanding and letting go of the past and any negative feelings associated with it, you can gain compassion for your parents and attempt to forgive them, which helps your own well-being. Even if you can't genuinely forgive your parents and others, it's important to try to accept what has happened in your past, and we'll guide you through how to do that.

For example, Marisa, age forty-nine, is a loving, compassionate woman who suffered through a painful childhood, a father-daughter wound, and an abusive first marriage. She's been abused, neglected, and cheated on, but she's a resilient woman who believes in forgiveness and healing. Therapy and a determined spirit have allowed her to leave an abusive relationship and to lead a well-balanced, happy, and successful life. Learning to become a more forgiving person has enabled Marisa to repair the broken pieces of her heart and restore her faith in life.

When Marisa was very young, her parents moved from New England to the West Coast because her father, who was a naval officer, was transferred. During her childhood she recalls many loud disagreements between her parents—mostly due to the fact that her mother was a substance abuser with mental health issues. Suddenly, when she was eight years old, her mother packed her and her five siblings into their station wagon, and they traveled across country without the luxury of stopping at hotels or solid meals. Marisa developed a strong yearning to be with her father because her mother was verbally abusive and struggling to support her six children. Marisa suffered from feelings of abandonment and low self-esteem. Throughout her teen years, she was permitted to visit her father in the summer months—a time when she felt happy and carefree.

With the help of a skilled therapist, Marisa was able to understand her divorce experience from an adult perspective and forgive her parents and herself. She was able to ask questions about her mother's mental health issues and put things in a better perspective. Gaining awareness about the emotions associated with her pain helped her come to terms with it. In order to make peace with her parents, she developed realistic expectations for herself and others and began to realize she couldn't change the past or other people. When Marisa began focusing on those things that she could control, such as the amount of time she spent feeling upset, she was able to accept her parents and become a more forgiving person.

Most crucially, Marisa needed to examine her thoughts, attitudes, and beliefs about relationships so that she could open up her heart and be receptive to the love and security she craved. She had a tendency to pick partners who were emotionally and physically abusive. Due to low self-esteem, she didn't feel worthy of love. Marissa had to focus on loving and nurturing herself before she could enter into a mutually rewarding and intimate relationship.

Marisa's positive intention of building healthy relationships allowed her to set personal goals and change self defeating behavior patterns. She replaced self-defeating patterns with healthy ones—a gradual process that is often beset with many setbacks. Being patient with herself during this journey of self-discovery and growth, she eventually met her husband, Dan, and has been happily married for over a decade.

Step 3: Examine your relationship with your father and attempt to repair any father-daughter wounds.

Establishing a close bond with your father may take time but is worth the effort, and in chapter 5 we'll show you how to do that. If you can't, we'll guide you through how to come to terms with the fact that you can't improve or repair your relationship with your father at this time and help you to move on. If your relationship with your mother has been negatively impacted, the action steps in this chapter can help you repair that as well.

Catherine, a professional in her late thirties, struggled through a series of unhealthy, short-term relationships and avoided commitment due to feelings of mistrust and fear of ending up like her parents. She learned a strong work ethic from her mother and is a successful attorney who is recognized as a leader in her law firm. Catherine is also a wonderful mother and devoted wife. But for several years, Catherine had difficulty believing that her husband Ethan always had her best interests at heart, which caused her to feel mistrust and anxiety at times. After all, her father was unfaithful to her mother many times. Due to her family script, she was programmed to fear abandonment and betrayal. Nonetheless, she chose a partner who accepts and understands her, and can give her the devotion and reassurance she craves. Most of all, Catherine admires Ethan and can be vulnerable with him. She compares her marriage with that of her parents, saying, "My marriage is quite the opposite of my parents' marriage. My husband treats me with respect, trust, and consideration—and loves me for me. We have a bond just like I wanted for myself. Ethan has a problem communicating his feelings at times, but we resolve our conflicts. It seemed to me that my father wouldn't ever try to resolve anything; he would run away."

Most women would have crumbled with the childhood that Catherine endured. From an early age she was subjected to her father's chronic infidelity, alcoholism, and eventual absence in her life. Rather than letting these tragic losses crush her, Catherine identified with her strong, supportive mother and set her sights on finding a partner who could be a loving husband and father. A self-reliant woman, she stopped at nothing to achieve her goals. While her attempts to reconcile with her father have been unsuccessful so far, she hasn't let it stop her from achieving a happy marriage. Currently, Catherine is living the life she has always dreamed of and has come to terms with her father-daughter wound.

Step 4: Improve your self-esteem.

In chapter 6, we'll help you get to the root of the belief that you aren't good enough. It's time to stop letting your parents' divorce—or your own—define your self-worth. You are worthy of love and the best that life has to offer, and we'll show you how to get that.

Unlike Victoria, many women struggle with their divorce histories for several years or even decades before they are able to make peace with their pasts. They are actively seeking love and intimacy, but often pick the wrong men or push suitable partners away. For some daughters of divorce, uncertainty and anxiety in intimate relationships are a recipe for disaster. Penny doubted herself and lacked the skills needed to safeguard her relationships from unraveling. She didn't have the self-confidence to choose a partner—so the wrong one chose her. Accustomed to a lack of love, and willing to settle for less than she deserved, she was drawn to narcissistic, distant, or moody men, like her ex-husband Steven.

Like many daughters of divorce, Penny was the physical and emotional caretaker of her mother and her younger half siblings when she was growing up. She grew up fast in terms of her maturity level and was super empathetic when they needed her help. A people pleaser, Penny often felt that no one was there for her when she needed support, and she had trouble asking for what she needed or setting boundaries. "I usually felt like I had to be in a good mood or positive with everyone in my family even if that wasn't how I really felt," she reflected. "I'm working hard to get over this and to not judge myself so harshly when I'm having a tough time."

People who succeed in relationships know how to treat themselves with empathy. Such a concept sounds strange. The Merriam-Webster dictionary states that empathy is the feeling that you understand and share another person's experiences and emotions. So what does treating yourself with empathy mean? It means acting as if you were your own best friend, and treating yourself with compassion, care, and concern. If your sister or your roommate or best friend came to you with a heart-wrenching relationship issue, you would hopefully respond to her with a willingness to listen, a propensity for kindness, and the instinct to say, "I understand."

Those who enjoy healthy relationships have learned from their mistakes and have treated their wounds with compassion. Just like you would say to your friend, "I've been there too" or "I know how you feel. I've gone through the same thing." What would it mean to say the same thing to yourself? Remind yourself, "Everyone goes through hard times in relationships. I'm not the only woman to have made this mistake." Instantly, you start to feel less alone. With an empathetic attitude, you start to connect to the rest of the world, as you remember that everyone has missteps. And you start to realize that the wonderful thing about judgment is that it can be improved. You might not get a second chance at your relationship, but there is still redemption for those who have made mistakes.

With the help of a skilled therapist and support group, Penny has been better able to work on boosting her self-worth and trusting her judgment in relationships. At times Penny is skeptical and doubts her ability to find lasting love. But in spite of her tendency to be cautious and guarded, she is planning a wedding with Bill, who has earned her trust and is devoted to her and Jennifer, her ten-year-old daughter. It's not easy for Penny to believe that Bill has her best intentions at heart, but she's learning to extend trust to him and not let her fear of commitment stop her from giving love a chance. She understands that her low self-esteem and trust issues come from being raised in a chaotic, divorced family in which her mother had little time to devote to her care and nurturance. Since her father was absent throughout most of her childhood, Penny hungered for his love and felt undeserving of healthy relationships until now.

During our last conversation, Penny shared her innermost

thoughts: "I still fear the collapse of my upcoming marriage to Bill will come in time. I'm not sure that I'll see it coming, but I'll do my best to stop it! Unlike myself, I want Jennifer to grow into adulthood with two parents under the same roof." Working hard at defying the statistics that say her second marriage is doomed to fail, Penny is armed with caution but also insight and a realistic perspective about the challenges of marriage.

Step 5: Build trust in your relationships.

Here we'll explain how to operate from the positive viewpoint that your partner wants the best for you and won't hurt or abandon you. In chapter 7, we'll show you how to let your partner prove, through word and deed, that he or she is trustworthy. If you don't have a partner currently, we'll help you work on extending trust to someone who demonstrates consistency in his or her words and actions.

Elizabeth, age twenty-nine, is an articulate young woman who provides a powerful example of a daughter of divorce who was deeply wounded by her father, who moved to Florida following her parents' breakup. She became engaged shortly after our first interview and contacted me (Terry) post-wedding to show me her wonderful wedding photos. Currently, Elizabeth is happily married and the proud mother of two young children. She describes her husband, Zane, as devoted and committed to loving and cherishing her and their children. There is no doubt in Elizabeth's mind that Zane is trustworthy and that she has created the kind of marriage that eluded her parents. But their marriage hasn't always been easy. At times, she worries that Zane will leave, like her father did, after they have a disagreement. Yet Zane reassures Elizabeth every time that he's in it for the long haul. He shows her through word and deed that he is trustworthy. His gentle, mature approach helps Elizabeth restore trust and love.

Elizabeth is a smart woman who worked hard at repairing her ability to trust. With the help of a therapist, Elizabeth allowed her heart to heal from the past—so that she can live in the present and enjoy the kind of loving relationship she deserves.

At age nineteen, Elizabeth had sought counseling while in the military. After being discharged, she had continued therapy sessions for several more years to deal with her severe anxiety in relationships. Ten years later, Elizabeth speaks candidly about resolving her issues with her father. She continues to love and accept him in spite of the fact that he has disappointed her throughout her life. Wise beyond her years, she reflects, "I don't blame my dad, and I don't blame myself. I think that it's better not to blame anyone. My therapist helped me realize that." After our interview, Elizabeth wrote this heartfelt letter to her father, which she forwarded to us via email:

I love you more than words can express. Though I understand the reasons you left, I can't help but hold it against you—the lack of your presence not only in mine but my children's lives. When you left, you didn't just leave the house, you left the state, putting a thousand miles between us. As a preteen, I missed the father-daughter dances. It made me feel left out, but I understood. As a teen, I needed you, your guidance, your sternness, your approval. When I graduated from high school, your face wasn't in the crowd.

Elizabeth aspires to have a very different marriage than the one she witnessed in her childhood home. She remembers family life as chaotic and riddled with conflict. Elizabeth has come to realize that her trust issues stem from her struggle with making sense of her father moving away when she was a preteen and in need of his love and attention. What she didn't realize at the time was that her father moved due to a job opportunity—not realizing the negative impact it would have on their relationship.

Elizabeth's keen understanding of her parents' divorce from an adult perspective has helped her to be realistic about love. While there are no guarantees in any relationship, she hasn't let her fear of loss destroy her relationship with Zane. Elizabeth knows the best partner is one she can be vulnerable with. When she begins to feel mistrustful, she owns it, and Zane helps to diffuse her fears by reassuring her. Keep in mind, her faith in love has been restored by degrees, and she has learned to trust Zane over time. Most importantly, Elizabeth was a mature, autonomous person before she made a commitment to Zane. Here is how she put it: "I was proposed to four times but I married 'the one' and I was in a good place when we got together. We try to talk about our problems and we have a lot of family time together. If one of us is upset with each other, we take a break. When people are upset, they say things they don't mean. People that love each other don't say things that destroy their relationship."

Elizabeth lacked positive images of how adult men and women can live together in a stable relationship, which made her more prone to see divorce as an option. However, she chooses to trust that Zane has her best interests at heart and won't abandon her like she felt her father did when he moved out of state after her parents' divorce. While marriage isn't desirable for everyone, Elizabeth is a "nester" who craves the love and security of marriage. Over the past decade, Elizabeth has worked through many of her trust issues and selected Zane, who has shown her through his actions that he is a trustworthy partner. While their marriage is a work in progress, they possess the essentials of a successful partnership and are committed to defying the statistics that say their marriage is doomed to fail.

Step 6: Practice being vulnerable with your partner in small steps.

In chapter 8, we'll help you develop a positive interdependence with your partner and rein in your self-reliance with others, a crucial step to forging strong relationships (both romantic and platonic). We'll help you learn to allow your partner to come through for you. While self-reliance is one of your strengths, it can rob you of true intimacy. Opening up to your partner can make you feel vulnerable and exposed, but it is the most important ingredient of a trusting, intimate relationship.

Rachel fits the description of a competent-opportunist who learned from an early age that she could rely only on herself. Her early experience of being deserted by both her biological father and stepfather left her feeling mistrustful of men and their intentions. For good reason, Rachel admired her mother and felt loved by her but lost respect for her due to her decisions regarding intimate partners. It makes sense that Rachel would feel anxiety about the future of her romantic relationships. After all, she adored her stepfather as a young girl and he betrayed her mother several times over—leaving their family destitute in Las Vegas, where they were without vital support, after his business venture fell through.

When asked about the impact of her parents' divorce and the breakup of her mother's second marriage, she paused, saying, "I believe it has caused me to feel anxious, depressed, and to have a sense of emptiness in my life. I'm also upset that my mother could never really take care of herself even though she claimed to be so independent." But in spite of her ambivalence about commitment and marriage, Rachel accepted her boyfriend Nick's proposal recently and they are making plans for their future together.

Now that Rachel is beginning the journey into adulthood, she places a high value on independence and is terrified of relying on someone else to take care of her needs. A thoughtful young woman, Rachel realizes that being self-reliant can have both negative and positive aspects. She reflects upon how she craves intimacy yet feels fearful of letting go of control: "I've learned to be independent and I thank my mother for that. She went through some extremely difficult times in her life. If somebody wrote a book about her, it would probably be a bestseller." Rachel has a keen sense of where she's come from and grati-tude for the opportunities she's had. She appreciates that having a successful career and a loving fiancé isn't something she can take for granted. Rachel reminisces about her life so far: "There are positives and negatives in the story of my life, and I am still trying to determine who I am. I struggle with feelings of extreme anxiety and inferiority daily, and these feelings seem to conquer me. However, there are more positive outcomes than negatives. Although I don't have a perfect life, these experiences have made me a stronger person."

Being self-reliant, tough, or appearing unbreakable can stem from low self-esteem or feelings of shame—the intensely painful belief that you are flawed or unworthy of love and acceptance. It takes courage to risk being vulnerable, but it will transform your relationship with your partner or help you select a mate who is a good match for you. Brown writes: "Shame resilience is key to embracing our vulnerability. We can't let ourselves be seen if we're terrified by what people might think. Often 'not being good at vulnerability' means that we're damn good at shame."

Step 7: Make the commitment.

Here we will teach you how to examine your attitudes and beliefs about love, marriage, and commitment and overcome your fear of them. A healthy respect for commitment will enhance your ability to build love, trust, and intimacy. In chapter 9, we'll show you how to make choices that feel right for you and aren't dictated by others' behaviors or by your own fear of failure in committed relationships. If you are single, there are many things you can do to prepare for a stronger future, and we'll walk you through these. If you are in a committed relationship or married to a suitable partner, moving to a deeper level of intimacy is within your reach and will enhance your life, and we'll walk you through achieving that!

Let's end with the wise words of Bailey, twenty-three, a college student studying architecture and one of the youngest women in our study. Her parents divorced when she was seventeen—just as she was getting ready to start college in a nearby state. She tends to be somewhat guarded when she first meets someone new and approaches love with caution, but still strives to build a lasting relationship built on mutual interests and respect. Bailey doesn't want to lose herself in a relationship and strives to maintain plans for her future and strong friendships. She says, "I have a lot of friends who I'm close to and plenty of hobbies and interests. I'd want to make sure that anyone I live with or marry gets along with my friends and is at least open to sharing my passion for most sports—but especially tennis and skiing."

Overall, Bailey is optimistic about her future as an architect and sees herself moving toward professional success and relationship fulfillment. She doesn't see her sense of caution as a disadvantage. Instead, she views it as an important step toward finding the right partner. Bailey rests her hands on her lap and explains:

> *I learned that opposites attract, but it doesn't usually work out. Also, that communication and compromise are absolutely crucial. If either person lacks the ability to do either one, the relationship is extremely unlikely to last. I think everyone should have concerns (about divorce) based on the statistics of how many marriages actually work out, but I believe I have a good chance of working at a relationship enough so it lasts, as long as I find someone who feels the same way and can hold up their end of the deal.*

CHEMISTRY AND COMPATIBILITY

Both chemistry and compatibility are essential aspects of a successful romantic relationship. Bailey's parents had good chemistry, but they weren't compatible because they didn't share common values, life goals, and interests. They also had poor communication and were unable to heal from repeated arguments that left them both feeling chronically resentful and disappointed. Over time, these differences caused rifts between them and they began to live separate lives—lacking a solid friendship and a shared purpose in their marriage. Both chemistry and compatibility are crucial ingredients to a happy, long-lasting, intimate relationship and it's possible to have both!

To her credit, Bailey has taken the time to explore her own passions and interests and looks forward to sharing them with a partner who shares her values and respects her individuality. She's examined her parents' marriage as an adult and isn't likely to repeat their communication patterns because she's insightful and has set clear goals for herself. The benefits of not rushing into a romantic relationship have paid off for Bailey because she has a strong sense of herself and strives to venture into romantic relationships with her eyes wide open.

While love and commitment shouldn't be taken lightly, Bailey is a perceptive young woman who has a healthy respect for both. She is doing her best to avoid the pitfalls that will increase the probability of her relationships failing or ending in divorce. Although a happy, long-lasting marriage eluded her parents, she has tremendous hope that she can have a successful one. Bailey's divorce experience has made her stronger, more realistic, and better prepared for the requirements of love. She is taking the necessary time to develop her career and fine-tune her expectations for the kind of partner who will be a good match for her.

Marriage isn't necessarily for everyone, and many people reject the notion of it these days. However, it can bring love and security to those willing to withstand the inevitable hard times. Whether you choose to marry or not, you have it within your reach to create loving relationships and to achieve personal happiness. Keep in mind it's never too late to restore your faith in love. Now let's get started!

A Word from Terry: A Mother's Perspective

For me, restoring my faith in love is a daily decision to operate from the viewpoint that my partner wants the best for me and has my best interests at heart. As I mentioned in the introduction, I'm a "nester" who desires the security of commitment, marriage, and a family. But I've always marveled at women who had confidence in their partners, while I've been plagued with self-doubt and mistrust. At times, I'm simply not good at figuring out how much of my mistrust is based on reality and how much is a figment of my imagination. Exploring my past has helped me to see that growing up in a fractured home didn't leave me with healthy beliefs or expectations about intimate relationships.

Many of my painful feelings about love and security were deeply embedded in my childhood and needed to be examined before I could become a more loving, trusting partner. I've learned that my security has to come from within—rather than from financial means or my partner's assurances. Put simply, I need to trust myself in order to let my partner come through for me. Through this process of self-discovery, I'm hoping that my daughters will learn the value of interdependence. While I struggle with overcoming my past at times, I'm on the journey and my new life is brimming with exciting possibilities for restoring my faith in love.

A Word from Tracy: A Daughter's Perspective

Having the confidence to choose the right partner is one of the biggest challenges women face. Penny's story reminds me this is an ongoing process. When she was young, she married a man who brought out her weaknesses. He seemingly preyed on her low self-esteem and made her feel unworthy and insecure. Clearly, in this relationship, she wasn't her best self. But love, true, healthy love, demands our best.

For me, restoring my faith in love has meant working through painful memories of the past and choosing to not let them define me. Like many women, I've endured relationships that soon turned into nightmares, rife with tears, tensions, anxiety, and a longing to be heard. Although I'm still young, some of the most painful times in my life have been when I was with a partner who was all wrong for me. A bad relationship can amplify all that is wrong with your life, making it feel as if there is a hole in your heart that can never be filled. In a good relationship, any vulnerability you have suddenly doesn't seem as important. Your partner's strengths complement your weaknesses and make you believe in a limitless future.

3

Step One:

Revisiting Your Parents' Divorce as an Adult

....

"Truth allows us to reconcile disparate voices in our heads, and it helps us heal the breach in our hearts. Acceptance of the past allows us to untangle hidden loyalties to a parent whom we rejected or who we feel rejected us, and forgiveness allows us to repair our ability to love."

—*Mary Hirschfeld, JD, PhD*

....

The first step in healing is to understand your experience with your parents' divorce from an adult viewpoint. Thus, before you read any further, we highly recommend you complete the following survey. The questions you will be answering are the same ones given to the women who participated in our research study, and they are designed to promote self-awareness and insight about your parents' divorce. Filling out this survey may take more time and thought than meets the eye, but it's worth the effort. In fact, some of your thoughts and feelings may have been buried for some time, and answering the questions may surprise you. If this is the case, discussing your reactions with a trusted friend or therapist may be a good way to help you to process them.

Step 1 will set the stage for seeking advice on how to overcome your parents' divorce. Whether you talk to your parents, a relative, a close friend, or a therapist as you work through this may depend on your situation. While therapy isn't essential to healing from your parents' divorce, many daughters of divorce find it to be highly beneficial as a way to express their feelings in a safe environment and to heal from emotional pain and loss. You may ask: Why do I have to revisit my parents' breakup? They have been divorced for many years and their marriage was a nightmare—why do I have to go back in time? However, if you are struggling with your current or past romantic relationships, this is a necessary step to healing and developing a better understanding of how your parents' split has impacted your choice in partners. There is always hope that you can learn to trust again.

Note: In order to make the most out of Step 1 and subsequent steps in this book, keeping a journal is essential. It will help you document your reflections and map your process of healing from your parents' divorce.

INTERVIEW QUESTIONS

Please answer the following questions to the best of your ability, providing as much information as you can recall. If you need more space, feel free to jot down your answers on a separate sheet of paper or in a journal, as we recommend. Try to be as honest and candid as possible, even if it's painful to recall. The more truthful you are with yourself now, the more likely this exercise will help you to form healthy relationships in the long run. As you read this book and the suggestions at the end of each chapter, you may find that your answers will change and you may want to go back and edit them.

1. What is your first memory of your parents' divorce?_____
   _____
   _____

2. What is your understanding of why your parents got a divorce?
   _____
   _____

3. How did your life change as a result of your parents' divorce?
   _____
   _____

4. How did your parents' divorce affect you as a child or adolescent? As a young adult?_____
   _____
   _____

5. Did you ever attend a court proceeding about your parents' divorce as a child, adolescent, or young adult? If yes, please describe it._____
   _____
   _____

6. As a child or adolescent, did you feel that your parents' divorce was your mother's or father's fault or both?_____
   _____

7. As a child or adolescent, did you receive counseling or attend a support group?_____
   _____

8. What impact does your parents' divorce have on you as an adult?
   _____
   _____

9. How would you describe your dating history (duration of relationships, number of partners, quality, etc.)?_____

_____

_____

10. How has having divorced parents affected your adult romantic relationships?_____

_____

_____

11. What lessons did you learn about marriage from your parents' marriage?_____

_____

_____

12. What lessons did you learn from your grandparents' marriage, if any?_____

_____

_____

13. Did either of your parents remarry? If so, how many times?

_____

_____

_____

14. If you had one or more stepparents, please describe your relationship with them. Be specific._____

_____

_____

_____

15. If you had one or more stepsiblings or half siblings, describe your relationship with them. Be specific._____

_____

_____

_____

16. If you are married, or plan to marry, do you strive to make your marriage different from your parents' marriage? If yes, please explain._____

_____

_____

17. What is the most difficult part of a dating or intimate relationship for you (trust, communication, etc.)?_____

_____

18. Do you ever fear that people you love will leave and that you won't see them again? If yes, please describe this feeling for you._____

_____

_____

19. Do you have any concerns about your ability to have a happy marriage, now or in the future? If yes, please describe._____

_____

_____

20. If you are currently in an intimate relationship, would you describe this relationship as happy or unhappy? Why?_____

_____

_____

21. If you are separated or divorced, how old were you when you married and what were the reasons why you separated or divorced?_____

_____

_____

22. Do you believe you choose unsuitable partners or reject available ones? If yes, please describe (abusive, unavailable, etc.)._____

_____

_____

23. If you are currently single and avoid commitment, please describe the ways in which you avoid commitment in relationships and why._____

_____

_____

24. If you are married or in a committed relationship, but have avoided commitment in the past, please explain how and why.

_____

_____

25. Do you feel that your life would have turned out better or worse if your parents had stayed together? Please explain how and why._____

_____

_____

26. Is there any other information you would like to share about your parents' divorce or the impact that it has had upon your life into adulthood?_____

_____

_____

Many of these questions were adapted from Elisabeth Joy LaMotte's survey in Overcoming Your Parents' Divorce: 5 Steps to a Happy Relationship.

Now that you're done, take stock of how you feel. Was it a relief to get this all out on paper? Did it stir up feelings of anger or fear or sadness? Did answering these questions help you recall something you'd forgotten or see your parents' divorce in a different light? Whatever your reaction, we hope that taking the survey was a meaningful experience, and we congratulate you on taking the first step toward healing yourself and your relationships.

As we noted earlier, it's common for daughters of divorce to bury their emotions about challenging events from the past as a way to cope with them. If taking the survey elicited strong feelings regarding your parents' divorce, don't worry; that is completely normal. However, we can't stress enough how important it is to be honest and open about those feelings. If you've repressed important facts from your past, it can lead to distorted thinking and hinder the healing process. That's why it's also important to discuss your survey with one or both of your parents (if they are available or willing to), and perhaps someone you trust, such as a family member, close friend, or therapist. This is your golden opportunity to question your parents—or possibly a sibling if your parents aren't available or willing—and clear up anything about their divorce that may be bothering you or that you can't remember. Getting these answers down on paper and sharing your experiences and feelings with them is the first step to letting go of the past, so you can heal. Remember, even if your search meets with resistance from others or makes them uncomfortable, you are worth the effort.

Another purpose of this exercise is to help you gain some perspective on your parents' decisions and actions. One of the most essential steps in healing from your parents' divorce is to develop expectations of them that are similar to those you would have for other people. For instance, you might be more objective or forgiving if you learned one of your friend's parents remarried someone with children of their own than you would be if your mother or father did that. Author Jeffrey Zimmerman, PhD, writes: "By recognizing your parents' humanity you can set your expectations of them in a manner that is more akin to their actual strengths and weaknesses."

In the end, by examining your parents' divorce from an adult perspective, you can gain a more realistic view of it. It will allow you to let go of anger and blame and learn to forgive yourself and others. Throughout this book, we'll help you realize you don't have to define yourself by your parents' marriage or breakup. We'll also show you the many lessons you can learn from their divorce, including how to break the cycle of destructive romantic relationships by picking a partner who is a good match for you, or how to achieve a happy relationship with your current partner. And that all starts with the exercises you're doing in this chapter.

> At times, therapy or a women's group can be a tremendous support to you in your efforts to heal the past and make healthy relationship choices in the present. Getting a better handle on the past will allow you to follow the remainder of the seven steps and move forward with your life. We wish you all of the happiness you deserve.

Now that you've completed the survey, try some of the following action steps, which will help you assess your situation objectively and prepare you for a strong future. Regardless of whether you're single or in a relationship, you can start doing them today.

ACTION STEPS

* **Gain awareness of your own history—dating back to childhood.** If you are able to, ask each of your parents the reasons why they divorced. Even if you think you know

55

their reasons, hearing their separate perspectives and discussing it with them as an adult may shed new light on their breakup. If you don't feel comfortable doing this or don't have access to both of your parents, attempt to ask this question of a grandparent, aunt, uncle, or trusted family friend who may have an objective view of the situation. Feel free to use the questions from the survey in this chapter to help facilitate this process. Obtaining information and feedback from your parents or others can aid your healing

* **Acknowledge any damage done by your parents, but shift to a perspective that's focused on understanding and healing rather than blame.** Ask yourself: Can I practice forgiving my parents even if I don't condone their actions? This viewpoint will allow you to feel more empathetic toward them. It will also empower you to turn any wounds into wisdom and difficulties into opportunities for personal growth.

* **Take responsibility for your actions and work toward letting go of any anger and resentment you may have toward your parents or stepparents.** Ask yourself: What is the reason for holding on to any negative emotions? What purpose do they serve? Find a way to forgive and dislodge yourself from resentment by letting go of lingering hurts and slights. Writing your feelings in a journal can allow you to release negative emotions, give you a space to write down things you are grateful for, and help you keep track of your goals.

* **Forgive yourself and your parents for any mistakes made in the past.** Ask yourself: How does living in the past help me to thrive in the present? Forgiveness is a conscious

decision that takes intention and effort. It's not something we do for other people. We do it for ourselves to heal and move forward with our lives. It takes time and patience. (You'll learn more about practicing forgiveness in chapter 4.)

※ **Focus on the things you can control, such as your own perspective and actions toward others.** Developing a growth mind-set will allow you to adopt the belief that, with effort, you can change and improve and reach your personal goals. Having a fixed mind-set just perpetuates the idea that you are a victim. Or, as Winston Churchill said, "A pessimist sees the difficulty in every opportunity; an optimist sees the opportunity in every difficulty."

※ **Discuss your survey results with your partner if you are in a relationship.** Even if it feels difficult to be vulnerable, it is important to share your journey with him or her. Not only will this give your partner crucial insight into who you are and your responses to different situations, but it may also help you both communicate better as you'll each understand where the other is coming from. Try to engage your partner in a dialogue about how you can mutually work toward a fulfilling relationship that will support both of your objectives.

※ **Write a new narrative or story for your life that outlines what you would like to achieve.** It should be one that includes taking your time to pick a partner who is trustworthy and willing to work on a creating a healthy, committed relationship together through good times and bad. As you do this, make sure you aren't comparing your intimate relationships to your parents' and simply saying that you want the opposite of what they had. If you are, stop and separate it from your own goals. Focus on what *you* want, not what you've experienced or seen fail in the past. Attempt to see yourself as learning from the past rather than repeating it.

A Word from Terry: A Mother's Perspective

Writing this chapter with Tracy was a meaningful experience, and it brought back a multitude of memories for me. Shortly after I wrote it, I made a trip from my home on the East Coast to the West Coast, where I was raised. Sitting on the porch of my older sister's ranch-style house, sipping iced tea and lemon in the hot summer sun, I had truly healed from my parents' divorce some fifty years previously.

With the support of two of my sisters, I realized that I was not alone and could find acceptance. As I interviewed them, they asked me questions in return. And even though we had drastically different takes on our parents' divorce, we all struggled to find love, trust, and intimacy in our relationships. My sisters' tenderness and heartfelt stories filled me with love and hope for a bright future. After all this time, I came to understand how we had each come to terms with our childhood in our own way and saw that it wasn't too late to strengthen our bond as sisters—even across thousands of miles.

· · · · · · · · · ·

A Word from Tracy: A Daughter's Perspective

When my mother asked me to write this chapter with her, I wasn't prepared. I wondered what I, as a writer, had to contribute. After all, she's the one who works as a therapist and researcher! But in her usual way, she nudged me to come up with action steps, and I grudgingly agreed. Then as time wore on, I realized that I had something to offer as a daughter of divorce: my experience and insights.

My mother and I hope that filling out this survey helps you get in touch with lost memories and feelings about your parents' divorce. That's what happened to me and the countless women I interviewed with my mother. As the women we met with shared their stories, I could see some of myself in each one of them and realized that none of us is truly alone. Now let's get started on the journey of restoring our faith in love!

4

Step Two:

Face Your Ghosts from the Past

"I have a lot of issues that I feel stem from or were exacerbated by my parents' divorce. I really didn't know how to have a healthy relationship with a man. I either pick the wrong one to fall for or push the good ones away out of fear of rejection. I never got to see or observe my parents getting along with each other or another partner. What goes on in a household with two parents who are partners? How do they interact daily and solve problems together?"

—Emily, age 32

When I (Terry) began the research for this book, I embarked upon a long journey that took me somewhere I never intended to go—into the hearts and minds of women who are a lot like me. Since I had carried around baggage from my parents' divorce for decades, I became passionate about helping other women overcome the legacy of divorce. I believe that it's never too late to mend from past wounds and enjoy healthier intimate relationships, and I want to show you how to do this. At first, my goal was to understand the epidemic of divorce and to figure out how to help women get past the pain of their parents' breakup. What I didn't realize until recently was that, in the process of growing up and trying to survive, I had built a wall around myself. Competent-at-a-cost, I took pride in my ability to deal with crisis and adjust to new situations, but I also lived with self-doubt, fractured trust, pessimism about love, and brokenhearted self-reliance. No matter how hard I tried, I couldn't hide from my past.

Only recently have I come to terms with the fact that, at age twenty-three, I married too young and picked a partner who was utterly wrong for me. My first husband gave me financial security but was unable to give me the intimacy I craved and needed to survive in the marriage. For reasons that are clearer to me now, I fully participated in a relationship that was doomed from the start. Like many daughters of divorce, I found it simpler to ignore my feelings of uneasiness and red flags because I desperately wanted love and was unconsciously hoping my ex-husband would help me to exorcise ghosts of my past.

I've come to learn that sweeping things under the rug and hoping nobody will discover them never works. Yet it wasn't until I cracked through the surface of my own past that I realized my view of life and particularly my concepts of love and marriage were forever altered by my parents' divorce some fifty years ago.

Two years after my divorce, in 1997, my need to love again surfaced and clashed with my feelings of hopelessness and despair. The way I resolved this conflict was to reach out and get support from friends, family, and a divorce support group. After a while, I began the process of healing and was fortunate to meet my husband, Craig, who had experienced divorce in his thirties and was eager to get remarried. Craig and I found we had the same hopes, desires, and hesitations. After many intense late-night discussions, we decided to give love a chance and were married in a beautiful Victorian church with my two children, friends, and family there to cheer us on. Less than two years later, our beautiful daughter Catherine was born. During the past eighteen years, I've discovered that creating a stepfamily is an opportunity to learn more about myself and to stretch my ability to love. During this process, my self-confidence has improved and my expectations of marriage are more realistic. Most of all, I can be truly vulnerable with Craig, and we are committed to making our marriage work.

Honestly, I didn't remember the details of my parents' breakup for nearly fifteen years, until I was in college. Like most adolescent daughters of divorce, I was preoccupied with living between my parents' two worlds and struggling with my own identity crisis. But as I got older, the prospect of intimacy, dating, commitment, and even marriage sent me into a tailspin. Fortunately, a skilled therapist was able to help me put my childhood into perspective. But understanding how my past affected my choice in intimate partners and relationships was a longer, more in-depth process, and I am still on that journey.

My hope is that by reading this book, you will examine your ghosts from the past, gain insight, and avoid unnecessary pain. And that's exactly what we'll cover in this chapter. I firmly believe that you can't heal from the pain of your parents' breakup until you work through the intense emotions associated with it. Rather than cutting yourself off from your feelings, you need to confront them directly. While you can't change the past, you can gain a new perspective and outlook on love and relationships.

Over the past several years, I interviewed dozens of women who, like me, were unable to unlock the pain related to their parents' split for decades. Many of the women I interviewed talked about having a delayed reaction to the powerful impact of their parents' divorce during young adulthood. A lot of them recounted details of their parents' divorce as if it occurred yesterday; they were still freshly reenacting that pain from their past. Often those women ended up repeating patterns from the past.

WHEN GHOSTS FROM THE PAST ARE RESURRECTED

When I first read Wallerstein's popular book *Second Chances* in 1994, I remember feeling frustrated and skeptical. Like other therapists and researchers, my assumption was that the pain of parental divorce dissolves after a few years. My training in psychology led me to believe that most children are resilient, deal with loss relatively quickly, and rarely look back—especially if parents are well-meaning, cooperative, and tuned in to divorce-related issues. However, my assumptions were challenged both by the publication of Wallerstein's book *The Unexpected Legacy of Divorce* and, around the same time, my young adult daughter's experience of a delayed reaction to my divorce, which had occurred when she was eight years old. As a young adult, Tracy had hit a wall in relationships, experiencing the "sleeper effect" described in Wallerstein's book. While Tracy's transition into womanhood was marked by many successes, including graduating from college, she began to doubt herself and was apprehensive about love and commitment as she attempted to create adult relationships of her own.

Meanwhile, while shopping for used books at my local library, I picked up a copy of Mary Pipher's book *Reviving Ophelia: Saving the Selves of Adolescent Girls*, and I felt as if I were struck by a lightning bolt. I realized that psychologists and therapists alike had been ignoring adolescent girls all along and that they really do slowly bury their authentic selves as they enter adolescence. According to Pipher, "Girls become female impersonators who fit their whole selves into small crowded spaces. Vibrant, confident girls become shy, doubting young woman. Girls stop thinking, 'Who am I? What do I want?' and start thinking, 'What must I do to please others?'"

While in the midst of my own crisis as a mother trying to help my daughter, it hit me that many girls seem to breeze through their parents' breakup during childhood, but that doesn't mean they've successfully overcome this painful experience years later. Often we submissively accept our parents' divorce, due to our tendency, as women, to repress unpleasant feelings. As a result, we may suffer from a stormy adolescence or young adulthood when our issues begin to emerge. As Tracy discusses in the preface, many young women begin doubting themselves and losing faith in love and commitment when they are young adults. Many parents and therapists underestimate the powerful effects of a disrupted family on the social and emotional development of girls. We minimize the pressure and expectations they feel as they try to distance themselves from their parents—especially their moms—at a time when their sense of trust, love, and security is fractured.

Why do we find gender differences in the reaction of adults to their parents' divorce? In her landmark book, *In a Different Voice*, renowned researcher Carol Gilligan posits that females value emotional connection more than males for personal growth because of their socialization. Girls begin to foster their relationships early on by being empathetic and verbally expressive. However, girls also learn that the expression of anger is often met with social disapproval and that mothers are generally more accepting of their sons' anger—while ignoring or advising their daughters to inhibit negative emotions such as anger or sadness.

I've come to realize that girls begin to hide their feelings at a young age because they believe they'll be perceived negatively by others. Often they learn to mask certain emotions, such as anger or fear, because they are criticized or described by others as overly emotional. Raised to be "good girls," many girls and young women then become adept at concealing their negative emotions to preserve their relationships. This would explain why so many daughters of divorce may appear fine on the outside while feeling emotionally upset or depleted on the inside.

Studies show that girls have a tendency to undervalue their strengths—such as enhanced verbal ability and emotional attunement. Compared to boys, girls have better developed vocabularies, greater word fluencies, and superior reading abilities, but they may not realize that these are advantages. So they might bury their true thoughts and feelings about stressful events—such as their parents' divorce—but hold on to the memories longer than boys do.

In *The Female Brain*, Louann Brizendine, MD, explains that females store more emotional memories and have a stronger reaction to emotional and stressful events than males do. She writes, "Part of the reason that her memory is better for emotional details is that a women's amygdala is more easily activated by emotional nuance. The stronger the amygdala response to a stressful situation, such as an accident or threat, or a pleasant event, such as a romantic dinner, the more details the hippocampus will tag for memory storage about the experience."

Brizendine concludes that because women have a relatively larger hippocampus, they have better memories for both pleasant and unpleasant experiences—including details surrounding an event—leaving them with a fairly precise, three-dimensional, sensory snapshot of experiences such as family disharmony or breakup.

For daughters of divorce, a delayed reaction or sleeper effect is often triggered by the activation of certain catalysts—such as new romantic feelings for someone—during late adolescence or adulthood. The familiarity of certain situations may cause old issues from earlier relationships or memories of her parents' divorce to surface. In fact, she may find herself inadvertently reverting back to her childhood reactions in some respects, such as avoiding conflict by shutting down or fleeing a situation that triggers a fear of being left behind.

Pipher reminds us, "Adolescence is such an intense time of change. All kinds of development—physical, emotional, intellectual, academic, social, and spiritual—are happening at once. Adolescence is the most formative time in the lives of women. Girls are making choices that will preserve their true selves or install false selves. These choices will have many implications for the rest of their lives." Just as daughters of divorce are grappling with their complicated relationship with their mothers—filled with love, longing, and both closeness and distance—they have the added stress of dealing with living in a divided home. Meanwhile, they are questioning where they stand with the first men in their lives—their fathers who may be distant, absent, or preoccupied with their new lives.

Like many daughters of divorce, you might find that your parents' breakup has had a powerful impact on your adult relationships. For instance, if you avoid memories of your parents' divorce, you might blame yourself, or project inaccurate feelings or intentions onto your current partner, such as fearing that your partner is cheating when he or she is simply running late. Or you might be burdened with thoughts of losing out on love and respond by clinging to your mate or refusing to become attached. If you don't take the time to face your ghosts from the past, you might be vulnerable to playing out the pain and hurt you experienced in your childhood home.

REPEATING PATTERNS OF THE PAST

Penny barely remembers her parents' divorce when she was three years old, but acknowledges she had a delayed reaction, reenacting the pain of her parents' breakup in adult relationships. As a young child she was a good-natured people pleaser who vividly describes witnessing her mother being preoccupied with trying to make her second marriage work. Her father has been married three times and has been absent for most of her life. Penny has a clear memory of her adolescence as a time of turmoil and inner conflict when she felt like an outsider in her own home. Pausing between her words, she described a particularly painful experience: "As an adolescent, I think that it hit me the hardest, that's when my mother had just borne my two stepsisters to my stepfather. Both parents (mom and stepdad) whom I lived with basically never 'got' me, and unconsciously treated me as a third wheel. I remember the time they took us all to Sears for Christmas photos. They displayed Sophie's and Ana's on either side of their beds and sent mine to my grandmother. The pain of that realization stayed with me for years."

Penny worked hard to please her mother and stepfather but rarely saw her father when she was growing up. "As an adolescent, mainly when I was sixteen—on my sixteenth birthday—I saw my biological father and he admitted that the divorce was his fault," she says. "My mother always told me that my dad was a skirt chaser. He was the love of her life and that kind of traumatized her. However, my mom's jealous tantrums didn't help the matter much." Like many daughters of divorce, Penny felt she didn't have permission from herself or her parents to grieve at their breakup, so she became every parent's dream of the ideal daughter—smart, pretty, and responsible. No one in her family predicted the stormy young adulthood that lay ahead.

At age eighteen, Penny made a bold attempt at self-reliance and moved to New York City from a small town in Rhode Island. Living with her maternal grandmother at first and attending a large inner-city college, Penny became obsessed with the notion that neither of her parents had shown much concern for her growing up. Going to extremes, she cut off all contact with her parents for several years. Attempting to leave her former identity as a perfect daughter behind, she found herself attracted to troubled, distant, and moody men. Accustomed to a lack of love, and willing to settle for less than she deserved, Penny was drawn to men with problems. By becoming enmeshed in their issues, she achieved a false sense of control—and avoided focusing on her responsibility to herself.

Penny's story can be understood through Sigmund Freud's theory of repetition compulsion, the tendency to repeat traumas or patterns from the past as a way to gain mastery over them. Freud (1856–1939) was the founding father of psychoanalysis, a theory which explains human behavior. He believed the unconscious mind governs behavior to a greater degree than the conscious mind. According to psychoanalytic theory, some daughters of divorce tend to pick adult partners whose behaviors resemble their fathers' when they were growing up, without conscious awareness. When Penny met her first husband, Steven, she was filled with self-doubt and lacked the confidence to choose a partner who was right for her. Penny wasn't aware at the time that she was repeating a relationship pattern she observed in her parents' marriage. With strong emotion in her voice, Penny describes her struggle to hold her marriage together and to retain her sense of self-worth:

I had a fragile sense of myself, a lower sense of myself as a child and teenager. I never had the guts to choose a boyfriend—so he chose me. I was never good enough for Steven. He was charming, handsome, the life of the party. He treated everyone great but me. From the beginning, I questioned why a nice-looking guy like him would want to be with me. I was twenty and I never thought that he would be interested in me because my self-esteem hit rock bottom. At the time, I was gorgeous and slim, but I didn't feel beautiful. It was a rocky five-year marriage. After I got pregnant with our daughter, Jennifer, things got worse and he was gone for long periods of time. When he was around, he put me down a lot and directed a lot of his insecurities toward me.

In love with the idea of marriage and looking for the nurturing and intimacy she lacked as a child, Penny committed herself to someone who bore a strong likeness to her emotionally distant, unfaithful, and selfish father. "My dad is a musician and his pattern was to marry (three times) and be happy at first. Then he went out to play the guitar, and he didn't come home for several weeks. As I said earlier, he wasn't a family man and should never have gotten married," she says.

Like her mother, Penny was self-sacrificing and married someone who was her opposite—self-absorbed and unwilling to make a commitment to work on their marriage. Ignoring the signals and cues given off early in the relationship, she was primed to re-create the patterns of the past. "The sleeper effect is particularly dangerous because it occurs at a crucial time when many young women make decisions that have long-term implications for their lives," explains Wallerstein.

Eventually, competent-caring Penny found a good therapist and is working on her self-esteem, as well as her tendency to get stuck in the approval trap. Her efforts have already paid off: she is now engaged to Bill, who appears truly committed to their relationship and the opportunity of being a stepfather to Jennifer, a vivacious ten-year-old. Taking things slowly, Penny and Bill are hopeful that their relationship will endure the test of time. As Penny has become more conscious of the filters of past relationships through which she views current ones, she has learned how to accept and love herself, and forgive others.

This is a critical aspect of achieving success at incorporating Step 2 into your life—forgiving others and moving on from the past. Despite Penny's signature strengths—being a gourmet cook, artist, and great mother—it has taken time and plenty of work for her to deal with the ghosts from her past that tell her relationships are doomed to fail. Like many daughters from disrupted homes, she was stuck in the approval trap until she gave herself permission to heal, set boundaries, and break away from the patterns of the past. (You will read more about Penny's quest to gain self-worth at the end of chapter 6.)

FEAR OF FAILURE IN RELATIONSHIPS

Emily from chapter 1 is a loving and capable woman who has struggled with feelings of loneliness and low self-worth through-out her life. To this day, she doesn't quite understand why her father left when she was six years old since it was her fourteen-year-old sister who broke the news to her. "I remember a vacation that never happened, helping my dad pack, and him driving off in his red Renault," she says. For many years she spent weekends with her father and younger brother, trying to distance herself from her mother, until she had an argument with her father over something silly when she was fifteen. For several years, Emily was estranged from her father and had a stormy relationship with her mother, who began abusing alcohol during the divorce. As an adolescent, Emily remembers going to extremes and resenting both of her parents—her dad for leaving and her mother for not giving her nurturance. Emily became rebellious toward both of her parents and the visitation schedule they set up for her when she was a child. These feelings aren't uncommon for many adolescents who may have been compliant as a child but now want to assert their autonomy. Here is how Emily put it:

I was mad at my dad and wanted to piss him off. He wasn't there
for me so I decided to do whatever I wanted. I even skipped school

because good grades were important to him. I was the quiet kid that sat in the back of the room and then one day I just let it all go. I was irresponsible as an older teenager and did a lot of partying. Then at age twenty, my sole focus was to meet someone because I didn't want to be alone. I met Justin and thought that we would be a great match. Since his mom had left (and my dad left), I believed we would complement each other. I wanted to be the opposite of my mom and showed him complete trust, but it totally backfired.

Emily's story provides another example of the sleeper effect. Like Penny, Emily appeared to be the ideal daughter—self-reliant, studious, and compliant. She had a strong craving for security after her father left, but her mother was unable to give her the support she needed. As a child, Emily appeared confident and secure—until anxiety surfaced later on when the task of finding a mate triggered a fear of rejection and betrayal.

Emily's parents' divorce left her with a deep-seated sense of anxiety about relationships that haunts her to this day. Competent-at-a-cost, she is a devoted mother and preschool teacher, but she is afraid she'll get involved with the wrong man and be duped again. Emily answered my questions easily and directly, reflecting on a ten-year relationship with Justin that was doomed from the start: "We only knew each other for a few months when we moved in together. I had a child with him and I tried to make it work. Then all of a sudden, he revealed who he really was—he was a cheater and he started to do drugs." Because Emily grew up with an emotionally unavailable father, she assumed that's how it should be with all men. She expected to lose and had become accustomed to it.

The fear of loss and betrayal Emily felt is characteristic of many daughters of divorce who feel abandoned by both parents. In fact, children not only identify with both parents as separate individuals, but with the relationship between them. In Emily's case, her parents divorced when she was so young, at age six, that she didn't have a template for healthy intimacy. It isn't uncommon for young women with her background to stay in relationships too long, unable to break away due to fear of rejection or being alone. Some women like Emily who fall in love quickly are convinced they've found their soul mate after only a few short weeks, ignoring red flags. Emily says, "I have a lot of issues that I feel stem from or were exacerbated by my parents' divorce. I really don't know how to have a healthy relationship with a man. I either pick the wrong one to fall for or push the good ones away out of fear of rejection. I never got to see or observe my parents getting along with each other or another partner. What goes on in a household with two parents who are partners? How do they interact daily and solve problems together?"

Self-doubt and anxiety can be particularly strong for girls who, like Emily, have buried their feelings of anger and fear over many years. In *Daughters of Divorce*, Deirdre Laiken writes, "Past, present, and future are all tangled together in a confusing jumble. The images are unforgettable: cars pulling out of driveways, doors slamming, disputes over the dinner table, mothers crying over emptied closets, and our fathers' backs as they walk out on our lives." Fearful of entering the kind of relationship in which her parents failed, Emily asks herself, "Am I going to make the right decision of who I am going to let into my life?" She doubts her ability to keep a relationship going due to ghosts from the past that have been imprinted in her memory.

Now single and dating, Emily reports: "The first thing that I think when I start getting to know someone is—they're just going to pick themselves up and walk away." Emily has examined her parents' divorce and knows it wasn't her fault, but unlike Penny, she continues to struggle with ghosts from the past and is currently unable to forgive her parents, which is preventing her from achieving Step 2.

SABOTAGING RELATIONSHIPS

Abby, in her late thirties, spent more than two decades struggling with ghosts from her past and experiencing turmoil in romantic relationships. Like Penny and Emily, she found herself reenacting the painful memories of her parents' marriage and subsequent breakup. But in her case, her fear of loss translated to an intense fear of commitment. Abby's parents divorced when she was about nine years old, and she struggled through a series of unhealthy, short-term relationships until she met her current fiancé, Rob, at age thirty-five.

Prior to meeting Rob, Abby didn't have a serious relationship for years. While attending college in upstate New York, she had fallen deeply in love with a young man who seemed like a perfect match in all ways. But she admits she sabotaged the relationship by being unfaithful several times during their three-year courtship, explaining, "When I was eighteen, I had a relationship that lasted for three years, but I cheated on him. He was great—smart, mature, and came from a well-respected family. Conner was wonderful to me and didn't deserve the treatment I gave him. I would cheat with guys who were the opposite of him for some reason. It ended when he caught me red-handed with another guy. After that, I dated a lot of guys but didn't have a serious relationship for many years."

For nearly two decades, Abby avoided relationships because she was mistrustful and fearful of ending up like her parents. Like many adult children of divorce, Abby doesn't remember much of her childhood, but she does remember precise moments that continue to inform her perspective on relationships today. "There was the time my mom woke my brother and I up in the middle of the night to go hide in the car. I remember us in the back of the car, both of us in footed pajamas," she says. When her parents split, it meant moving to her grandparents' house and losing most of her childhood friends. She also recalls a painful adolescence when she moved between two homes (her dad lived in a small apartment) and feeling ashamed about her parents' divorce because she was raised in an affluent community where divorces weren't talked about much. Here is how Abby put it: "When back-to-school time came around, I began to fret about explaining how my parents divorced. I felt ashamed and embarrassed, as no one I knew had divorced or separated parents."

Abby, who recently returned to college to pursue a career in education, describes her adolescence as a time of turmoil and going to extremes:

By the time I reached junior high school, my relationship with my mom had become quite stressed. I wanted to spread my wings and have a bit more freedom in my social life. In the eighth grade we began to experiment with drinking alcohol. We were a good group of kids, but we were thirteen and some of us were getting drunk on a weekly basis. It was around this time that I started getting into trouble for breaking curfew, declining grades, and being defiant of my mother. This was also around the time that I had a fight with my mother and she told me that if I didn't like her rules, I could go live with my father...so I did.

Like many daughters of divorce, Abby needed special encouragement to grieve the loss of her family after her father moved out. In the absence of this support, she began to engage in risk-taking behaviors, which she told me continued until she was in her early thirties. In *Meeting at the Crossroads*, Brown and Gilligan write, "For over a century the edge of adolescence has been identified as a time of heightened psychological risk for girls. Girls at this time have been observed to lose their vitality, their resilience, their immunity to depression, and their sense of themselves and their character." While moving in with her father at age thirteen helped Abby restore her equilibrium somewhat, it was the beginning of a very strained relationship with her mother.

During our recent interview, Abby stated that she hadn't seen her mother in four years and was questioning whether she would invite her to her upcoming wedding. Fortunately, she maintains a close bond with her father and stepmother, who have been happily married for twenty-five years and raised her since she was an adolescent. However, the rupture in her relationship with her mother is preventing her from attaining Step 2. Abby is seemingly unaware that this estrangement has started to affect her relationship with her fiancé. Since she never expected good things from her mother, she never expects good things from Rob.

Even though Abby is currently planning her wedding, she fears that her marriage is doomed to fail like her parents' marriage did.

"Forever is a long time, and as uncomfortable as it was to go through as a kid, the last thing that I want to do is go through a divorce as an adult. Actually, the last thing I'd want to do is go through it (divorce) as an adult while watching children of my own go through it. I definitely have a fear that I will end up like my parents," she says. When I asked Abby what the most difficult parts of intimate relationships are, she stopped and nodded.

Trust and intimacy aren't my strong suits. I hope that my marriage isn't anything like my parents'. I hope that it will be based on commitment and communication, which Rob and I have been working on. But I can be standoffish and have serious issues with intimacy and trust. Every day, Rob wants to get close to me, and I push him away. Right now, we are in counseling to get to know each other—even though my friends think I'm crazy since we aren't even married yet!

We love each other and want to get married, but I have this block and we need to undo it. He wants to get closer but I won't let him because it involves trust. I'm fearful that Rob will leave. Trust is my biggest issue and it's becoming pretty exhausting. I finally have a therapist who is helping me deal with my past and the shame I felt when my parents divorced. I always had this feeling that I just have to stand on my own two feet, and brush myself off and move on with my life. Put on my big girl pants and move forward.

Establishing a healthy level of trust in a relationship is possible, but takes time and effort. Abby recognizes that she has a ways to go to learn to trust Rob and be vulnerable enough to let him get close. But first she must begin to trust herself. After all, how can she trust Rob when she questions her own judgment? Rather than playing it safe, Abby is beginning to allow herself to be vulnerable and take risks—two crucial steps in developing intimacy and restoring her faith in love.

As Abby began to take steps toward forgiving her parents for their high-conflict divorce, she began to feel more confident in her ability to trust Rob—believing that he had her best intentions at heart and was truly worthy of her love and devotion. Smart women extend trust to deserving partners.

LEARNING TO TRUST YOURSELF

A crucial aspect of achieving Step 2 is learning to trust yourself and extend trust to others enough so that you can practice forgiveness. But it's a lot easier said than done. Like Penny, Emily, and Abby, you may have unrealistic expectations about love and relationships—more focused on your dream of how a relationship should be rather than the reality of how it is—and inadvertently bring about the disappointments you fear the most. Trust issues can be activated anytime someone or something triggers an emotion or painful memory from your past. For instance, your boyfriend or husband may arrive late to meet you somewhere and forget to call you. Maybe you'll start an argument when your partner comes home a little late or forgets to call. Or you may feel anger that's disproportionate to a situation, so you hang up the phone.

In a study conducted by Candan Duran-Aydintug on several college campuses, 82 percent of college students whose parents had divorced disclosed that they had trust issues. In chapter 7, you will learn more about how experiencing parental divorce can trigger trust issues, as well as ways to overcome them.

How are ghosts from the past and trust connected? Every child exposed to divorce experiences a trust wound. If this initial injury isn't addressed and resolved, it will fester into adulthood. In Abby's case, she was unable to maintain a committed relationship until she reached her midthirties, and still struggles mightily, because she hasn't been able to heal the severed relationship with her mother and forgive both of her parents for splitting up. Step 2, which is forgiving others and moving on from the past, is impossible without first repairing the trust wound.

FORGIVENESS: BURYING GHOSTS FROM THE PAST ONCE AND FOR ALL

Practicing forgiveness is one of the most powerful actions you can take to come to terms with the ghosts from your past. Forgiveness is more of a perspective and a practice rather than a single action. It is a way to let go of your old baggage so that you can heal and move forward with your life. Forgiving someone doesn't mean that you are saying what they did is all right; rather, it's about a gift you give to yourself. Deep down you probably know that in order to forge healthy relationships, you need to let go of resentments from your past. When you forgive, you give yourself permission to live an abundant life and to free yourself from the powerful fears that trigger you (either consciously or unconsciously) to react in unhealthy ways.

The action steps below will help facilitate your journey toward understanding your parents' divorce so you'll be able to make accurate assessments and healthy choices in romantic partners. It's also important to remember that there was good in your past because that awareness can give you a sense of pleasure and strength.

Through understanding and letting go of the past and any negative feelings associated with it, you will gain compassion and release any resentment about your parents' actions, which is necessary for your own well-being. Again, this doesn't mean you're condoning, excusing, or minimizing what happened. It doesn't mean you are going to let people walk all over you. Rather, it will give you the strength to stand up for yourself and for what you want. And if you can't genuinely forgive others, at least try to accept what has happened in your past.

ACTION STEPS

* **Write down three crucial ways that your parents' divorce has impacted (or is still impacting) your life.** These might include low self-esteem or a negative mind-set about your abilities or your future. We will show you how this information can be used to set goals shortly—so hold on to it!

* **Make a conscious choice to practice forgiveness.** Adopt the mind-set of a forgiving person by making a decision to live fully in the present. Avoid holding a grudge and declare out loud that you are free to let go of resentment. After all, we are all imperfect. Practicing forgiveness signifies

breaking the cycle of pain and giving up the belief that other people should suffer as much as you do.

* **Strive to let go of the past.** This isn't the same thing as absolving someone who intentionally hurts or abuses you. But it does mean trying to let go of things that happened in the past and are out of your control—including infidelity and the selfish behaviors of parents, ex-partners, and others. You will gain strength to forgive those who have wronged you not by what they do, but by what you do. You don't forgive to abdicate the offender, but to bring peace to yourself.

* **Write down three personal goals to address any ways your parents' divorce is affecting you negatively.** Keep in mind that the objective here is to focus on pain from your past that may be carrying over into the present.

* **Attempt to pick goals that are attainable.** It's always wise to enlist the help of a close friend, family member, or therapist. Since it typically takes at least twenty-one days to see any progress when trying something new, be patient with yourself along the journey.

* **Use positive intentions or affirmations daily such as "I am capable of having loving and trusting relationships."** Repeat them to yourself often and post them on your desk or mirror. You can repeat the same intentions and affirmations or add new ones as you desire as long as you feel enthusiastic about them. Writing them down for several days is a good way to keep track of them and monitor your progress on your goals.

* **Accept that people do the best they can and attempt to be more understanding.** Again, this doesn't mean that

you approve of the hurtful actions of others. You simply come to a more realistic view of your past and give it less power over you.

❋ **Make recovering from your parents' divorce a priority and accept that you can benefit from support.** Achieving self-love, acceptance, and forgiveness is a daily practice, and sharing your experience with a women's group, therapist or coach, and possibly a close friend are key to developing healthy relationships.

There are many reasons why people have difficulty letting go of the past and reversing the painful consequences of their childhood, writes Fred Luskin, PhD, a psychologist and recognized expert on forgiveness. He posits that they may take on the pain of their parents' mistakes because they take their offenses personally. Subsequently, some people create a "grievance story" that focuses on their suffering and assigns blame. A grievance story is similar to a grudge. Luskin notes, "Grievance stories describe the painful things you have endured but not healed from. You will know these stories because telling them makes you mad or hurt all over again." He explains that grievance stories are the ones you tell when you want to give details to a friend about why your life has not turned out the way you hoped or to make sense of your unhappiness.

Luskin explains that individuals heal best when they are able to acknowledge the damage done and shift to an impersonal perspective. The next step is crafting a new story by creating a positive intention—a way of transforming a grievance story into a positive goal. For instance, Marisa's intention was building strong and supportive relationships. You might recall that Marisa is a resilient woman who was in an abusive relationship for many years, and she suffered through a father-daughter wound when her mother left her father and moved across the country. Fortunately Marisa made peace with both of her parents and forgave them for the painful childhood she endured. Luskin also writes, "Forgiveness isn't a focus on what happened in the past and neither is it remaining upset or holding on to grudges. You may have been hurt in the past, but you are upset today. Both forgiveness and grievances are experiences that you have in the present."

The following are five steps to becoming a forgiving person adapted from Luskin's model:

1. **Identify any emotions you have about your past.** Reviewing your survey from chapter 3 can help with this. Honestly addressing these feelings will allow you to move forward. It's likely you have developed a grievance story because certain things happened as a result of your parents' divorce that you could not control.

2. **Take steps to lessen the impact the loss or trauma has on your relationships.** Repair the damage by finding ways to soothe hurt feelings. This might include writing a new grievance story, perhaps exploring your parents' split from their point of view. Once you do this, you have begun the process of positive change!

3. **Make a choice to feel hurt for a shorter period, rather than letting yourself stew about it.** Challenge your thinking and let go of "unenforceable rules"—Luskin's term for unrealistic expectations and standards we hold for ourselves and others that ultimately lead to feelings of disappointment or distress. In Marisa's case, she finally understood

that she couldn't change the past, so she made a decision to minimize the time she spent feeling upset in the present.

4. **Focus on those things you can control.** Things began to make perfect sense as Marisa gained self-awareness and focused on the things she could control—including the amount of time she spent feeling angry. She realized she didn't cause her parents' divorce and didn't need to take on the burden of her parents' pain or allow others to push her buttons.

5. **Learn to think like a forgiving person.** During our last conversation, Marisa shared that recently she had been spending time with her mother, and while she was still resentful, she was able to feel compassion for her mother. Her new story became this: though she didn't always have Marisa's self-interest at heart, her mother had survived an abusive childhood and married very young. For once, Marisa was able to build healthy relationships and to focus on love and forgiveness rather than anger and blame.

CRAFTING A NEW STORY

As a child and young adult, Marisa's grievance story was one that included blaming both of her parents for their divorce and identifying with the role of victim. She was caught in a vicious cycle of self-blame and anger, which resulted in her reenactment of patterns from her past. Marisa chose needy, troubled partners with whom she played the caretaking role to her own detriment. However, she learned that controlling and caretaking don't lead to intimacy.

Even though Marisa endured a painful childhood, she was choosing to create a happy marriage in the present, which included two children and a supportive husband. As an adult, she was able to transcend her childhood by unlearning unproductive thinking and behavior while adopting healthier habits—such as good communication skills and practicing self-care. Marisa was able to stand on her own two feet and live with intention rather than parroting the past or other people's agendas.

As Marisa proceeded through Step 2 and gained insight about her emotional heritage and the triggers that activated her ghosts from the past, she was ripe to meet Dan, who could give her the love and intimacy she had been craving. Marisa gained understanding about issues that contributed to the demise of her parents' marriage, and she began to let them off the hook—thus lessening the impact their divorce had on her. Marisa has established goals for herself and her marriage. Most of all, she has learned to be gentle with herself on her road to recovery.

A Word from Terry: A Mother's Perspective

In hindsight, repeating patterns of the past was my way of trying to gain mastery over them. As a young woman, I was attracted to partners who bore a strong resemblance to my father—who was unavailable at times during my childhood and unable to give me the love and security I craved. However, what I didn't realize until decades later is that by passing on the legacy of divorce to my daughter, Tracy, I also passed on my pessimistic view of love and marriage. Embarking upon the long journey of writing *Daughters of Divorce* with Tracy has allowed both of us to come to terms with our heritage, gain self-worth, and restore our faith in love.

A Word from Tracy: A Daughter's Perspective

Sometimes you find yourself repeating patterns of the past—not only your own, but those of your parents. Other times, you find yourself fighting furiously against their example by picking partners who bear little or no resemblance your family of origin. My mom and I have very different expectations and attractions in our relationships. I'm not attracted to men like my grandfather, my father, or my mom's current husband. Even though our tendencies are different, my mom and I share the same legacy. We both desperately want to avoid divorce in our lives. Although we might have different "ghosts," our struggles are the same.

5

Step Three:

Longing for Dear Old Dad

OVERCOME YOUR BROKEN (OR MISSING) RELATIONSHIP WITH YOUR FATHER

> "I don't blame my dad for leaving and I don't blame myself. I think that it's better not to blame either of my parents. My therapist helped me to see that."
>
> —Liza, age 27

The quality of the father-daughter relationship—good, damaged, or otherwise—profoundly impacts daughters in multiple ways. A girl stands a better chance of becoming a self-confident woman if she has a close relationship with her father. A dad's presence (or lack of presence) in his daughter's life will affect how she relates to all romantic partners who come after him.

Studies show that if a girl grows up with a damaged relationship with her father, her self-esteem will be lower than one who does not. In fact, she may seek out partners who confirm her low opinion of herself. Women who have a wound in the father-daughter relationship may gravitate to mates who treat them poorly because they are unaware of the root of their issue. However, when it is brought to their attention, they can reverse this pattern and pick partners who honor and respect them.

Many of the women we've interviewed talked about being attracted to or marrying someone like their father. Sandra, a software engineer, age twenty-six, reflects: "I've had several partners who were like my dad. I guess I felt that the way my dad treated my mom was the way I deserved to be treated. I've been in many bad relationships where there was physical and emotional abuse."

According to author Peggy Drexler, PhD, awareness of the father-daughter wound and willingness to accept responsibility for changing is key to healing any damage. She writes: "Likewise, even the most troubled, overwrought, baggage-laden relationship is not without hope—if not of reconciliation, then at least of the daughter finding a new way of seeing her father that might help her make sense of the forces and motivations that shaped him and his actions."

Many experts believe that adults unconsciously repeat unhealthy patterns from parent-child relationships—for example, picking partners who are unavailable in ways that are similar to how a parent was unavailable. Therapist and author Jasmin Lee Cori writes: "In these cases healing is often a matter of becoming more aware of the pattern, working through these childhood wounds in therapy or other places, and making new choices in terms of love relationships."

Sandra's story illustrates the importance of repairing damage done to a father-daughter relationship and working through any wound that exists. Sandra was eight years old when her father moved out suddenly, leaving her with a mother who had difficulty coping. When her father left, Sandra felt confused and stopped believing in herself.

Growing up without a father's emotional support, Sandra

developed a strong yearning for male attention, and she jumped headlong into relationships with men in need of rescue. Filled with self-doubt and anxiety about finding a partner, she endured a series of brief, failed relationships with partners who were wrong for her. She had difficulty setting boundaries and so the men in her life took advantage of her kindness. At times, she sabotaged relationships that had good potential by being mistrustful and controlling.

Sandra lacked the self-confidence to ask for what she needed from partners because she felt unworthy of love. She explains: "When I felt like a guy was getting too close, I would push him away. That way, it wouldn't hurt so much when he left." With the help of a therapist, Sandra gained insight into the source of her issues, and she has learned to trust her judgment and pick partners who are a good match for her.

Due to the caretaking role she played with her mother, Sandra was attracted to men with problems. She became accustomed to measuring love by the amount of pain she felt, and she developed codependent tendencies—causing her to love too much and to become obsessed with her partner's well-being. By becoming absorbed in their problems, she neglected her own problems.

However, Sandra is learning that loving someone doesn't mean you have to control or change them. Ultimately, she's come to realize that she can only truly work on herself. To be able to heal her wounds from the rupture of her relationship with her father, Sandra is letting go of the past and creating a life filled with hope for a bright future.

Jungian analyst Linda Schierse Leonard says that for many girls and women, the root of their difficulty in romantic relationships stems from a damaged relationship with their father. "If the father isn't there for the daughter in a committed way while she is growing up," Leonard writes, "she may lose confidence in herself, and a wound may occur."

The "daddy game," a phrase coined by Laiken, refers to the fact that most girls see their fathers infrequently after their parents' split, or not at all. Consequently, they tend to idealize their dad and fear losing his love. This pattern often follows daughters of divorce into adulthood—making romantic relationships shaky as they get into the nitty-gritty of dealing with issues and resolving conflicts with partners. After all, women learn about intimate relationships through their relationship with their fathers and observing their parents' interactions.

WHEN DAD'S MISSING IN ACTION

In a divorced family, there are many ways a father-daughter relationship may suffer. Based on her research, Nielsen discovered that divorce often damages a daughter's relationship with her father more than a son's, as boys tend to spend more time with their dads after a family dissolves than girls do. Nielsen posits that while most daughters of divorce are well adjusted several years after their parents' divorce, many have damaged relationships with their fathers years later. Unfortunately, if the damage is severe, a girl can grow into adulthood with low self-esteem and more troubled relationships with men.

What a girl needs is a loving, predictable father figure—whether married to her mother or divorced—in order to help her shape a confident sense of herself. Some dads are better able to relate to their daughters and make them a priority, rather than vanishing or distancing themselves. Joshua Coleman, PhD, a recognized expert on parenting, explains that one of the predictors of a father's relationship with his children after divorce is the mother's facilitation or obstruction of the relationship. In his book *When Parents Hurt*, he writes, "Mothers who feel wronged in the marriage or divorce, who believe that mothers are more important than fathers, or who have psychological problems may directly or indirectly interfere with the father's desire to have an ongoing relationship with his children."

Whenever possible, divorced mothers need to encourage their daughters to have regular contact with their fathers and facilitate a close relationship with them. Even if they didn't have happy childhoods, fathers can unlearn the negative patterns of the past and develop healthy, loving relationships with their daughters. Many fathers may not know how to relate to their daughters due to their own upbringing. Coleman found that a mother may be able to bridge the intimacy gap that might exist between a daughter and father in an intact family, but this isn't as easy to accomplish in a divided home. Coleman explains, "Studies show that a father's relationship with his daughter is the most vulnerable to disruption with a divorce."

Certainly a strong father-daughter connection is a challenge when it comes to post-divorce relationships. This is especially true during adolescence when many fathers have a tendency to distance themselves or feel rejected by their daughter's preoccupation with her appearance and peer relationships. What daughters need most from their dads is plenty of affection, tenderness, and intimacy. The results of many studies, including my own, show that the amount of contact that a girl has with her father after divorce and her feelings of closeness with him are related to her post-divorce adjustment and self-esteem. A rupture in the father-daughter relationship is associated with risk factors for daughters of divorce such as early marriage, trust issues, lowered self-esteem, reluctance to commit to a romantic partner, and a heightened sense of pessimism about marriage.

In recent years, divorced or single parent fathers have become increasingly aware that they are the key to teaching their daughters to become confident and assertive women. Since a father-daughter wound can impact a daughter's future, it's important not to blame fathers (many of them had damaged childhoods) but to encourage close bonds between fathers and daughters after divorce. At the end of this chapter, you will read about Liza, who provides a good example of a woman who suffered from daddy deprivation as a child but healed her wound with her father and successfully worked through Step 3.

In order to prepare yourself to accomplish Step 3, it's important to examine the particular pattern of your dad's involvement in your life and whether there was a rupture in your relationship after your parents divorced. The following patterns were designed to help you on your journey to gain insight and to give you tools to improve your relationship with your dad.

RECOGNIZING THE PATTERNS OF A FATHER'S INVOLVEMENT

First we will identify various patterns of father involvement and then we'll offer you strategies to heal a damaged father-daughter relationship. The following categories of a father's involvement with his daughter emerged from the in-depth interviews of more than three hundred women who participated in our study. The term "distant father" will be used to describe dads who were there in body but not in spirit. "Absent fathers" tragically desert their daughters, either by gradually drifting away after a divorce or by leaving suddenly. Based on our research, the term "remarried dad" will be used to describe fathers whose relationship with their daughters seemed to be altered primarily due to their subsequent remarriage.

While only a handful of women interviewed for this study identified that they were involved in a healthy, balanced relationship with their dads, we added the "competent father" category to examine how a mutually respectful father-daughter relationship can shape the way a daughter grows into womanhood and relates to intimate partners. At the end of this chapter, you'll learn how a close connection with your father can help you to emerge a confident woman.

The Distant Father: Passive and Emotionally Unavailable

For most women, their fathers are beyond reach—mystery men who work and fix the car, and who may even leave the family without looking back. Distant fathers, in retreat from their daughters, may create a longing or hunger for male attention due to their absence. Of all the themes that emerged from the interviews conducted for this book, the distant father was the most common. For the sake of simplicity, distant fathers have been categorized into two types: passive and emotionally unavailable.

The main distinction between these two types is that daughters usually feel emotionally close to the passive dad, yet he keeps a low profile and will pay any price for peace. Passive fathers tend to be underachievers either at home or at work and avoid conflict at all cost. Emotionally unavailable fathers are either unwilling or unable to express their emotions—appearing remote or disengaged. These dads usually believe they are doing their best. They may even pay child support and have regular contact with their daughters, but they have an amazing ability to use denial to avoid dealing with pain or conflict, and so they become adept at tuning out their children's emotional needs.

The Passive Father

Until participating in therapy, Brooke had little understanding of how her dad leaving when she was an infant affected her development and feelings of insecurity as a young adult. A week after our interview, Brooke forwarded this letter to me via email:

> It scares me that after twenty-two years I have such a weak connection with my dad. I feel guilty for the way that things have turned out between us. I know realistically that I was a baby when he left and it didn't have anything to do with me, but I feel it (guilty). I fear the future and I want to do better. I want to give my children the things that I never had, like security and trust. I hope that I can give myself to others and treat them as I want to be treated.

On the surface, Brooke's life seemed to be going along all right after her father left. She lived with her mother full-time and her dad came on Saturdays for weekly visitation. She remembers weekends spent with him at the park or beach—meals shared and some good memories of their time together. But Brooke also remembers being a young teenager and feeling let down when he would call to cancel or invite his girlfriend to join them. Brooke desired a stronger connection with her father and yet felt like a burden to him. "He never said much, but I felt his indifference. He would take me along on camping trips with his friends, but he never had much time for me. I usually felt like an afterthought," she says. These outings made Brooke feel worried and lonely, but she rarely complained to anyone, not wanting to risk upsetting her father or her mother, who was clearly overwhelmed with the life of a single parent.

Passive fathers, perhaps more so than emotionally unavailable ones, are uncomfortable with intimacy. They tend to look to others to direct their mood, and they may disappear into the woodwork. Brooke recalled sadly, "My grandma would tell me how selfish he was, but I idealized him—he would take me to the park and do fun things with me. Now I see how selfish he was. I never thought about it that way when I was young. He always spent a lot of time on himself, on his hobbies and lifestyle. He tried to be my friend but I never respected him."

As Brooke entered adolescence—a pivotal time in female development—she suffered emotionally due to their fractured relationship. Her father was not there to provide a buffer between her and her strong-willed mom, who she says had an "Irish temper." Brooke believes that her dad disappeared in order to evade conflict with his ex-wife at all costs. Consequently, he didn't assert his rights as a parent—even missing visits with Brooke.

Though smart, thoughtful, and attractive, Brooke needs to repair her broken relationship with her father so she can restore her faith in love. She admits she has a tendency to pick boyfriends with the same passive personality as her father, which leaves her feeling disappointed and unloved as she settles for less than she deserves from her partners.

Hetherington, in *For Better or For Worse*, notes that daughters of divorce who are raised in a family with passive or distant dads are more at risk for becoming "pursuers" in their own intimate relationships. A pursuer, typically a woman, chases or clings to her partner, while he withdraws from her advances or overly needy behavior, creating a "pursuer-distancer" dance. The problem develops when this pattern becomes ingrained, and one behavior provokes and maintains the other. If you chase a distancer, it's likely he'll distance more. Couples with this dynamic tend to feel chronically dissatisfied because they have vastly different needs for closeness and space. In her study, Hetherington found that couples who adopted the pursuer-distancer pattern were the most divorce prone and thus most likely to pass on the legacy of divorce to their children.

The Emotionally Unavailable Dad

Victoria, age fifty-one, grew up in a female-dominated home. Raised with two younger sisters, she was a good student, studied ballet, and participated in the town swim team. After her father left for another woman when she was twelve, he lived in the same town and provided for most of their financial needs, but kept her at arm's length. In retrospect, Victoria says, "I adored my dad, as a girl I had a special affection for him. He was a hands-on dad and would take us to amusement parks. I had a strong connection with him before he left but that changed—visits every other weekend weren't the same. My mom never really got over him leaving, and I guess I withdrew and lost my spunk."

Over lunch at a local restaurant, Victoria described herself as close to her father before her parents' breakup but as aware of his remoteness when they no longer had daily contact. Emotionally unavailable fathers tend to be there in the flesh but distant and out of touch with their daughters' emotional needs. Some are psychologically unavailable to their daughters, and others may even be oblivious to their needs for love and attention. In her popular book *The Unavailable Father*, psychologist Sarah Simms Rosenthal writes, "When a father makes it clear to his daughter in every way that he loves her unconditionally, just for who she is, he lays the foundation for her positive self-concept." She explains that when girls experience disinterest or rejection from their fathers, they may assume it is the result of some flaw within themselves. Victoria reminisces about her adolescence:

> *The year of the divorce was 1971; I was twelve and entered the seventh grade in a new school. It was a very traumatic experience for me with my father leaving home, moving to a different home, and beginning junior high in an unfamiliar environment. Whereas in grammar school, I had been a leader and outgoing, I now pulled into a shell, became less confident, less competitive, and more withdrawn. Although I remained an honor student throughout junior and senior high, I became more aloof and reserved and*

participated less in class and school activity. I became more self-conscious and unsure of myself.

In spite of her difficulty adjusting to her parents' breakup during adolescence, Victoria maintains a strong faith in marriage and is determined to make her marriage last. Competent-caring, she has devoted her life to her husband, children, and career as a teacher. "I never allowed myself to stop trying, or to let my background stop me. After a while, I chose to accept my dad's limitations, and to rebuild our relationship," Victoria continued. "I know that my dad could have behaved better after the divorce, but my mom had issues with depression and my dad just couldn't deal with it."

Victoria, radiant and hopeful, isn't allowing her parents' divorce to define her view of marriage. She contacted us prior to the publication of this book, excited yet nervous about her upcoming trip to Florida, where she plans to visit her father. She is coming to terms with the fact that, while she still feels a lot of resentment toward her father, a "good enough" father doesn't have to be perfect. Victoria has successfully worked through Step 3 because she has examined her relationship with her father and hasn't let her past stop her from achieving a happy marriage.

The Absent Father

Tall and stylishly dressed, Diana, age twenty-four, is a college graduate. She describes herself as a straight-A student from elementary school through high school. "I was an overachiever, but I didn't focus on being happy. We were all suffering because of my dad's controlling ways. Anytime I saw through him, he would put me down and try to control me," Diana explains.

"Finally, when my dad left, I realized that my mom had detached from him years earlier and we were all very unhappy." Diana says she was sixteen years old when her father moved to Colorado, and she hasn't seen him since. Prior to her father leaving, her parents had rarely spent time together, and Diana had begun to distance herself from him years before he left. Diana explains, "He was a very selfish person and I never felt close to him. My mom was the nurturing one who took on the role of mother and father."

Author Victoria Secunda writes, "It is a tragic and unavoidable reality that once a marriage ends, a great many fathers simply vanish." Surprisingly, this parental neglect isn't due to the vindictiveness of ex-wives. In her research, Secunda found that very few mothers deliberately withheld their daughters from their fathers. She writes, "In the end it was indifference and inertia that kept these fathers from finding their daughters. And if the reunion was to be effected, it was almost always the daughters who did the legwork, broke through the silences."

A bright young woman with a successful career, Diana has many female friends, yet she comes across as tentative when she talks about her intimate relationships. "I'm not very committal because I don't want to get hurt. I know that this is because of my parents' divorce. I'm deathly afraid of a relationship dissolving with a guy, because then I have to go through all that divorce pain again," she says. Diana describes herself as pessimistic about marriage for good reason, since her father vanished suddenly. She is mistrustful and leery about committing to men—always waiting for the other shoe to drop.

At sixteen, Diana was on the road to finding her identity and on the outside it appeared that all was going fine. She didn't consciously blame herself for her father leaving. Yet, like many other daughters of divorce, she experienced the sleeper effect. Some girls, like Diana, repress anxiety at the time of their parents' divorce, yet become anxious, depressed, or even rebellious during late adolescence or young adulthood. Here is how Diana put it: "I went to extremes—from not drinking any alcohol at all in high school to overdoing it in college big time. I was looking for attention from men and became very flirtatious. I think that I was trying to make up for the void that I felt from the absence of my dad. I don't trust men, and I always assume that things are going to turn out awful."

After years of convincing herself that she was unlovable, Diana is dealing honestly with her father wound and feelings of abandonment. Author H. Norman Wright, a counselor and certified trauma specialist, concludes that abandonment is a common theme for adult daughters of divorce. He writes, "In a divorce, adult needs often take priority over a child's needs. Caretakers aren't as available, life is disrupted, and losses increase, but they aren't identified as losses. Yes, there's often physical as well as emotional abandonment. You feel unworthy to be loved, and you fear being left on your own."

Diana's fear of abandonment appears to be a direct result of her father disappearing just as she was emerging as an older adolescent. Pipher describes adolescence as a vulnerable time when girls are supposed to distance themselves from their parents—just at the time when they are most in need of support. She writes, "As they struggle with countless new pressures, they must relinquish the protection and closeness they've felt with their families in childhood." Pipher points out that divorce is particularly hard on adolescents, who suffer if divorce brings multiple losses—including the loss of a loving relationship with both parents and financial resources.

For girls and young women like Diana, this struggle is amplified by the absence of their fathers when they are dealing with the challenges of adolescence. During the teen years, a father makes an important contribution to his family, since he provides a sense of balance and accountability. Because girls naturally distance themselves from their mothers during adolescence, it is the father who can validate their femininity. Study after study shows that fathers set up their daughters to achieve success in intimate relationships. Naturally, young women like Diana, whose fathers vanish, often experience trust issues. Diana explains, "I don't trust men; I always assume that they are going to turn on me because my parents' marriage turned on me. I hide things and I am deathly afraid. I want to run but yet I keep trying. I can't give up because there is always a chance that things might work out."

Diana fits the description of competent-at-a-cost: competent in most areas of her life, yet mistrustful in her relationships with men. She is intensely afraid of relationships ending and yet has a tendency to sabotage ones that might lead to commitment. Identifying with her rejected mother, as most daughters of divorce do, has had far-reaching effects on Diana's attitudes toward men. In her acclaimed book *Father Loss*, Elyce Wakerman concludes, "The girl who was abandoned by her father enters adulthood in a pervasive state of doubt. She longs for a man, distrusts all men, feels powerful enough to have ended a marriage, utterly powerless to sustain a relationship. She strives to prove herself lovable, shies away from intimacy."

Several months after our interview, Diana called to share her good news. She met someone she cares deeply about and, while fearful, she is willing to extend trust. "The scariest thing is that there is no foolproof relationship, so it's a risk no matter what. My boyfriend says that there are no guarantees, he is aware of my trust issues, and is still hanging around." She also told us that after our meeting, she decided to call her dad on his birthday. Diana took a big risk and was pleased that the conversation went fairly well. She continued, "There were a lot of awkward pauses, but he actually listened when I told him about my life, and said that he realized the damage that he had done—that he had messed up and wanted to be in touch."

Other daughters, who are abandoned by or separated from their fathers, suffer such a severe wound that they make a decision to terminate the relationship. When this happens, these fathers mostly suffer from either psychological problems or they lack an emotional connection to their daughters. Secunda explains, "My own research has led me to conclude that divorced fathers who abandon their children, either wholly or in part, share one primary characteristic: they don't appear to have a paternal identity. Abandoning fathers are essentially immature, stuck in the primary narcissism of early childhood, unable to feel anyone's pain or joy but their own."

In her recent book, *Longing for Daddy*, author Monique Robinson recommends that fatherless women examine their attitudes, beliefs, and identity. She writes, "Daughters experience an emotional, psychological, and spiritual death when a father's actions shatter their image. In the past I associated grief primarily with physical death. But death isn't the only loss we grieve. We need to grieve the loss of relationships, jobs, homes, dreams. The absence of a father is worth grieving." There are many ways that a father can leave a daughter. The following story from Patricia illustrates how some dads abandon their daughters because they are preoccupied with a new marriage. However, these issues can usually be dealt with and resolved, and it's worth the effort!

The Remarried Dad

Through our interviews with women whose fathers remarried after divorce, we discovered there were two outcomes for daughters with a remarried dad. In most cases, the father-daughter bond suffered when the dad started devoting most of his time and attention to his new family. In some cases, when daughters have just begun to settle down after a divorce, they are faced with becoming part of a new family. This family might come with a new stepmom and possibly her children, or even one or more half siblings. It's understandable that daddy's little girl may feel abandoned by a dad who is preoccupied with his new life. But in other cases, some of the women we spoke with acknowledged that their fathers' remarriage brought out the best in them. By ending a dysfunctional marriage and starting with a clean slate, many men become better dads—even when a stepmom was brought into the mix. In this section, we illustrate this point with the stories of two women who experienced very different outcomes when their fathers remarried.

Patricia, in her late fifties, met us for breakfast at her favorite restaurant and spoke candidly about her parents' divorce as if it happened yesterday, even though her parents divorced fifty-one years ago. She explained how her relationship with her father changed after he met and married her stepmother, shortly after her parents' breakup. Patricia, a sales executive, was the middle child of three sisters—each with their own personality and take on their parents' divorce. She sympathized with her mother after the split even though it was her mom who left. "My mom was a controlling woman and unhappy with our father because he didn't work much to help support us four girls. She took care of the bills, had all of the responsibility," she says.

But looking back, Patricia blames both of her parents for the divorce, saying, "It takes two people to get a divorce." What Patricia couldn't predict was that her father would remarry very soon after her parents separated and gradually distance himself; he didn't even attend her wedding. She remembers experiencing loyalty conflicts because she perceived, rightly or wrongly, that her mother needed her allegiance—causing her to reject her stepmother. Soon after our interview, she wrote her father a letter.

I need to tell you that it really hurt me when you wouldn't come to my wedding and give me away. You did this for your other two daughters. I think there was an excuse that you couldn't leave the restaurant, but I'm sure Alison could have run it for one day (if you felt it was important enough). I know that Alison didn't want or trust you to be alone with Mom. Her jealousy of Mom and us has always reared its ugly head during your entire marriage. I lost so much respect for you over the years to see that woman run your life. I guess it was hard for me to understand why you always put her needs first. It just hurt and split us apart so much to let a new stepmother make decisions in regards to YOUR daughters.

Hetherington's research underscores the challenges that daughters face when their parents remarry after divorce. She writes, "Divorce and remarriage are usually very stressful situations and transitions. How well adults and children deal with these transitions is related to the balance between risk factors that undermine their ability to cope with stress and their well-being, and protective factors that help buffer them from adversity." In Patricia's case, one of her risk factors was the lack of a harmonious relationship with her stepmother, Alison. From Patricia's perspective, Alison felt threatened by her husband's need to spend time and money on his children, so she rarely made an effort to be friendly or supportive.

Certainly, Patricia's family had several protective factors such as her mother's occupation as a teacher, giving them access to good income and education. But they also had many stressors, including her father Henry's sporadic income as the owner of a small restaurant. Henry also married Alison within one year of the divorce—and they had their son, Grady, shortly afterward. Just as Patricia and her sisters were adjusting to the loss of daily access to both of their parents, they had to deal with the presence of a new stepmother and a half sibling. It makes sense that Patricia would be hurt and experience resentment toward her father because she felt displaced by her dad's new family. We found this reaction to be common among daughters whose fathers remarried soon after divorce— especially if they had one or more children soon afterward.

Rivalries: Moms vs. Stepmoms

According to Hetherington, some remarried fathers may lack the financial resources to support two families. She concludes, "Some men just disappeared; others tried to be responsible but lacked the financial resources to support two households. Remarriage or making paternal visits difficult could cause a man to stop or reduce child support." Other common stressors on remarried families include rivalry and competing loyalties. Hetherington notes, "Rivalry between first and second wives is often intense in the early stages of remarriage, and sometimes continued for decades."

The rivalry between Patricia's mother and stepmother caused a lot of inner conflict, because Patricia felt like she had to choose sides. Being the faithful daughter to her mother meant that Patricia couldn't express affection or love to her stepmother. Many daughters of divorce can relate to being stuck in the middle and feeling the intense stress of divided loyalties. This conflict is made worse when parents remarry too soon after divorce, because children and parents don't have adequate time to heal from the initial loss of the breakup of the family. In her case, Patricia also perceived her stepmother as a rival for her father's attention, since he had less time for her after his remarriage.

By filling in the blanks of her father's inattentiveness with fantasies of how he would be a better father to her if she were more lovable, self-blame gave Patricia an illusion of control. It was preferable for her to think she wasn't "good enough" rather than imagine there was no feeling from her dad at all and no possibility of ever gaining his love. But while self-blame solved one problem, it created another. As the years passed, she wondered how any man would ever love her and internalized feelings of shame that she still hasn't healed from. "I know that my dad loves me and my sisters, and of course I love him. But our relationship was changed forever after he married Alison. His words and actions crushed me. My dad made it clear to me that I would never be more important than this woman who hated me," Patricia says.

Patricia married right Rick out of college, and they had a passionate but stormy relationship. Unfaithful during most of their brief marriage, Rick was a substance abuser and deserted Patricia and their son. Currently single for over two decades, Patricia has good reason to mistrust men and fear commitment and hasn't yet embraced Step 3.

During one of our Building Healthy Relationships Seminars,

Patricia acknowledged that she has trust issues with men as a result of the wound in her relationship with her father and betrayal by her ex-husband. She has put a protective shield around herself, denying any need for love in adult romantic relationships. Many women like Patricia are successful at their careers and good at taking care of others, but relatively poor at letting others nurture them. Patricia explains, "My family was split apart after the divorce. I lived with my mom and yet we all had to take sides. When my dad married Alison, it made matters worse because I knew that I couldn't trust her. She would look through my stuff when I came for weekend visits. There was a lot of conflict and Dad picked her over me. She hated me because I was close to my mom. Then they had a son, and he took all of my dad's time."

Money Wars

Susan Shapiro Barash, psychologist and author of *Women of Divorce: Mothers, Daughters, Stepmothers—The New Triangle* describes how bad feelings between stepmothers and stepdaughters can go on for years. She writes, "On top of their parents' split, daughters of divorce must deal with living in two homes, custody arrangements, and not long after, parents' boyfriends and girlfriends, stepparents, and stepsiblings. With men remarrying at a greater rate than women, often within three years of their divorces, the likelihood of having a stepmother in a daughter's life is great." Barash also cautions us that money is a large issue in many second marriages and something that mothers, daughters, and stepmothers have strong feelings about.

Eileen's story provides an example of how money can put a wedge between mothers, stepmothers, and children. She has a "good enough" personality style and was barely seven years old when her father moved out but stayed in the same town, living with a woman whom she knew well. She remembers many arguments between her parents about money. Her father frequently asked her to give support checks to her mother. In her late twenties, Eileen is a single special education teacher who is successful at her job. After her mother died two years ago, she decided to make peace with her past and began resolving the issues from her family of origin. Like all smart women, Eileen knows that repairing her wounded relationship with her father will allow her heart to heal. She speaks matter-of-factly about her parents' divorce: "I don't think of my parents' divorce as a bad thing. I have a crazy family background, but my sister and I are close and we see our dad often, in spite of the tension with our stepmother. My dad instilled in me a work ethic and I work two jobs—as a teacher by day and tutor after school. Having money in the bank is very important to me; it makes me feel secure."

When she was twenty-two, Eileen inherited $10,000 after the death of her paternal grandmother. She vividly recalls her stepmother's resentment toward her, expressing anger that she received the money at all, feeling that her husband was entitled to all of his mother's inheritance. Joshua Coleman writes in *When Parents Hurt*, "I have heard many stepparents (mostly women) talk about feeling wounded by their stepchildren. The rejecting behavior of the child, brewed from the volatile feelings of disloyalty, loss, and anger resulting from divorce, can put stepparents at the center of the conflict in ways that they have neither the experience or stomach for. These dynamics may explain why a very small percentage of adult daughters of divorce say that they have a close relationship with their stepmothers." Eileen says, "My stepmother Jeanne taught us a lot and helped raise us, but she didn't show us much love and affection. Her two daughters always came first."

In her landmark study of divorce, Wallerstein reminds us that there are a lot of problems in remarried families. The continued tension between ex-partners and stepparents is often conveyed directly to daughters. She writes, "Relationships with daughters were heavily influenced by live-in lovers, or stepmothers in second and third marriages. Some second wives were interested in children, and some wanted no part of them. Some fathers were able to maintain their love and interest in their children, but few had time for two or sometimes three families."

It's clear that Eileen's relationship with her father has sustained her through rough times and has helped her to overcome much adversity. Eileen says of her father: "My dad is an amazing father. My mother has mental health issues, and he just couldn't stay married to her. But even after he left, he always made me feel special—would check on me and make sure that I had what I needed. Caroline and I moved in with him when I was in middle school, when our mom was hospitalized, and he was always there for us."

As Eileen's story illustrates, divorce and remarriage may create an opportunity for a disrupted father-daughter relationship to heal. Eileen and her father have stayed connected throughout her childhood, even maintaining their ritual of a Friday night supper out every month. Eileen has also worked at establishing a closer relationship with her stepmother over the last several years. She isn't bitter toward her father and she doesn't place all of the blame for the divorce on him. Eileen has successfully worked on Step 3 because she is working on self-acceptance and forgiveness, which will enable her to make peace with her past.

The Competent Dad
According to psychologist and child development expert Kevin Leman, fathers are the key to their daughters' future. He notes,

"Evidence shows that a father's relationship with his daughter is one of the key determinants in a woman's ability to enjoy a success-ful life and marriage." In *Always Dad*, author Paul Mandelstein advises divorced fathers to find ways to play a crucial role in their daughters' lives. He suggests that newly divorced parents call a truce with their ex-spouse to put an end to active fighting and to collaborate. While this is a challenge at times, collaboration with an ex-spouse paves the way for greater cooperation in the future. Even several years after a family dissolves, the father–daughter connection is heavily influenced by consistency in contact, the quality of the relationship, and the experience a daughter has with a stepmother, stepsibling, or multiple remarriages.

Megan is a young woman pursuing her dream job and loving life, and she can partially thank her competent father for her success. After her parents divorced when she was six years old, her parents had joint custody. She reflects, "Until I was sixteen, when I got a car, I spent almost every weekend with my dad. When I was young, my dad would pick me up from school every Friday afternoon and drop me off every Monday morning. Even after he moved to a nearby state, he would arrive early to my dance shows, bring flowers, and stay after to take me out to dinner."

As Megan reflects on her experience growing up in a divided family, she remembers her parents trying to be civil and cooper-ative. She also has fond memories of vacations and holidays with both of her parents (separately), spending close to equal time with each of them. Megan's parents' ability to adapt to their new roles after their divorce helped her to adjust. Coparenting expert Constance Ahrons, PhD, reminds us that even though divorce is never easy for a family, it doesn't have to destroy children's lives or lead to a family breakdown. She recommends that parents become cooperative colleagues rather than angry associates or fiery foes after a divorce. Since Megan's parents worked hard at keeping her out of the middle, she was able to escape the intense loyalty conflicts that some children of divorce experience. Her parents also helped her to deal effectively with family transitions. A competent-opportunist, Megan explains her divorce experience growing up, saying,

> *Spending every weekend away from my mom was sometimes hard. Living in a split household, and being an only child, caused me to be a "good daughter" because I was with adults almost all of the time and I wanted their approval. To my cousins, I was a "goody-two-shoes." But looking back, it was the best situation for all of us. My adult relationships with my parents are great. I just had my twenty-fifth birthday party and both of my parents came with their significant others and my extended family.*

Ahrons concludes, "Holidays, graduations, weddings, and births of grandchildren were the occasions where having parents that get along mattered most. Clearly, being able to have both parents together for special occasions without worrying about whether they would get along brought a sense of relief for many. When parents were able to get along, it increased the adult children's sense of family." Patterns of parenting after divorce that lessen conflict and encourage open communication are beneficial for daughters emerging into adulthood. By all accounts, Megan's parents are cooperative colleagues who have helped her maintain a sense of family. After our interview, Megan forwarded us a brief note that she sent her father after her twenty-fifth birthday party. It was also a celebration of his upcoming fiftieth birthday. She writes:

I wish to express my deepest gratitude, for I wouldn't be who I am today without you as my father. In many ways, I feel as though I have watched you grow as much as you have watched me grow. We have both learned that life can be full of setbacks and lessons; however, success is measured from how we deal with those setbacks and learn from those lessons. I am extremely proud to have such a witty and intelligent man as my biggest fan, and even better, as my father.

SUCCESSFUL COPARENTING OR SHARED PARENTING MAKES A DIFFERENCE

Megan's story illustrates how dads can make a tremendous difference in the lives of their daughters. Leman notes, "Fathers leave an indelible imprint on the lives of their daughters. They shape their daughters in ways so profound that many women live unwritten rules they've never thought to question. These rules were ingrained into them so deeply, many women don't realize that though they may graduate from college, get married, and even give birth to a half dozen males, they'll never stop being Daddy's Little Girl." Megan exudes a sense of confidence common among women who have a strong bond with their fathers into adulthood. In spite of her parents' divorce, she is well adjusted and accomplished—a woman with inner strength and resilience that will help her to navigate the challenges of intimate relationships.

When we last met up with Megan, she had just accepted a marriage proposal from Tim and was beaming with optimism. One thing that stood out when we interviewed Megan over the course of several years was that she consistently reported that her parents had a friendly yet businesslike relationship after their divorce. Competent-caring Megan has a healthy view of intimate relationships and a close bond with both of her parents. She never witnessed intense conflict and her parents were able to provide her with the stability, security, and parental love needed in order for her to thrive. Unlike many of the women we interviewed, Megan has an optimistic view of marriage and is willing to take a chance on love, trusting her own judgment. While there aren't any guarantees, she appears to have picked a partner who is a good match for her.

What's in the best interest of children after divorce? Joan Kelly, PhD, a well-known psychologist and parenting researcher, confirms that the outcomes for children of divorce improve when they have equal access to both parents. These outcomes include better psychological and behavioral adjustment and enhanced academic performance. Recent studies show that shared parenting post-divorce increases the chances of children to have positive outcomes on a variety of psychological variables.

In fact, Richard Warshak, PhD, a leading social science researcher, posits that, given normal circumstances, even young children (under the age of four) benefit psychologically from overnight stays in both parents' homes. He concludes that depriving the young child of overnights with her father could compromise the father–child relationship. The research demonstrates numerous benefits to children of divorce when their living arrangements enable loving fathers to be actively involved in their lives on a weekly and regular basis.

Many women underestimate the importance of their fathers in their lives. Like other researchers, we found out that the women in our study were profoundly affected by the quality of their relationships with their fathers. Some fathers were preoccupied with their new lifestyle or family or lacked the financial resources to support two families. Some were devoted fathers who spent a lot of time with their daughters. Others didn't have the benefit of shared parenting or lived at a distance. A daughter's relationship with her father is the first one that teaches her how she should be treated by a romantic partner.

Whenever possible, divorced parents need to encourage their daughters to have regular contact with their fathers and facilitate a close relationship. This includes promoting phone calls, special occasions, and a child-centered parenting plan. Whenever possible, parents can better nurture their daughters by establishing a child-centered parenting plan that allows a continuing and meaningful relationship between a daughter and both of her parents. Liza's story provides an example of a courageous woman who worked hard to heal her wound with her father and is leading a successful life.

REPAIRING THE FATHER-DAUGHTER WOUND

What if your parents didn't coparent well or at all after their divorce? There are still many things you can do to repair your relationship, as Liza's story illustrates. When Liza, age twenty-seven, was nine years old, her father moved out on Christmas Day, leaving her with a workaholic mother who turned to alcohol for solace. To make matters worse, her father quickly remarried and had two children. Even though Liza visited her dad once or twice a week, she remembers feeling resentful because she became the caretaker of her mother, who succumbed to alcoholism. "I missed out on a lot as a teenager—mostly because I was worried about my mom being alone," Liza says.

Growing up without a father who could support her emotionally, Liza developed a strong yearning for male attention, and she jumped headlong into relationships with men in need of rescue. Filled with self-doubt and anxiety about finding a partner, she endured a series of brief, failed relationships with unsuitable partners. Needless to say, intimate relationships were a huge challenge for Liza during her college years. She had difficulty setting boundaries, and so the men in her life took advantage of her kindness. Liza lacked the self-confidence to ask for what she needed from partners because she felt unworthy of love. With the help of a therapist, she gained insight and learned the importance of allowing herself to be vulnerable and to rely on her partner for love and support.

Liza's need to control her partners comes naturally. As a child, she felt responsible for so much and had little or no control over her mother's alcoholism and her father's absence. However, by adopting Step 3, Liza has started to focus on her own healing and embraces the idea that she deserves a rewarding relationship. She's no longer caught up in the feeling that love brings pain. Liza knows that she doesn't have to prove anything to her partner about her self-worth. As a result, she's not obsessed with the well-being of others, and she's better able to concentrate on getting her needs met in a healthy relationship.

After several years passed, Liza met her husband, Ben, and they are approaching their fourth anniversary. While her relationship with Ben isn't perfect, it was born out of trust and vulnerability. For once in her life, Liza was honest with Ben, sharing her fears and insecurities. She recognizes that a good marriage is about respecting each other's dreams and making a commitment to work on communication and trust issues. Liza is devoted to Ben but, at last, not at a cost to herself. Over time, she has learned to be gentle with herself and Ben—who has earned her trust by demonstrating congruence between his words and actions. He has Liza's best interests at heart and reassures her when she loses faith in him. In return, Liza is learning to ask for what she needs emotionally rather than bottling up her feelings.

A turning point for Liza was the awareness that her fear of commitment was intertwined with her fear of intimacy and closeness, as well as feeling unsafe in relationships. And that all boiled down to her troubled relationship with her dad. Only when she faced her unresolved issues of trust and resentment toward her father could she achieve balance in other intimate relationships. Liza had the right to feel angry, but she needed to actively deal with her anger in order to let go of it and genuinely forgive her father. Author Melody Beattie writes, "Yesterday's smoldering coals—the unresolved feelings and unexamined messages—create today's fires. We work it out, or live it out. What we deny from yesterday, we'll be blind to today. And we'll have many opportunities to deny it because we'll continue to re-create it. Unfinished business may be buried, but it is alive and breathing. And it may control our lives."

Like Liza, it is important that you examine the beliefs you have about your father and his ability to change if you are going to heal. Let's look at Liza and how she ended the vicious cycle of self-blame, anger, and resentment toward her dad.

Misconceptions Daughters May Have about Improving Father/Daughter Relationships

❋ **My father isn't capable of changing.** It may be true that your father is resistant, but it could be that you haven't tried the right approach. Liza realized, for example, that talking on the phone wasn't an effective way to connect with her father. So she suggested they have lunch at a restaurant where they could talk freely. They began to have lunch regularly, and her father told her he was unaware of the extent of her mother's alcoholism.

❋ **My father will reject me because he was absent or distant in the past.** Liza believed that her father abandoned her and was aware of her mother's alcoholism. Her father shared that he regretted not fighting for custody of her when she was young but feared that it would harm her to testify against her mother. He also feared that Liza would reject him because he thought she preferred living with her mother.

❋ **My father didn't want to spend more time with me when I was growing up.** In some cases, fathers are separated from their daughters due to distance or not being aware of the importance of their role in their daughters' lives. As in the case of Liza's father, many dads aren't fully informed of their daughters' wishes for contact or their view of their living arrangements.

❋ **There's nothing my father can do at this point to improve our relationship.** Your first question should be: have I identified what I want to change about my relationship with my dad? Once you know this in specific terms, you'll be able to come up with a plan of action. Liza decided she needed ongoing contact and emotional support from her father. Once she let go of blaming him for the neglect she suffered from her mother, she realized she craved her father's nurturing and love. This set the stage for healing and a loving relationship between them.

HEALING THE FATHER-DAUGHTER CONNECTION

Once you have examined your beliefs about your father's ability to change, you are ready to begin changing your relationship with him. Holding on to the past and resentment will only cause you and others pain. The following guidelines for healing were adapted from H. Norman Wright's *Healing for the Father Wound* and Robin Casarjian's book, *Forgiveness: A Bold Choice for a Peaceful Heart*.

So now it's time to examine your relationship with your father and attempt to repair any father–daughter wounds through the action steps below. While parental divorce often alters the father–daughter connection, remember that it's never too late to attempt to heal this relationship. The first step is to acknowledge that there is damage and be willing to take a risk to examine the issues. If your bond with your father doesn't improve, acceptance of your situation is a worthy goal. If your relationship with your mother has been negative, these action steps can apply to her as well. Let's get started!

ACTION STEPS

※ **Let go of the "blame game" and attempt to forgive your father and yourself for thoughts or actions in the past.** Be honest with yourself about any wounds that exist and how you participate in the reality that you continue to experience.

⁎ **Explore your intentions and desires.** When you think about building a relationship with your father, what does it look like? Is it realistic for him to make up for what you lacked in the past? Accepting your dad for who he is will help both of you to reestablish a new bond, based on who you are today rather than on your idealized image of your father from the past. Counseling and talking to close friends can assist you in this process.

⁎ **Look at ways you may have accepted relationships that weren't healthy to fill the void your dad left.** For example, you may have dated or committed to unavailable partners or ones who were all wrong for you. Perhaps you repeated familiar patterns from your family blueprint in intimate relationships or marriage. Or you might have used denial to accept relationships that were self-defeating.

⁎ **Identify what you want from your father and attempt to be specific.** For instance, you may decide that a phone call once a month would be beneficial if you live at a distance or aren't ready for face-to-face contact. On the other hand, you might prefer to meet at a restaurant or neutral spot once a month. Write him a letter or call him and explain your intention. You need to take some control over this decision!

⁎ **Express your needs clearly and calmly to your father.** This could be verbally, in a letter or a written release. If you are requesting a change in your relationship, try to make one request at a time so he doesn't feel overwhelmed. Writing a statement can help you release any leftover negative feelings from the past. For example, one possible release is: "Dad, I release you for not spending as much time with me after you remarried. I still feel some resentment about this, but I'm working on letting it go." You may decide not to share your letter with your father, but this step can still be therapeutic. Or you may decide to write a letter to your father and include your release in it. This strategy can be used if you had a damaged relationship with your dad and you didn't have a chance to heal before he died.

※ **Be patient and adopt realistic expectations of your father.** After all, it may take time to reconnect after being distant for some time. Give up your dream of a perfect relationship with your father. Accept that tension may exist between you and know you can work through it. By giving her father some time, Liza reestablished the bond they had during her early childhood. "In the past, whatever I felt he wanted me to be, I tried to be—but not now. I can tease him, make fun of him, if I feel the need. He has come around from being very stern to showing emotion, but it took time," she says.

※ **Create healthy boundaries.** It may not be necessary to dredge up past hurt every time you meet. Since you can't change the past, you may be better off focusing on the present and the future. On the other hand, in some cases, you may need to ask questions to continue connecting in a loving way with your father. Liza felt the need to get factual information from her dad since she couldn't trust some of the things her mother told her about him.

※ **Seek professional help to deal with your wound with your father if your relationship doesn't seem to be**

improving (or if it is impossible to repair, as in cases where you don't know where your father is now). Many women find support groups highly beneficial because they can share experiences and learn positive strategies to deal with daddy deprivation.

⚹ **Accept the fact that even if your relationship with your father doesn't meet your expectations—or he is absent in your life—you can still let go of the past and write a new story for your life by developing other positive relationships.** It can be therapeutic to talk to a trusted friend or therapist about your disappointment.

> If you feel remorse because your father died before you had a chance to heal, be gentle with yourself. Remember, you can't control the past, but you can choose to take control of your life today. In some cases, you may make a choice not to be in a relationship with your father, and writing a release or a letter to him can help you to deal with unfinished business and move on with your life.

During our recent interview Liza says, "I don't blame my dad for leaving and I don't blame myself. My therapist helped me to realize that." Liza acknowledges that things don't always go smoothly, but she no longer blames her father for the divorce. When her father left, she was at a pivotal age in terms of observing her parents' relationship and forming beliefs about love and intimacy. At times, she is flooded with triggers, such as a negative comment, and she feels like a hurt little girl. But for the most part,

Liza no longer feels like a victim who is helpless to control her fate. This is proof positive that she has incorporated Step 3 into her life. Liza is learning to tell a new story about her life, in which she is surrounded by a loving husband, friends, and family. By examining her relationship with her father, Liza corrected faulty assumptions and beliefs, which allowed her to build trust in him and ultimately restore her faith in love

A Word From Terry: A Mother's Perspective

As I mentioned in the introduction, the breakup of my parents' marriage had a profound impact on my relationship with my father. As a young child, I was daddy's little girl and knew I held a special place in my dad's heart. In retrospect, the biggest factor that altered my relationship with my father was his remarriage. Like most divorced men, my dad remarried quickly after my parents' divorce—actually a year later—which didn't give me adequate time to adjust to the loss of our family. Another key element of my childhood was that my stepmother had a young son when they married. Consequently, I was forced to share whatever time I had with my dad with a new stepmom, stepbrother, and my three sisters.

Examining Eileen's story allowed me to gain insight into both the positive and negative aspects of my relationship with my father. I've always felt my father's love sustained me through some tough times. On the other hand, I remember questioning my dad's willingness to support me since my mother complained that he didn't pay enough child support. After he remarried, his time and resources were spread thin after he took on a new wife and stepson. As a result, having money in the bank has been a source of control and security for me throughout my life. Writing a letter to my dad facilitated a therapeutic experience wherein I was able to release hurt feelings and forgive him even though he died almost two decades ago.

The process of exploring my own father-daughter wound has been influential in helping me gain insight into the importance of the place Tracy's father has in her life. Consequently, I've been working on not interfering with their connection, even though I admit to feeling jealous of it at times. I believe that by honoring Tracy's bond with her father, I will be supporting her growth as a woman and ultimately helping her to restore her faith in love.

· · · · · · · · · ·

A Word From Tracy: A Daughter's Perspective

To say that a woman has "daddy issues" is usually considered a disparaging term. It means that she has low self-esteem and is looking for her romantic partners to fill the void left from an unhealthy relationship with her father. But the truth is that all women have "daddy issues" in varying degrees. No person has a perfect relationship with his or her parents, but a woman's relationship with her father is critical. He provides the first example of what she can come to expect from all other men. If he provides a poor example—if he is unkind, distant, or chooses other priorities—it can damage the father-daughter bond and adversely affect future relationships.

Some women have severely broken relationships with their fathers. Many aren't in touch with them at all. Some women were subject to abuse or neglect. Others have experienced blowout fights or long-standing hostilities. It would be easy to say these women have daddy deprivation because their situations are on the more extreme side of the spectrum. If your relationship with your father wasn't as extreme, it doesn't mean you are exempt from issues. If your parents divorced when you were a child, it is nearly impossible for your relationship with your father to have been unchanged. The hope is that this daddy deprivation can be satisfied. By doing the work to reconcile this important bond, all your other relationships will be nourished.

6

Step Four:
Building Self-Esteem

LET GO OF YOUR
CHILDHOOD HANG-UPS

"Inexperience can so often be your undoing. I accepted bad behavior too often in my past relationships, and stayed too long. Now, when I see a red flag, I confront it."

—*Theresa, age 25*

For daughters of divorce, childhood experiences run the gamut. Perhaps you grew up in a chaotic household, marred with substance abuse or other addictive behavior. Perhaps domestic abuse or infidelity tainted your childhood. Maybe a new stepfamily forever changed your quality of life and the way you see the world. Or perhaps you experienced an inner conflict living between two worlds if your parents had joint custody. No matter your experience, you undoubtedly endured some degree of disruption, even if your parents coparented as well as they could. Regardless of your circumstances, one truth remains: the way you feel about the woman you are today is a direct result of how you felt about yourself as a child.

Your relationships and the responses you receive from others have helped create your self-esteem. This started very early on within your family as your parents' divorce experience forever altered your sense of self-worth. As an adult, when you attempt to create romantic relationships of your own, you acquire a different sense of self. In *The Psychology of Romantic Love*, the late Nathaniel Branden, PhD, indicates that you experience who you are in the context of your relationships. He writes, "When we encounter a new human being, our personality contains, among other things, the consequences of many past encounters, many experiences, the internalization of many responses and instances of feedback from others." Negative experiences in relationships can change who you are as an individual, including what you expect from the world and what you expect from your romantic partners.

Sarah is a tall, attractive, athletic college basketball player. Her parents divorced when she was sixteen, and she describes her father as a verbally abusive alcoholic. As a result, competent-at-a-cost Sarah says she has learned not to rely on men. "I feel uncomfortable with men," she says. "My relationship with my dad caused me to seek approval in the wrong way. I don't know how to keep a guy without sleeping with him. I've had depression and anxiety and a sense of not being worthy of love. My friends have more self-confidence and better relationships than I've had." Her lack of self-esteem isn't unique or uncommon for a young woman with her past. Sarah's story rings true for so many daughters of divorce. She hasn't yet achieved Step 4, getting to the root of the belief that she's not good enough.

Before a woman can begin to build successful relationships, she must have healthy self-esteem. If your parents' divorce left you with a limited ability to see yourself as lovable and valued, you must build a positive sense of self on your own. Although your childhood experiences have helped create the woman you have become, it is up to you to carve out a new story for your life. Take the time to examine how your relationships have played themselves out and what role your self-esteem took.

Many daughters of divorce consistently put others' needs before their own and end up in one-sided relationships. The consequences can be profound, with girls and women dismissing their own needs and ending up with a depleted sense of self, according to author Jill P. Weber. She posits that many girls learn to tune out their own inner voice due to their family experiences, and this prepares them for one-sided relationships in adulthood. Weber writes, "As a woman develops a strong core sense of self, fulfilling relationships will follow."

Rather than submerging yourself in the lives of others and always thinking of ways to make them happy, you can build healthy self-esteem by respecting your personal limitations and recognizing your own gifts and talents. In *The Psychology of Self-Esteem*, Branden defines self esteem as "the experience of being competent to cope with the basic challenges of life and as being worthy of happiness." He goes on to say that the two basic essentials of self-esteem are self-respect and self-efficacy. Self-respect is the confidence in our right to be happy and achieve fulfillment, while self-efficacy is confidence in our ability to make appropriate choices and change.

Self-esteem means believing in yourself and trusting that you did what was best in any given situation. Self-esteem is based on your belief system—which is a blend of the way you feel about yourself and the way you believe others see you. Your view of yourself influences your perception of what you can do, how you get along with others, and how you cope with problems.

People don't acquire self-esteem all at once, and it fluctuates throughout their lifetimes. They may see themselves positively in one domain but negatively in others. Some daughters may feel confident in school, for instance, but lack confidence in relationships. Unsurprisingly, most of the women we interviewed reported more confidence in school and work than in intimate relationships.

Studies show that children of divorce are at increased risk for psychological, social, and academic problems compared to their counterparts in intact homes. However, it's important to recognize that these risks are moderate and can be affected by many factors. A recent British study reported that a quarter of young girls with absent fathers grow up to be depressed teenagers if their fathers leave before they are five years old, and that boys cope better than girls with parental separation. These findings suggest that girls are more vulnerable to negative life events than boys are.

My research published in 1996 found that daughters of divorce, but not sons, have low self-esteem when children didn't have access to both parents. Parental conflict—before and after divorce—was also associated with low self-esteem in females, but not males, in my study. An essential finding to consider is that harmonious relationships between parents post-divorce greatly reduced a daughter of divorce's risks for low self-esteem. As a result, it's important for parents and stepparents to model good communication, problem-solving, and conflict resolution skills.

Perhaps one of the most important factors in the development of self-esteem is the way a child sees her parents interact with one another. By and large, when two people divorce, they haven't been treating each other very well for a while. Without a healthy model to follow, a daughter may not know how it feels to forge a relationship based on kindness, mutual trust, and love.

As we saw in the previous chapter, the father–daughter connection is a key element of a woman's self-esteem. In fact, there is some evidence that a father can be a girl's ally in her struggle to establish a firm sense of identity. A girl's relationship with her father and/or stepfather can help her grow into adulthood with confidence in her ability to love and be loved. Author Meg Meeker, MD, writes, "It's important for every good father to know the impact of divorce on his daughter. Only then can he help her." After all, a daughter's relationship with her father is the first one that teaches her how she should be treated by romantic partners.

Below, we've listed identifiable characteristics of an individual struggling with low self-esteem. Certainly this list isn't exhaustive, nor do these qualities apply to everyone. Furthermore, one can have these feelings in varying degrees at different times. But as you read this list, identify which you recognize (or have recognized) in yourself—or which others have observed in you. The more honest you are, the more successfully you'll be able to tackle any self-esteem issues so they don't hold you back.

CHARACTERISTICS OF LOW SELF-ESTEEM

- You are too agreeable. You find yourself agreeing with others even if you truly don't feel the same way they do.
- You avoid confronting those who have treated you badly.
- You believe other people have it better than you do.
- You feel ashamed of your family or your upbringing.
- You feel guilty or ashamed of being angry. Perhaps you try to contain your anger.
- You often make disparaging comments about yourself or feel you "should be" doing something else.
- You are insecure about any contributions you make.
- You have been too clingy or needy at times. Conversely, you may not ask enough of your partner.
- You never feel like you deserve to be number one in anyone's life.

LOW SELF-ESTEEM AND PEOPLE PLEASING

Why do many women who have low self-esteem become people pleasers? As we've explored already, experiencing parental divorce can alter a girl's self-worth and make her feel damaged, even if her parents tell her it's not her fault.

In order to preserve relationships and be accepted, daughters of divorce may become overly compliant and even self-effacing. If they take on the role of caretakers, because one or both of their parents aren't coping well, this can set the stage for becoming a people pleaser. For many women, the underlying belief behind their being a people pleaser is that they aren't worthy—causing them to put others' needs before their own.

According to Gilligan, girls are socialized to seek approval from others, and they look to social connections to give them a sense of self-worth. Because women thus tend to derive their self-worth from relationships, they may be more vulnerable to the losses associated with having a divorce in their family.

> Learning to love yourself is an inner journey that involves examining your past from a fresh perspective. Take the time to investigate any carry-over from the past that might impact your current relationships. At times, people might resent you as you start to set boundaries and take care of your needs. But rather than giving in, it's important to embrace loving relationships without giving up part of yourself.

In order to improve your self-esteem, it's important to make a commitment to get rid of self-sabotaging guilt and fear. You can learn to assert yourself in relationships because you are worth it, even though you might believe you have no rights at all. Asserting your needs with others and setting limits may seem harsh. You may feel guilty expressing your needs—especially if this is a fairly new experience or you aren't sure what your needs are. Keep in mind, you deserve to have your needs met and you are worthy of love.

OUR FIRST RELATIONSHIP IS THE BASIS FOR ALL OTHERS

All children need continuity and predictability in their lives. A perfect example of this is the life of an infant. Competent parents provide security for their babies. If you have ever been around a baby, you know that if they aren't on a regular schedule for feeding and sleeping, they become irritable and hard to manage. This same principle applies as children grow. Once infancy passes, feeding and sleeping become less crucial. But all children still need the structure of a family life to help them feel grounded. The continued physical presence of both parents within a family unit provides the security kids need to thrive.

As children try to make sense of the world around them, it is important that they are able to predict the behaviors and responses of important people in their lives. If children experience a great deal of upheaval and unpredictability, they'll be wary of the world around them. They won't know what to expect, and they'll be unsure of their own actions. Furthermore, parents must continually validate their children's abilities in order for them to feel self-confident and sure of themselves and their place in the world. If this reinforcement is absent or inconsistent from parents, children won't develop healthy self-esteem.

WE'RE SOCIALIZED TO BE CARETAKERS

Girls growing up in this environment may take on a caregiver role. Some girls who were leaned on too much by their parents during or after a divorce develop a sense of helplessness and may ask themselves why they can't solve problems in the family. This kind of helplessness could lead to low self-esteem if it goes on for a while. In *For Better or For Worse*, Hetherington explains that girls with this profile tend to grow up fast and suffer from "parentification," where the roles of parent and child are reversed. If the parent is lonely or overburdened, the child may be asked to perform household tasks or emotional support beyond her capacity. How well parents and children cope with the transition from intact family to divided home determines their ability to weather adversity and maintain a healthy sense of well-being.

Those of you who were raised to be "good girls" learned to take care of others and to defer your own needs. Family therapists Claudia Bepko and Jo-Ann Krestan refer to this syndrome as "too good for her own good." They write, "In fact, most women suffer from the problem that has no name. While outwardly their lives may be changing, inwardly women still feel trapped by a deep conviction that their lives are on loan to them, borrowed from creditors, all those external arbiters who set standards for goodness and to whom they then feel responsible." Women are socialized to be caretakers. Typically this means putting others first and saying yes when they mean no. Harriet Lerner, PhD, writes in *Life Preservers*, "Historically speaking, women have learned to sacrifice the 'I' for the 'we' just as men have been encouraged to do the opposite, to bolster the 'I' at the expense of nurturing other family members."

THE WAY YOUR PARENTS FIGHT AFFECTS YOU

Children soak up everything they see, feel, and hear. Parents may believe they are giving their children all the love they need, but they send a conflicting message when they fail to reconcile their own relationships with their partners. Growing up, a child may see her parents fight constantly, but sleep in the same bed every night. They might complain about one another, but act upset when the other went away. Sometimes parents don't fight openly in front of children, but tension and anger seethe beneath the surface. These contradictions play a powerful game with a child's head. When a child is left with unexplained contradictions, she'll try to explain them to herself, often coming up with incomplete or incorrect conclusions. Thus when girls can't understand the turmoil around them, they tend to internalize this pain and blame themselves.

Sarah's insecurities are far more than that of an average college girl. They reveal the deep anxiety and low self-worth of a woman impacted by a being raised in a high-conflict divorced home. Sarah remembers growing up she always felt like she was walking on eggshells. Her father would blow up at her over little things, like leaving papers on a table or leaving a light on in a room. "It's so sad when I look back," she says. "I missed out on a lot. I've learned not to rely on men and that is why I'm so independent." There was also a large age difference between Sarah and her younger brother, leaving her without a buffer to shield her from conflict in the household. Hetherington's research indicated that having a female sibling can protect girls from disharmony in the family. Perhaps if Sarah had a sibling, particularly a sister, closer to her own age, she may not have taken the brunt of her father's problems. Sarah's mother was also weak and cautious, fearful of leaving her husband. All of this contributed to what Sarah calls her "independence."

But this independence has also robbed her of her ability to be vulnerable with others, assert herself in relationships, and love herself. With hesitation in her voice, she explains, "I'm learning to be more comfortable with being intimate and close with a guy, but it feels hard. I don't know how to interact with a man in a way that will make him stay." Sarah reveals that although she is working on herself and her ability to maintain an intimate relationship, she finds it difficult to be affectionate or kiss and hold hands with her current boyfriend. The shame from her childhood and the contentious relationship with her father has been a barrier for Sarah in building a healthy relationship.

Shame

Did you grow up believing that you weren't good enough or that others are responsible for making you feel safe and worthy? In her groundbreaking book, *Daring Greatly*, Brown explains that love and belonging are essential to the human experience. During her research, she noticed one factor separated those who felt a deep sense of love and belonging from those who seemed to be struggling for it. She writes, "Wholehearted living is about engaging in our lives from a place of worthiness. It means cultivating the courage, compassion, and connection to wake up in the morning and think, *No matter what gets done and how much is left undone, I am enough.*"

According to Brown, the root of our unworthiness is shame, which she defines as "the intensely painful feeling or experience of believing that we are flawed and therefore unworthy of love and belonging." She goes on to say: "Shame is a fear of disconnection—it's the fear that something we've done or failed to do, an ideal that we've not lived up to, or a goal that we've not accomplished makes us unworthy of connection. *I'm not worthy of or good enough for love, belonging, or connection.*" Being resilient to shame is about sharing our story with others who respond with empathy and understanding—shame can't survive when we reach out and connect to others. By doing so, we begin our journey toward loving ourselves and learn to practice self-compassion.

Self-Blame

Divorce leaves children with the ultimate feeling of rejection. Many girls internalize the breakup of their families and feel it is their fault. Logically, many girls understand that the dissolution of their parents' marriage didn't have to do with them. Often, parents take great pains to make sure their children understand they aren't to blame for the breakup. But girls often experience a disconnect between logic and emotions, leaving them feeling shameful, worthless, and damaged. Because of the way they grew up, they feel something is wrong with them. Deep inside they feel they aren't enough. Although they are lovable, they don't feel nearly as lovable as they are. It doesn't seem natural or normal for someone else to love them unconditionally, because they have been abandoned before. Although their heads tell them they ought to be loved, their hearts feel differently.

Feelings of Rejection

Cori is attractive, kind, and intelligent. Easy to talk to, the young professional doesn't come across as having low self-esteem. But upon further conversation, it becomes clear that her childhood greatly affected her self-worth. As a child she felt trapped by a strict and controlling father, and she remembers how scared her mother was to leave him. She describes her father as emotionally distant, never showing affection. "Other people always thought I had the perfect life because I was always going on vacation and always had the newest toys," she says, "but they didn't see what happened behind closed doors. I never loved my father the way a daughter should, which also had me experience mistrust. I believe that is why I pulled away from people. I felt that if I got too involved with someone, they would ultimately end up betraying me and not provide me with the love I needed." The connection between self-esteem and trust is an important one to make. Those who struggle with trust inevitably struggle with self-esteem. They are inextricably linked. In order to trust, you must love yourself. With damaged self-worth, it is impossible to build a healthy, trusting relationship and to achieve Step 4.

Cori describes herself as a very shy child. She recalls being bullied in school. The combination of a troublesome home life and cruel peers did a number on her self-esteem. "I remember one day I was about to walk into homeroom and about six of the boys in my class were lined up in the hallway and they all started to bark at me as I walked by," she recalls. Years later, she remembers how the cruelty of others still affects the way she feels about herself. In her adult relationships, Cori says, "every time a guy would show interest in me, I would pull away so I didn't get hurt. I almost felt like when a guy said he liked me, he was lying and trying to scheme me. I didn't feel good about myself so I didn't understand how someone could think I was pretty." Because she didn't feel good about herself, Cori feared that when a guy really got to know her he would leave her. And so she would leave her partners before they ever got the chance.

Cori is working on her self-esteem, and has found that focusing on what she has, rather than what she lacks, has been of enormous help. Rather than focusing on the pain and rejection she experienced with her parents' divorce, she is choosing to emphasize what she has gained. After her strict and controlling father left, Cori says, "I had more freedom to do the things I wanted. My stepfather is an incredible man. He took me in like I was his own and would do anything for me. I look at him as more of a father than my real father." Cori also highlights that her divorce experience has made her more selective about who she dates so she doesn't end up with a man like her father. Although she still struggles with feelings of low self-worth, Cori is aware of her issues, and she's making a concerted effort to maintain balance in her relationships.

Depleted Sense of Self

Nathaniel Branden makes an important distinction between those who have healthy self-esteem and those who don't. When meeting a new person, an autonomous individual will ask themselves, "What do I think of this person?" A dependent individual, or one who has low self-esteem, will ask, "What does this person think of me?" This is the classic problem many women encounter in relationships. Often, they are more worried about their partners than themselves. They seek validation, support, and love from their romantic partners because they don't feel it within. Branden writes, "But because the problem is essentially internal, because the person doesn't believe in him or herself, no outside source of support can ever satisfy this hunger, except momentarily. The hunger isn't for visibility; it is for self-esteem. The purpose of romantic love is, among other things, to celebrate self-esteem— not to create it in those who lack it." It is clear that an individual must possess healthy self-esteem before they can create a satisfying and healthy relationship. The problem is that women's previous relationships have changed who they are and how they relate to others. This makes it difficult to develop balanced relationships when they have no template to follow.

Women with low self-esteem often find it hard to assert themselves in relationships. They are afraid if they truly ask for what they need, their partners will reject them. Most daughters of divorce are hesitant to classify themselves as having low self-esteem, but in fact, battle with it every day. Most would be hard-pressed to say they consistently believe in themselves, maintain a healthy balance in their relationships, and feel confident in their abilities to get their needs met. The truth is, everyone struggles with self-esteem at one time or another. But there is hope for those who deal with this important issue. Although coming from a divorced home comes with a higher risk of damaged self-esteem, it is possible to improve and repair past damages.

LEARN TO LOVE YOURSELF

Theresa, a successful professional in her midtwenties, knows all too well the difficulties of asserting herself in a relationship. Her experiences prove that individuals feel most at home with partners whose self-esteem matches their own. She recalls falling in love and developing her first serious relationship when she was twenty-one years old. "I loved everything about Jeremy," she says. "Any outsider could have seen what a flawed person he was. He was older than me, he drank too much, and never really treated me the way I deserved to be treated. But he was my first love and I was determined to make the relationship work. I felt as long as I loved him the best way I could, he would love me back with the same purity and intensity." Theresa remembers that they had some good times, but he was always emotionally unavailable to her. Whenever she felt he was really opening up to her, it was always short-lived, and his drinking would continue or he would clam up again the next time they were together.

When Jeremy would reject or mistreat Theresa, she took it personally. As their relationship progressed and his alcoholism and depression became more apparent, she realized he had inner demons that existed before she entered the picture. Yet although

Theresa knew his problems weren't her fault, she took his failure to love her as the sign of a defect within herself. To fight against that feeling, she tried to be the most loyal, caring, and loving girlfriend imaginable. She was going to be the best partner anyone could ask for, because then Jeremy would have no reason to leave her.

None of this mattered, and Jeremy continued to mistreat her. So deeply in love and determined to make it work, Theresa could never leave him. They would break up and get back together again, with Jeremy always hoping for another chance, never adequately giving Theresa an explanation for his bad behavior, leaving her always wondering if there was something broken inside her. Through therapy and a great deal of self-work, Theresa's self-esteem improved, and she realized she could no longer be in a relationship that wasn't meeting her needs. Once her self-esteem rose to be greater than Jeremy's, Theresa found the strength to move on.

After Jeremy, Theresa quickly fell into a new relationship with someone her own age who adored her. James showered her with affection and affirmed his loyalty to her at all times. She never had to question his love for her. She felt this was exactly what she needed in the wake of her last disastrous relationship. They moved quickly in their romance, and after several months of dating, James revealed his dependence on prescription pain medicine. Their relationship quickly unraveled as Theresa found herself in a codependent relationship with a drug addict and then endured another painful breakup, wondering how she found herself in this place again.

"I learned a lot in those relationships," says Theresa. "Inexperience can so often be your undoing. I accepted bad behavior too often in my past relationships, and stayed too long.

Now, when I see a red flag, I confront it." Theresa is currently in a relationship with Michael, and feels it is healthy. "I bring up things with him when I am feeling scared or nervous or unsure. If there is an aspect of his life or his behavior that I am uncomfortable with, we talk about it. I'm trying to make sure we are working toward common goals. He is the most open, loving, caring, and nurturing man I have been with. He makes me feel safe." But Theresa is also careful to point out that she maintains her independence from her boyfriend, and she has taken the pace of their relationship rather slow.

Theresa admits that she is in no way a complete success when it comes to relating to men. But her own self-work and therapy have helped her to gain perspective and tools to cope. She is working hard to achieve Step 4 and is functioning in the "good enough" range of adjustment compared to many women her age. She recalls how her therapist explained her situation:

I know that total healing will come in time. After college, I saw a licensed psychologist who said that I had it all together mentally but not emotionally. He told me that my heart and my head were in conflict, that my emotions weren't there yet, that they hadn't healed. In my head, I know what's going on, but deep inside I feel something's missing. Psychologically and intellectually, I understand what happened (with my parents' divorce), but my heart hasn't completely healed. I feel that since all these bad things have happened, it's because of something I did. Something's wrong with me. And I know those thoughts are wrong, but my heart still feels it.

This is the insidious nature of low self-esteem. Most daughters of divorce are completely aware that their parents' divorce was no fault of their own, but emotionally, this hasn't sunk in. And so, like Theresa, they may appear to have their lives together, but inside they remain scarred, and their relationships suffer. In his book, *The Learning to Love Yourself Workbook*, Gay Hendricks, PhD, explains, "Most of us grew up around people who didn't feel loving toward themselves. They were burdened, or distracted, or hardened by life's catastrophes; discouragement was a backdrop, fear an undercurrent." It is important to understand that when others harm you, it is because of their own shortcomings, not yours. For the most part family members aren't malicious; they are dealing with life's stresses the only way they know how. Unfortunately, their inability to effectively deal with these challenges ricochets into other people's lives.

Theresa reflects that after her parents' divorce when she was eighteen, she rarely heard from her father. Then, on her twenty-fourth birthday, he called. "We had a very civil conversation," she says. "My dad reached out first because I think he realized that it's already done. The damage has been done. He screwed up." Theresa realizes her parents' divorce left her with a damaged bond with her father and low self-confidence. But forgiving her father for the pain of the divorce has been life-changing. She knows that more than anything, the forgiveness wasn't to absolve her father of any responsibility but to free herself from the pain. No longer would she let childhood wounds deprive her of the ability to enjoy a happy intimate relationship.

TRUST YOUR OWN JUDGMENT

Theresa says the most important part of her healing has been deciding who to let into her life. She knows she had bad judgment in previous relationships, and she has trouble trusting her judgment now. Sometimes she overlooked negative qualities in her partners because she wanted the relationships to work so badly. In her current relationship, she has taken a different tack. "I make it abundantly clear what I want," she says, "and he likes to know what I want." Theresa reflects that in the past when she and Michael would have a disagreement, she would cry and want him to apologize, but he didn't know the words she wanted to hear. Now she communicates, telling him exactly what she needs, and he is happy to comply. "I tell him exactly what I want and how I want it. So next time, he can do it," she smiles. Theresa is asserting her needs in the relationship, because she knows she is worth it. She knows she deserves to have her needs met. After all, feeling worthy of love is the cornerstone of accomplishing Step 4.

Although as a daughter of divorce you are at greater risk of having low self-esteem, it is possible to improve. Psychologist Virginia Satir encourages: "One of the kindest things we can do for ourselves at this moment is to take a look at everything we believe in and ask ourselves if it really fits or if it's something that we were told should fit. Is it a carryover from the past that we have accepted without any critical investigation?" Let there be no carry-over from the past. As Satir writes, "The beginning of new possibilities starts when you believe that there are no fixed, permanent sets of roadways inside you, that they are all capable of being resurfaced, reshaped, reconstructed, bypassed, and built anew." Although your childhood experiences have helped create the woman you have become, it is up to you to forge a new way forward.

LET GO OF HANG-UPS FROM THE PAST

Penny, age thirty-six, spent many years paralyzed by the pain of her childhood divorce experience. You might recall that her father was an adulterer and married three times. Instead of feeling the intense hurt associated with his rejection, Penny buried her pain and experienced emotional numbness. Tied into her numbness were feelings of guilt and shame because she believed that something was wrong with her. A sign of true healing is the ability to deal with the emotions about the loss of your parental home, grieve it, and move on to accept yourself and others.

During our second interview, Penny reflected on her divorce experience, saying, "I was very confused. I didn't know any other kids from divorced families. Somehow I was ashamed that my family was messed up." Clearly, she experienced a disconnect between her head and her heart. Although her head told her she was lovable and not to blame for her parents' divorce, her heart felt differently and she blamed herself. Shame and rejection were the precursors to Penny's low self-esteem.

As you might recall, Penny was drawn to Steven, who tried to control and dominate her. Perhaps she had an unconscious need to master unresolved issues with her father due to her feelings of shame and low self-esteem. Shame isn't easy to recognize or name, according to Marilyn Mason, PhD, a renowned expert on shame. She writes, "Shame carries strong injunctions; we can't say we're wrong, we made a mistake. With guilt, the self says, 'I made a mistake.' With shame, the self says, 'I am a mistake.'" Mason concludes that since shame is born within relationships, and women are more sensitive about relationships, they are prone to experience higher levels of internalized shame than men.

Let's examine Penny's view of herself and her relationships. Competent-caring, Penny was raised to please others and struggled to be on the good side of both parents. As a child, she began putting others' needs before her own—and became stuck in the approval trap. As an adult, Penny's self-esteem doesn't yet match her accomplishments. A human service professional, she is raising a daughter on her own. Penny is very successful at work, extremely self-reliant, and yet doubtful about love. In spite of her achievements, she has spent many years questioning her ability to trust others and find lasting love. Her marriage to Steven—who was ten years older—lasted five years and was a reenactment of her parents' troubled marriage, marred by emotional abuse and abandonment. With great self-assurance, Penny says,

Well after my divorce, now nine or ten years ago, and prior to my current relationship, I gave myself time to rebuild my personality and self-esteem. My mother made me feel that my divorce from Steven was brought about by something I lacked. Now I know better; my marriage didn't end because I did something wrong. It didn't end because I wasn't good enough for him—not a good enough cook, housekeeper, or whatever.

My self-esteem took a huge downward spiral (during my marriage), and things got worse when my ex-husband ridiculed my every move. My self-esteem has increasingly grown from the time of my first marriage and divorce in comparison to now.

Penny's comments reflect those of a woman who has worked on releasing these bottled-up feelings of shame and inadequacy. She realized she was unconsciously following a family script that was preventing her from achieving self-worth. Penny is going through a process Martin Seligman calls "shedding the skins of childhood," which often occurs during early to middle adulthood. This means she is becoming less focused on what others expect and learning to assert her needs—thus making changes in her life that make her happier and more in control. Rather than being a victim, Penny is setting boundaries in relationships and changing her beliefs about her role in them.

* * *

Why might parental divorce cause some women like Penny to develop diminished self-esteem and to lose confidence in themselves? This is a complicated question and should probably be explored during individual and group therapy sessions. However, what is known is that your relationships and the responses you receive from others help create your self-esteem. This starts early on, within your family and community. Nathaniel Branden, an expert on self-esteem, explains that negative relationships can alter who you are as an individual. He writes, "The process of growth presents many challenges to a child; every day presents him with new opportunities to expand his knowledge and skills, to explore the world around him and gain greater proficiency in dealing with it."

As a child, Penny was faced with many challenges—including her father's infidelity and absence, as well as a series of transitions after her mother remarried. She has worked hard to shake off insecurities and to keep people out. "I put up an unbreakable shield that didn't allow much of my significant other in," Penny explains. She questions herself and doesn't always feel good enough about who she is and what she does. But Penny strives to know and care about herself. She is working on finding self-worth that doesn't depend on others' view of her. The root of Penny's problem with low self-esteem was her belief system about her divorce experience.

Once Penny began to view her parents' divorce from an adult perspective, she began thinking differently about herself and relationships. Penny realized she blamed herself for her parents' pain and subsequently disrespected herself. She's learning an important lesson—how to give love without giving up part of herself. Today Penny is eager to begin the journey of self-discovery, and she is on the path to higher self-esteem. As your read through the action steps for Step 4 below, visualize yourself healing from the wounds and stresses from your childhood and taking charge of your life!

ACTION STEPS

* **Examine your divorce experience as a child or adult and identify any self-defeating messages that derive from it.** Strive for self-awareness, positive self-talk, and setting realistic goals.

* **Write an intention to achieve each day; boost your confidence by setting a goal.** For instance, take a risk and try something new such as practicing ten minutes of stretching or yoga in the morning. Or promise yourself you are going to reach out to that friend you've lost touch with. The intentions can be small, but they can have a huge positive impact on your self-esteem. Then follow through on them.

* **Use positive intentions to express how you feel and what you want.** For example, "I felt happy to be reading for thirty minutes today." You can use the same one for many days or set a new intention every day. Keeping your intentions and writing them down for twenty-one days can be inspiring and motivating. Adding a phrase about something you are grateful for can further enhance your intentions. For instance: "I am grateful for the sunny day."

✳ **Keep track of any negative automatic thoughts that pop into your head and cause you to feel distressed.** Words have power, so whenever you realize you're thinking a negative thought, replace it with a positive affirmation such as "I am learning to love and accept myself each day." Keeping a daily journal can help you with this process. It may seem unnatural at first but will become second nature after a while.

✳ **Change persistent negative thoughts to positive statements or self-talk in a more formal way.** For instance, if you tell yourself you don't accomplish enough, start a daily success journal and write down three things that you accomplish each day. Your self-worth will grow as you accumulate evidence of your accomplishments.

✳ **Make a list of happy thoughts.** Start by taking about fifteen minutes a day to list all the happy thoughts you can think of. List the people, places, and things that make you happy—such as good friends. The next step is to refer to your list of happy thoughts when you feel unhappy or unworthy. Make a personal commitment to think positively and to replace negative thoughts with happy ones from your list.

✳ **Create a vision board.** Post quotes, positive intentions, affirmations, goals, and photos of images that inspire you to feel good about yourself and your potential.

✳ **Cultivate partnerships with people who help you grow.** Healthy relationships are about mutual respect and reciprocity—they're not one-sided. The best partner will bring out your very best. When you are with him or her, you will begin to see untapped possibilities in yourself and in the world. This may mean shedding self-destructive relationships that bring you down. A significant other who truly cares about you will boost your self-esteem.

※ **Focus on your uniqueness and potential rather than your limitations.** Practice positive intention and take up a new hobby or interest. Nothing builds confidence like experiencing yourself learning a new skill. Remind yourself of how far you've come. For instance, you may not be a strong writer but you are a great cook. Keep practicing those things that you believe are your gifts. Persistence pays off!

With self-awareness and patience, you can turn your negative beliefs about yourself into power-packed positive thoughts. You don't have to let your parents' divorce dictate the decisions you make today or your view of yourself or relationships. Over time you will learn to trust your own judgment and replace feelings of failure with optimism about your future. Like all challenges in life, greater awareness and willingness to work on an issue can spark change.

A Word From Terry: A Mother's Perspective

Penny's story is a powerful reminder to me of my own issues with self-worth. On the outside she is competent and intelligent, but on the inside she doesn't feel good enough. I remember experiencing a similar disconnect between my head and heart that Penny described during our interviews. However, I can also relate to Penny's sense of self-reliance and inner strength. It is her determination to succeed against all odds that inspires me. Like Penny, I'm learning to love myself and set boundaries in relationships. Speaking up when people treat me unfairly is still a struggle, but writing in a journal and dialoguing with close friends has been healing. As a mother, I strive to communicate the importance of personal power and choice to my daughters. I remind myself every day that I don't have to define myself by my parents' mistakes and that I can surround myself with people who support my journey toward self-worth.

As a young girl, I was often unable to trust my own experience and can remember feeling numb and detached from any true expression of emotions after my parents' breakup. For most of my childhood and young adulthood, I prided myself on agreeing with others even when I didn't agree with them. In my childhood home, I was the people pleaser and strived not to make waves. Consequently, I avoided people who treated me badly and remember experiencing a knot in my stomach when I felt like standing up for myself but didn't. To this day, I am often insecure about my contributions and have difficulty naming my accomplishments or accepting praise. Penny's story illuminates the importance of not letting your parents' divorce define who you are as a person. My hope is that my daughters will recognize their inherent value and craft a new story for their lives.

· · · · · · · · · ·

A Word From Tracy: A Daughter's Perspective

Writing this chapter has crystallized two issues for me. A woman with healthy self-esteem will assert herself in a relationship and ask for what she needs. She'll also trust her own judgment about who to let into her life. Theresa's story exemplifies how self-esteem is an evolving process. Through trial and error with a few relationships, she has learned to ask for what she wants from her current partner. Experiencing the ups and downs of relationships and coming out stronger on the other side has helped her to be confident about her decisions. I know this has been true in my own life.

One thing my mom and I found to be universally true among the women we interviewed is that they were all hesitant to classify themselves as having "low self-esteem." Most women don't view themselves that way. A hallmark of low self-esteem is that a woman's head and heart are detached from one another. She may tell herself, "I'm smart. I'm capable at work. I'm a good mom. I'm a good wife." She may have people around her who love her and tell her so. But inside, she remains scarred, fearing the abandonment she experienced in childhood. No matter how many times people tell her otherwise, she feels at fault for all the pain she's endured. My hope is that the stories contained in this chapter provide greater insight for women looking to make improvements in their lives. The ultimate goal is to engage both the head and the heart, so that when a woman says, "I love myself" her heart actually feels it.

7

Step Five:
Learn to Trust Yourself and Others

Many women who grew up in divorced families wonder why they continually seem to pick the wrong guys. Even if they find themselves in a reasonably healthy relationship, daughters of divorce still may be unable to completely trust their partners. Sometimes, their partners are simply untrustworthy based on their past actions, so they have reason to feel leery. Other times, the initial breakdown in childhood has caused women to lack trust in their romantic partners.

When women mistrust their partners, they aren't simply distressed at the thought of becoming victims of infidelity. Mistrustful women hold the fundamental belief that their partners don't have their best interests at heart. Daughters of divorce may doubt their partners truly love them. They may believe the person they fell in love with will waver in his or her devotion. They may think their partner will change, and they'll be left wondering what happened to the person they fell in love with. Most of all, women who mistrust their partners are filled with a fear of abandonment.

Mistrust comes in many forms, from suspecting partners of infidelity to fearing that they'll abandon you emotionally or physically. Some women become "relationship junkies," looking for men to be salve for their wounds. Others avoid the option of finding love entirely for fear of being hurt. Trust is an act of courage, but it is the most crucial step to building a satisfying and lasting relationship. It's also important to keep in mind that trust is a skill that can be learned.

The stories that follow illustrate different types of mistrust and how Step 5 can help you build trust in intimate relationships. While Haley, Jenna, and Hannah, the women featured here, are all unique, they share something in common—they fear the people they love will leave them. They are learning how and when to trust more wisely. With courage and persistence, you too can turn hurts from past betrayals into lessons. But remember, don't be hard on yourself as you are learning to rebuild trust in relationships.

TRUST ISSUES

We sat down for coffee with Haley one afternoon. An outgoing and lively twentysomething, she has found herself in an on-again off-again relationship with a guy she just can't seem to break away from. "I've always known I'm the way I am because of my dad," Haley says. We found her frankness refreshing, and so we asked her more questions. Her story, similar to so many other women, reflects the root issue of trust. One of her most searing child-hood memories was waiting for her father to pick her up from her mother's home, and he never came. Haley relates that her father constantly went out drinking and eventually cheated on her mother, which ended their marriage. She goes on to say her father was selfish and immature and incapable of maintaining a healthy relationship with anyone in his family.

Objectively, Haley knows this was her father's fault and didn't have anything to do with her or her mother. Yet she constantly doubts herself. "I always feel inadequate," she says. "I feel like I'm with guys I can only get so close to." In her current relationship, she puts up with being treated badly by her boyfriend, Troy. She thinks that if she is the most thoughtful, loving, and caring girlfriend she can be, Troy will naturally respond the same way. But she knows this thinking is futile, because he never responds in kind. Troy's father left when he was a teenager, and he has told Haley he doesn't believe any relationship will last forever. Because they both have trust issues, their romance has been defined by ongoing arguments that never get resolved.

When Haley's partner doesn't treat her well, or devalues her love, she wonders why she isn't worth fighting for. She wonders what is wrong with her that won't allow a relationship to work. Haley never wants to be responsible for a relationship ending. With great intensity, she describes her struggle with finding lasting love: "It all has to do with the person you choose." She is right. And she knows she is right, but she continues to cultivate her relationship with an unsuitable partner. She longs for a boyfriend who would offer her love, security, and respect. But she says whenever she runs across a man who could potentially give her those things, she isn't attracted to him. All she knows is the cycle of inadequacy and mistrust.

Haley lacks trust in her own instincts. Although she knows her current partner isn't a good match for her and mistrusts his intentions, she lacks the courage to end the relationship. While many of her friends are in committed relationships or have plans to marry, Haley remains frozen and unable to make a decision due to her cycle of mistrust—staying in a relationship that's all wrong for her but lacking the skills to trust herself or others. While she acknowledges the connection between her divorce experience and current relationship dysfunction, she hasn't yet chosen to follow Step 5.

LOOKING FOR INFIDELITY IN ALL THE WRONG PLACES

Jenna has a similar story. A warm and engaging twenty-six-year-old, her close-knit Hispanic family unraveled when her father left her mother for another woman. Her parents divorced when she was fourteen, when she was just starting to blossom as a young woman and make relationships of her own. She recalls, "I remember Valentine's Day. That was the day my family began to fall apart and all that I knew no longer existed. That evening, my dad was going to a party and left my mom at home. It turned out he took another woman to the Valentine's Day party." Jenna was the first person her father told about his infidelity. Not long after the party, her father sat her down and said, "I slept with her," meaning his mistress. "No matter how many years pass or how many therapy sessions I have," Jenna explains, "my disgust for the whole thing will never go away."

Family life as she knew it drastically changed from that point. Like many other daughters of divorce, Jenna grew up fast since she became a shoulder for her mother to cry on and a second mother to her siblings. She recalls being left alone a lot with her younger siblings when she was in high school, even overnight a couple of times. Carrying around the burden of her father's infidelity put an abrupt end to her childhood: "I turned upside down. Everything safe and comforting was taken away. I became vulnerable and untrusting. I was fourteen years old and I was no longer a child."

During adolescence and young adulthood, Jenna experienced several unhealthy relationships. Her boyfriends cheated on her, even at times inflicting physical abuse. With great intensity, Jenna says: "I picked one bad boyfriend after another. I was attracted to bad boys, abusive physically and emotionally. I never believed I was good enough for anyone decent to stick around for. I was afraid to be alone." Then one day on an impulse, after a boyfriend punched her in the face during a heated dispute, she packed her belongings and booked a flight to Florida. In her case, Jenna wasn't looking for a vacation, but a fresh start in a new city where she knew no one and could fade into the crowd.

After several years of therapy and attending a community college to pursue a degree in nursing, Jenna met her current boyfriend, Trevor. After avoiding commitment for many years, Jenna met Trevor through a friend and began dating him. At first, Jenna feared that Trevor would leave or cheat on her. It makes sense that Jenna was hesitant to trust Trevor since she was betrayed by her father and previous romantic partners. Here's how Jenna put it: "My biggest issue is trust, not being able to control the other person the way I want to. I know I need to take one day at a time and give Trevor a chance. But even though he's my best friend, I fear that one day he may be gone."

Trevor hasn't given Jenna a reason not to trust him. He has never cheated on her, and he always reassures her of his love for her. All in all, he treats her quite well. But the scars from her past continue to plague her. When she thinks about her parents' divorce, she says it has almost cost her current relationship. "Several times I almost lost Trevor because I was mistrustful, overly jealous," she says. Jenna would question Trevor about where he was going, who he was going to be with, and when he would be home. Even if Trevor had given her no reason to suspect anything was wrong, her first thoughts were always colored with doubt and fear. Her anxiety would rise when he left, because anything could happen when he was gone.

FEAR OF INFIDELITY

Infidelity is a key issue for many daughters of divorce. "I don't trust men," Haley says. "I firmly believe that all men cheat. I don't think there is a man out there who hasn't or wouldn't cheat. I also have a tendency to be cold or withholding with men who really like me and would treat me well." When girls like Haley witness their father cheating on their mother, it shatters their view of men. A girl's father is her first template for what to expect from all other men, and no matter how far she is from her childhood, this expectation never seems to fade.

"Just look at my parents," Jenna says. "They were together since age thirteen. Men are bound to be curious. I worry that I'm going to look older. Maybe that's why I work out, so I look the best I can for Trevor, so that he doesn't want to look at other women." Haley also focuses on her appearance and works out religiously to maintain a nice body. Just like Jenna, this is all tied into her self esteem. By working out extra hard, Haley tries to prove just how worthy she is. What she craves is security, love, and respect. What she wants is a man who embodies, in her words, "I'm there for you." She wants everything her father wasn't, but she can never seem to find it.

It's understandable that Jenna's perspective on relationships is also skewed. Her parents were once childhood sweethearts. This is the sort of history so many people crave but are rarely blessed to experience. Her parents had it, and her father walked away from it. This cruel fate has influenced how she views all other relationships. Ultimately, cheating is so much more than an act of physical betrayal. It is a choice to abandon a life you have built with someone. It is a broken promise, a revocation of love. And when a woman has been the victim of such an offense, she is never the same again.

FEAR OF ABANDONMENT

Infidelity isn't the only trust issue for daughters of divorce. Mistrust, at its origin, is really the fear of being left. A woman can be afraid her partner will abandon her in all sorts of ways, and it doesn't always involve him or her leaving with another person. Sometimes the biggest betrayal is when a partner leaves emotionally. Many women fear that when someone truly to gets to know her, really know her, he'll ultimately leave her. She questions if the words her partner tells her are true. One day this person might change his mind. One day he might stop loving her, and there will be nothing she can do to stop it.

Proving trust is so much more than catching your partner in a lie. To trust someone, you must have faith in them. You must have a strong belief and conviction that you won't be hurt by your partner. You must believe your partner is honest and dependable, and that you are his or her first priority. Can you say that you are truly confident in your partner? Are you confident that your partner is truthful, faithful, and in every way present in your relationship? Cultivating this sort of relationship is the greatest challenge for many daughters of divorce.

No person is perfect, but the best partner is the one who is willing to go on the journey with you. "The moment he would tell a small lie I would be ready to be done," says Jenna of her boyfriend. Although Trevor wasn't perfect, he was always open. And any transgressions he made weren't so large that he and Jenna couldn't work through them. "You think the worst in every possible situation. Thankfully, he has been very patient, the only patient person who I have dealt with. And he's helped me to be [more trusting]. In the beginning, I didn't realize how fearful I was until I was with Trevor. Because he was worth me working on myself and being aware of what I was doing wrong," Jenna says. "Before that, no one was ever worth it."

Although every relationship is different, it is important for you, as a daughter of divorce, to realize how you can be your own saboteur. Love is a leap of faith, and there are no guarantees. This is true for all people, whether or not they grew up in divorced families. When your first reaction is to act from a place of mistrust, this shows a lack of confidence in your partner.

The scariest thing about falling in love is living with the knowledge that it might end. You are faced with a choice. You can come at relationships from a place of love and trust, or you can choose to be suspicious, doubtful, and wary. The most important thing to consider is whether your partner is worthy of trust. Have his or her actions matched his or her words? Does your partner treat you with respect? Is your partner reliable? Is your partner faithful and truthful? If the answer to these questions is yes, you must choose to trust. It is possible you might end up getting hurt. But if your partner has shown you trustworthy behavior, you should reward him or her by showing trust in return. Jenna's story illustrates how it is possible to work through Step 5 if you extend trust to those who are worthy of it.

AVOIDING ABANDONMENT BY AVOIDING COMMITMENT

Some women take the opposite tack of Haley and Jenna. Hannah, an information technology specialist in her late twenties, has sworn off relationships altogether. Competent-at-a-cost, her parents' divorce made her lose faith in others. "I want commitment, but I don't trust someone else to commit," Hannah says. "I long for commitment but don't believe what I want is possible." Her experiences have made her skeptical of others' true emotions and intentions. Even if she had a relationship where her partner professed his love and devotion, he could just as easily change his mind. Living with the risk of getting hurt is just too much for her to bear.

Hannah has every reason to feel this way. Her parents' marriage and subsequent divorce was shrouded in secrecy and masked intentions. Hannah recalls that her mother and father never even told her they were divorcing. Her father's things simply started disappearing from their house over a period of several weeks. Her grandparents, whom she started spending more time with, were the ones to explain her parents' separation. Perhaps cheating has never been an issue in her life, but the fear of being left is an even greater deterrent to trust.

At the very root of mistrust is the fear that when your partner truly knows you, he'll leave you. When these thoughts permeate your mind, it may become difficult to be emotionally intimate and vulnerable with him. It is the uncertainty of love that scares you. Relationships can fade away or end abruptly. Faced with this reality, you may try to control your partner's behavior for fear of losing him. Or as in Hannah's case, you may avoid attachments altogether to avoid the prospect of losing love all over again. Hannah operates from a viewpoint that a prospective romantic partner wouldn't have her best interests in mind. She has chosen not to embrace Step 5. If Hannah continues to let her fears consume her, she'll most likely close herself off from the opportunity to find real love and intimacy with a partner.

LEARNING TO TRUST

In adult relationships, daughters of divorce have a tendency to reenact the pain of their childhoods. The love a child has for her parents is meant to evolve into a love for an adult partner. Our parents model what that love should look like. If that model is unhealthy or absent, it is only natural to feel like a ship lost at sea, losing direction but desperately seeking a straight course. The most satisfying type of love is the kind that endures time and temptation, the kind that endures life's hardships and comes out stronger on the other side. Since you haven't experienced this kind of love in your own family, you may not believe it is possible.

Think back to your parents' divorce. You may feel a potent sense of rejection from it, which is a common emotion. It's the same feeling evoked by the heartache of a breakup.

While many daughters of divorce would like to think they seek out partners who will be good for them, they may choose ones who will bring them some sort of pain or unavailability because that's what they know from their parents' divorce. After all, security and fulfillment weren't in their realm of experience as children, so why should it be as adults? Like them, you may not feel confident in your ability to create a satisfying and lasting partnership. The goal, then, is to overcome the mistrust first experienced in childhood.

Take a moment and consider this: your partner isn't solely responsible for creating mistrustful feelings. You must take equal responsibility for creating an atmosphere of safety and security in your relationship. In order to begin the process of overcoming mistrust, ask yourself:

* Does my fear of loss and abandonment cloud my perspective and cause me to overreact to my partner's actions?
* Do I bring my best self to my interactions with my partner?
* Do I feel comfortable asking for what I need and allowing myself to be vulnerable?
* Do I possess self-love and expect to be loved and respected?

While your relationships may not always have been resounding successes, you undoubtedly can claim achievements in other areas of your life. Perhaps your turbulent childhood made you self-reliant, and as a result you have always been hardworking and attained much success at work or school. Or perhaps you have always been a good friend and have held those relationships as important as family. Maybe you are already a mother, with children of your own, and take great pride in your ability and skill to nurture and care for your family. There are countless things you can be proud of. And in order to become successful, it was critical to be self-assured, positive, and confident in your abilities.

You must take the same tack in your relationships. Before you seek to trust your partner, you must first realize that you possess all the tools you need to create a healthy relationship. You must believe that within yourself, you possess the very ingredients necessary to build a lasting partnership. How is this possible, given your past and your innate hesitancy and doubt surrounding relationships? First you must identify the thoughts and actions that have sabotaged your ability to trust.

ELEVEN BELIEFS THAT SABOTAGE TRUST

Although Haley, Jenna, and Hannah have different experiences with parental divorce, they have all come out with similar presuppositions about love. Women with trust issues often doubt that a lasting partnership or marriage is possible, which sets them up for failure from the start. Check out the following list and see if one or more of the following beliefs has crossed your mind before.

1. Love is easily broken, and despite everything I try, it may disappear.
2. If I show my partner the true me, he probably won't like me and will go away.
3. I can't ask for what I need, because my partner will likely reject me.

4. If I show how much I want to be loved, it will scare my partner.

5. If my relationship fails, I am unlovable.

6. Marriages trap people.

7. All relationships end.

8. Marriages and relationships may work for a while, but they always end up souring.

9. Everyone I love eventually leaves me.

10. There is something wrong with me, and I don't know what it takes to make a relationship work.

11. I always pick the wrong partners, or the wrong partners always pick me.

All of these statements reflect a lack of confidence. If you truly want to have a lasting and satisfying relationship, you must first acknowledge and work to overcome your self-doubt and lack of self-acceptance. Trusting yourself will only happen when you are able to love others in a committed way and believe in your ability to find lasting love.

We can say this with certainty: there isn't one person on this planet who hasn't made mistakes when it comes to relationships. We can also say with certainty that some make more mistakes than others. But only the truly masochistic make poor decisions and relish the results. Most of us hope we are making good choices at the time, only to get badly burned later. If you've had your heart broken a couple times, you may start to lose trust in yourself. After all, if you've made bad choices in the past, how do you know you'll make the right ones the next time around?

SHAME: THE FOUNDATION OF MISTRUST

Many of the women we've spoken to feel a sadness or embarrassment they can't quite name when they talk about troubled
relationships that ended badly. But I'll put a name to it—shame.
Perhaps you survived domestic violence and are ashamed to admit
you were treated that way. Maybe your partner cheated on you
and you're embarrassed to say that, as it might make you seem
like you're not worth being loyal to. Maybe his or her critical
comments did a number on your self-esteem. Maybe he or she had
a substance abuse problem, which in turn inflicted its own sort of
abuse on you. Experiences like that can change you. Worse than
making you feel like you did something wrong, shame can make
you feel like you are something wrong.

Brown has taught us that empathy is the antidote to shame. But
I also believe that empathy can help restore faith in your ability to
make good decisions. After ending a distressed relationship, many
women find it difficult to trust the next man who comes into their
lives. They fear that in time, he'll change. After being hurt, many
women approach new relationships with caution and restraint.
They look back on the past and wonder how they could have
made so many mistakes. How can you know the next relationship
will be different?

Those who enjoy healthy relationships have learned from their
mistakes and have treated their wounds with compassion. Just
like you would say to your friend, "I've been there too." Or, "I
know how you feel, I've gone through the same thing." What
would it mean to say the same thing to yourself? Remind yourself,
"Everyone goes through hard times in relationships. I'm not the
only woman to have made this mistake." Instantly, you start to feel
less alone. With an empathetic attitude, you start to connect to the

rest of the world, as you remember that everyone has missteps. And you start to realize that the wonderful thing about judgment is that it can be improved. You might not get a second chance at your relationship, but there is still redemption for those who have made mistakes.

As a daughter of divorce, you likely don't trust others to love you because you don't fully love and believe in yourself. If your relationship ends, you may feel something is wrong with you. The uncertainty of relationships scares you, because you so desperately crave love, commitment, and a lasting partnership. As you embark on the journey to love and trust both yourself and others, it is crucial to remember that there isn't anything wrong with you if a relationship ends. It simply wasn't the right relationship.

Haley claims to want a healthy, enduring relationship. Yet she keeps her relationship going with Troy, who continually tells her he never wants to get married. Since Haley would like to get married one day, this relationship is clearly incompatible with her needs. Furthermore, he can never give her the emotional intimacy and reliability she craves. These painful feelings in her current relationship trigger the heartache and rejection of her childhood. And so her desires and her intentions don't match up. She hasn't yet gathered the courage to trust her ability to develop the type of relationship she needs. Uncertain and tenuous love is the only kind she has known, and so it is the kind she has perpetuated into adulthood.

At the root of Haley's mistrust and lack of confidence is shame. The breakdown of a marriage often makes a child believe something is wrong with him or her. As a daughter of divorce, you may believe there is something inherently flawed about you and where you come from. Since you weren't good enough to keep your family together as a child, how could you possibly be able to keep a happy and cohesive relationship as an adult? You might focus on your shortcomings rather than on your abilities. Most of all, you fear abandonment because of the unworthiness you feel.

Perhaps as a child you were embarrassed to tell your friends or other kids in school that your parents were divorced. This is a perfect example of how shame can start to permeate a child's heart. She may be told that the divorce isn't her fault, and logically she may know that she didn't do anything to cause it, but shame nevertheless grabs hold of her. This leaves her with a feeling that something within her is ugly or defective. As a daughter of divorce, you might have felt unwanted, unloved, or invisible. You may feel embarrassed by a divorce you didn't want, especially when you saw other children living in intact homes.

Brown believes that shame and vulnerability are connected. Shame erodes the piece of us that believes we are capable of change. She concludes, "We all have shame. We all have good and bad, dark and light, inside of us. But if we don't come to terms with our shame, our struggles, we start believing that there's something wrong with us—that we're bad, flawed, not good enough—and even worse, we start acting on those beliefs. If we want to be fully engaged, to be connected, we have to be vulnerable. In order to be vulnerable, we need to develop resilience to shame." Haley is freezing out the opportunity to let her authentic self shine and to share her innermost thoughts, feelings, and wishes with intimate partners. Her sense of shame and fear of being vulnerable has created a pattern of emotional disconnection with potential partners who might be a good match for her.

The most difficult part of feeling ashamed is that you, as a daughter of divorce, have done nothing to deserve feeling this way. You aren't guilty of any mistake. You have simply been on the receiving end of a difficult crisis. Ronald and Patricia Potter-Efron's work, *Letting Go of Shame*, highlights the following experiences. As a daughter of divorce, you likely have experienced shame, with varying degrees, in the following ways:

* ❋ You are hesitant to accept praise. You don't believe the compliments others pay you are true.
* ❋ You see yourself as a burden to others.
* ❋ You think others tolerate you being around. You find it hard to believe anyone really wants you.
* ❋ You are overly critical of yourself, or you are prone to criticize others.
* ❋ You feel empty and unworthy.
* ❋ You have difficulty letting things go.
* ❋ You apologize for things that aren't your fault.

Shame eats away at the core of your very existence. It is no wonder you may have found it difficult to sustain healthy relationships, because you live with thoughts of shame in your head. This may be why you find it so hard to trust your partner and to allow yourself to be vulnerable with him. It is exactly why you find trust so fickle, elusive, and difficult to maintain. "I think at first I trust someone until I fear them leaving," Haley says, "and then I lose trust for no reason at all." This comment reflects deep-seated shame. She loses trust for no reason at all because as a child, Haley's world shattered for no reason at all. No reason that she had any control over.

Like Haley, you may tend to lose yourself in love. Because of the childhood you endured, you might seek unconditional love from your partner but rarely receive it, or not recognize it when it exists because it's alien to you. Most of all, you may be attracted to the emotional qualities in others that you have refused to acknowledge within yourself. When you haven't fully worked through the pain of your childhood, you are bound to relive the turmoil of the divorce experience. Consciously or unconsciously, you find yourself in relationship patterns that mirror the unhappiness of your upbringing. It is only when you have broken free of the ashamed, hurt, and abandoned girl that you can become a strong, confident, and trustful woman.

Women who aren't yet healed seek partners who are as wounded as they are. Unhealthiness is contagious in relationships. But when you are fully healed, you remove yourself from any individuals who don't contribute toward your health. You will seek out those who love you, those whom you can share your feelings with, and those who provide you with comfort and security. Most importantly, a healed woman is one who challenges the deeply held negative opinions she has of herself and her childhood. This allows her to embrace Step 5 and extend trust to others who are trustworthy.

Jenna is working hard to rebuild trust in intimate relationships. She has found learning to trust, more than anything else, is about courage. When we caught up with Jenna later in our study, we were pleased to hear that she and her long-term boyfriend, Trevor, had gotten engaged. Like many daughters of divorce, Jenna dealt with feelings of mistrust and shame. Her prior boyfriends never treated her well.

"Until I met Trevor, I was one of those women who wouldn't let anyone get close to me. I didn't want to rely on anyone. I've fought with that for a long time. I'm learning to let Trevor help me," Jenna says. By her own admission, she felt ruined by her parents' divorce. "Until I met Trevor, I was the girl who didn't want to get married. Why put myself in that situation when I can prevent things from happening all over again? Why bother, just to get hurt?" Clearly, something changed for Jenna. And it wasn't that she simply got lucky by meeting a nice guy like Trevor. She found the courage to trust, and it took a lot of work.

First and foremost, Jenna challenged her thoughts of shame and mistrust. As cliché as it sounds, she learned to love herself. Learning to love yourself is an inner journey that involves examining your past from a fresh perspective. If you can't believe you are good enough, how can you believe a new partner would choose you? Take the time to investigate any carryover from the past that might impact your current relationships. Make a commitment to get rid of self-sabotaging guilt and fear. You deserve to have your needs met, and you are worthy of love.

FINDING A GOOD MATCH FOR YOU

While Jenna weeded through many unsuitable partners, she easily could have thought something was wrong with her. But she wisely realized something was wrong with *them*. When she finally found a loving, caring, and devoted partner in Trevor, she also found herself able to work through issues rather than being scared of them. "Being with Trevor has taught me that you don't run away from the problem; you deal with it head-on. You work through it together, as a team, and in the end it makes you stronger," Jenna says. She is a work in progress, like anyone else, but she is moving forward.

As a daughter of divorce, it is important to find a partner you can be vulnerable with. He or she needs to understand the source of your trust issues. And if your partner can't be reassuring and empathetic, he or she isn't the right one for you. As a rule, daughters of divorce are fiercely loyal, loving, and protective. Since you do your best not to be careless with other people's hearts, you shouldn't put up with people who are careless with yours.

Perhaps most crucially, Jenna worked through years of mistrust and painful experiences with her father. Because Jenna felt rejected by her father, she ended up building barriers in her relationships with men as an adult. Jenna, like so many daughters of divorce, saddled those feelings of rejection and inadequacy on herself. Due to her father's infidelity and her parents' painful divorce, Jenna's perspective on relationships was skewed, and she has struggled with trust issues for over a decade. Trevor has never given her a reason to mistrust him, but her father's infidelity had shattered her view of men. Finally, when she was truly able to internalize that her father's problems weren't her own, she could begin to heal. Jenna says,

> I was able to overcome my fear of cheating through counseling and reading, and through Trevor himself. It takes a special man to deal with a person who has trust issues. I was lucky and blessed to meet Trevor. His patience, understanding, and support have helped me cope with my trust issues. In situations where I was most vulnerable, Trevor reassured me of his love and commitment. He never turned his back and became frustrated with my repeated accusations.

He simply, devotedly gained my trust time and time again. He never missed a beat and with every promise, he delivered.

Although Jenna is working to overcome her trust issues, she must remember to be gentle with herself as she is making peace with her past. "Yes, I fear that people I love will leave me," Jenna says, "but not as much as I used to. I fear that one day I'll wake up and Trevor will be gone. But I try to live with that fear and try not to let it affect me. Good thing he's a great guy and every day says, 'I want you.'"

Jenna speaks candidly, sharing her innermost thoughts: "At one point I thought that it was impossible, but I no longer think this way. I'm actually excited to go on this journey with him and see where it takes us. We are very happy and most of the time we talk things out." But at times, Jenna withdraws or lets her fears get the best of her: "Trevor will say, 'Jenna, talk to me, you can't do that!'" In her relationship, Jenna has been able to communicate to Trevor her deepest needs, and he has been able to respond with kindness and a willingness to get to the bottom of any problem. This is important for all relationships, but even more so for women with trust issues.

As we sit in a quiet café near her apartment, Jenna reflects on a story from her early courtship with Trevor that illustrates her struggles with trust and intimacy. One night, after Jenna and Trevor enjoyed a dinner out, Jenna was struck by feelings of mistrust that almost ruined their relationship. As they sat in front of Trevor's computer screen surfing the Web, an instant message popped up from a female whose name Jenna didn't recognize. Rather than question Trevor, she froze her feelings and went into panic mode. Meanwhile, Trevor ventured into the kitchen to grab a snack—unaware of Jenna's mistrustful, hurt feelings. Overreacting without thinking the situation through, Jenna bolted out the door without saying a word to Trevor.

Fortunately, Trevor knew enough about Jenna's trust issues to text her immediately—stopping her in her mistrustful tracks. He reassured Jenna that the message was from a high school friend whom he hadn't seen in years. Jenna quickly regained trust in Trevor. This example demonstrates the importance of picking partners who understand your history and are willing to show you—through word and deed—that they are worthy of trust and that it's safe to show vulnerability. Reflecting on that story now, Jenna sees how far she has come. She almost doesn't recognize the petty, suspicious person she was at the beginning of her relationship with Trevor.

Jenna's comments highlight the importance of unlocking the past and examining thoughts, attitudes, and beliefs about oneself and others. Here is how Jenna put it:

I know that my mistrust of my fiancé is basically a projection of my parents' relationship and even more so, my previous relationships. I try to remember that Trevor isn't my ex and that he is loving and supportive. Most of my feelings of mistrust are self-conjured. We talk about the goals in our relationship and how to achieve them. My counselor suggested that we have a plan to achieve goals…personal, financial, etc….so we usually evaluate where we are within our plan about once a month.

The most important belief that you need to embrace as a daughter of divorce is that you are capable of change. You were born with a propensity to trust, but through life experience, you have become mistrustful as a way to protect yourself. Perhaps you are hesitant to trust others because you are afraid of being rejected. It may seem at times that you are wired to re-create the past. However with courage and persistence, you can learn to trust again and restore your faith in love.

Jenna's story is an inspiring one for all of us, and we're all capable of changing for the better like she did. As we've seen in this chapter, it's crucial to decide to build trust in your intimate relationships. Rather than always taking a reactionary stance, try to operate from a viewpoint that your partner wants the best for you and won't hurt or abandon you. Let your partner show you, through their behavior, that he or she is dependable. If you don't have a partner currently, work on extending trust to someone who demonstrates consistency in his or her words and actions (say a friend or coworker). Practice trusting others in small steps. Learning to trust is a skill that can be nurtured over time, and the following action steps will help you get started.

ACTION STEPS

* **Pinpoint how your parents' divorce may impact your feelings of trust in intimate relationships.** Self-awareness will enable you to identify current situations that trigger mistrust.
* **Learn to trust your intuition and instincts.** Have confidence in your own perceptions and pay attention to red flags such as inconsistencies between your partner's words and behavior. Don't beat yourself up over what

you perceive as your weaknesses or mistakes—or the mistakes of your parents.

* **Take responsibility for your own reactions and focus on changing your mistrustful mind-set.** Apologize when you jump to conclusions and overreact to your partner's behaviors that may not have been intended to be hurtful or deceitful.

* **Extend trust to partners worthy of trust.** When others have lost your trust, don't be quick to judge. Don't automatically assume that a failure in competence is a failure in character. Many mistakes aren't intentional; don't make them into something they're not. Listen to your partner's side of the story. Avoid blaming or criticizing your partner if you confront him or her with feelings of mistrust.

* **Challenge mistrustful thoughts.** Ask yourself: Are my mistrustful feelings a result of my past or present relationship? Be willing to take a leap of faith if you don't have all the information, and don't assume the worst of your partner.

* **Adopt a resilient mind-set and don't issue ultimatums to your partner.** You will be better able to withstand the highs and lows of an intimacy if you have a foundation of trust and avoid threatening to end the relationship. Ask yourself: Has my partner has been honest with me so far? Are they mostly reliable and dependable? If so, these are signs of someone who is trustworthy.

* **Be aware of "hot-button" issues**—a term coined by Seligman to describe topics such as money, sex, work, or in-laws that trigger feelings from past relationships and may cause you to overreact. You may recall that Kelly felt mistrustful when her husband, Mark, returned late

from work. Because her father had been unfaithful with a coworker, work relationships became a hot-button issue.

❋ **Practice self-compassion when you stumble and overreact** to something small that your partner says or does that triggers feelings of mistrust. Be gentle with yourself on your journey to becoming more trusting of others!

Daughters of divorce come from many different backgrounds, and their experiences have shaped them in singular ways. But nearly all of them have emerged with problems trusting others. Perhaps you are like Hannah, with a heart of stone. Your fears and insecurities have trapped you so much that you are afraid of ever loving anyone, because they might leave you. So you refuse love altogether, believing that freezing it out is far less painful than letting it in. Or maybe you are like Haley, who continually finds herself with an unsuitable partner who can never truly meet her needs. Her trust issues keep perpetuating themselves seemingly without end, because she hasn't yet worked through why she feels so damaged. Or you might be like Jenna, who has been cheated on, abused, and abandoned in a multitude of ways, but who nevertheless presses on, understanding that trust is a skill that can be learned and improved.

Most women raised in disrupted homes are in different stages of progress toward the same goal. They each have unique divorce stories, and in turn, their own unique relationship histories. Your heart may have been broken more times than you care to remember. But if these stories of trust have proven anything, it's that it is up to you to mend your life. You must do the work. And you must believe that you are worth resolving your pain. As you make steps toward this goal, you must be gentle with yourself. A healthy level of trust is possible but takes time. It is only available to you once you have recognized the hurt and shame within, and gathered the courage to stop it in its tracks.

A Word From Terry: A Mother's Perspective

As a young woman, I remember being clueless about why I often questioned my boyfriends' feelings toward me and the intentions of my ex-husband. What I've come to realize is that trust is a much broader concept and can be tricky in terms of how it plays itself out in intimate relationships. In my case, I didn't really worry much about infidelity since I picked guys who were loyal, but my mistrust always had more to do with questioning whether my partner had my best interests at heart and if he would come through for me.

I've gained a lot of insight as a result of researching trust, and I'm learning to be vulnerable and trust myself. Relationships can be complicated, but I've come to realize that communicating openly with my husband will help deepen my relationship with him. Ultimately, I believe my relationships will be healthier as I learn to have confidence in my own judgment. When I feel safe and allow myself to be vulnerable with my husband, I can be totally truthful about my thoughts, feelings, and wishes—without fear of rejection. A positive by-product of building a foundation of love and trust in my relationships is that my daughters will benefit from my example.

· · · · · · · · · ·

A Word From Tracy: A Daughter's Perspective

Mistrust can play itself out in unpredictable ways. It doesn't always mean that you're scanning your partner's cell phone for text messages from other women or checking his or her pants pockets for receipts or evidence of an affair. Usually, mistrust is just a lingering feeling in the back of your mind that your partner doesn't truly love you. If you believe that your partner truly loves you and wants the best for you, you will trust him or her. And if your partner hasn't done anything to betray your trust, shame is most likely at the root of the issue.

The child of a psychologist and social worker, I was eight years old when my parents divorced. They went to great lengths to assure me that their divorce didn't have anything to do with me. I was the product of a "good" divorce where my parents had joint custody, kept my life consistent, and did everything they could to encourage my emotional and educational development. Despite their best efforts, I still felt shame. I wanted my family to be together. And although I couldn't completely process these emotions as a child, my heart was broken and I felt there was something wrong with me.

Learning to trust is really about learning to heal a broken heart. It takes time. It's about bridging the gap between the head and the heart—the head that says you haven't got anything to be ashamed of, and the heart that feels otherwise. When you catch yourself mistrusting your partner, I've found it is most effective to stop yourself when these thoughts begin and challenge them. Does your mistrust have any bearing in reality, or is it a remnant of the past? Be kind with yourself on this journey, and remember that trust is a skill that can be learned and nourished over time.

8

Step Six:
Vulnerability

DISCOVERING THE KEY TO
LONG-LASTING LOVE

....

"I still feel like I have to take care of me. I feel like I
never want to depend on anyone because that's what
my mom did, and look what happened to her."

—*Rachel, age 28*

....

Growing up in a divorced home, a girl is forced to face life's realities
far younger than many of her peers. But on the flip side, the divorce
experience arms her with great strengths. The vast majority of women
from divided homes describe themselves as independent, steadfast,
loyal, and conscientious adults. They are hardworking, trustworthy,
and self-reliant—and pride themselves on these traits. Divorce caused
them to grow up fast, and as a result, they have become responsible
and resourceful women, able to handle the blows life gives them,
regardless of how painful they may be. They may feel self-assured
and autonomous—confident they can take care of themselves when
others can't. Truth be told, self-reliance is both an asset and a liability.
While it's important for women to be self-sufficient, it's also important to be able to rely on a partner for nurturance and support.

Self-reliance must not be confused with self-confidence. There are many self-reliant women from divorced homes who work hard, have successful careers, and competently raise their children, but their self-esteem remains low. Many women from disrupted homes are self-reliant to a fault, putting far too much pressure on themselves. They bring self-reliance to a new level because they are unable to rely on anyone, when in fact reliance on others can be healthy and affirming. But often a daughter raised by divorced parents felt when she was growing up that she had only herself to rely on, and so she may have become overly independent to compensate for what her surrounding environment lacked.

While self-sufficiency and autonomy can help you weather the storms of life, they can also prevent you from achieving the love and intimacy you deserve. For a relationship to be balanced, partners must be able to depend on one another and feel that they are needed and appreciated for the support they give. If you have been let down in the past, the prospect of needing someone can be frightening. Opening up to your partner can make you feel vulnerable and exposed, but it is the most important ingredient of a trusting, intimate relationship.

Vulnerability is often seen as a weakness, but it's actually a strength. Brown explains that it's really about "sinking into" the joyful moments in life—about daring to show up and letting ourselves be seen. She writes, "To let ourselves sink into the joyful moments of our life even though we know they are fleeting, even though the world tells us not to be too happy lest we invite disaster—that's an intense form of vulnerability."

It's unfortunate that we often equate vulnerability with weakness. In *Daring Greatly*, Brown explains that vulnerability is based on mutuality and requires boundaries and trust. She writes:

"It's not oversharing, it's not purging, it's not indiscriminate disclosure, and it's not celebrity-style social media information dumps. Vulnerability is about sharing our feelings with people who have earned the right to hear them." She describes vulnerability as an integral part of the trust-building process—which is essential to achieving emotional attunement with a partner.

The good news? You can stop sabotaging relationship after relationship if you get to the root of your fear of being vulnerable. If you are worried about showing weakness to your partner, for instance, you might not be aware that fear is preventing you from being totally committed to him or her. You may be limiting your ability to find lasting love if your fear of exposing your true feelings prevents you from being authentic with your partner.

WHAT DRIVES YOUR FEAR OF BEING VULNERABLE WITH YOUR PARTNER?

* Are you fearful of exposing parts of your personality that your partner may find unacceptable?
* Does keeping a distance make you feel safe and in control of your emotions?
* Are feelings of shame stopping you from exposing your true feelings or talking about tough topics?
* Do you fear that your partner will abandon or betray you?

For many daughters of divorce, a fear of intimacy may translate into testing a relationship by picking a partner who is wrong for them, picking fights constantly to get their partner to prove their love, or simply playing it safe by distancing themselves. If this is true for you, pause and ask yourself: "What is it that stops me from being vulnerable and intimate with my partner?" Notice I don't ask you, "What do you think your partner should do differently?" Surprisingly, most of the women I meet with answer, "I don't want to get hurt." My response to them is that it's time to examine their fear of vulnerability and the ways they might be sabotaging their relationships.

So what can you do if you are paralyzed by fear or unable to risk being vulnerable with your partner? First, you need to acknowledge it. Fear doesn't go away on its own—it tends to morph into something else. Did you ever notice that walking on eggshells never works, and instead just drains you of energy?

HOW CAN BEING VULNERABLE LEAD TO INTIMACY?

* Vulnerability increases your sense of worthiness and authenticity.
* It helps you to feel close and connected to your partner yet achieve your own sense of identity.
* Being vulnerable helps you to ask for what you want and to avoid stonewalling (shutting down or distancing yourself from a partner).
* It allows you to build trust in others and to become fully engaged in an intimate relationship.
* Being vulnerable allows you to open your heart—to give and receive love fully.

Trust and vulnerability are essential aspects of achieving intimacy in relationships. On the other hand, disengagement is the most dangerous factor that erodes trust in a relationship. The only way to avoid this is to risk being vulnerable with your partner by asking for help, standing up for yourself, sharing unpopular opinions, and having faith in yourself and your partner. The ultimate risk is allowing yourself to fall in love—which requires letting go of control and opens up the possibility of being hurt or abandoned.

"LITTLE ADULTS"

In some cases, your fear of dependence may be preventing you from being vulnerable with your partner and from expressing your needs in a healthy way. In other cases, you may have become extremely self-reliant or overly responsible as a way to protect yourself from the pain of being left or simply because you believed you needed to take care of yourself in your childhood home.

Why do women raised in divorced homes often describe themselves as being extremely self-reliant and responsible? Psychologist Diane Fassel suggests that many ACODs have an overdeveloped sense of responsibility. Even in the most amicable of divorces, the parents' needs supersede the child's. This can result in feelings of helplessness and despair for children. Feeling a total lack of control, they become overly responsible and take on a caretaking role. Fassel writes, "All this focusing on the needs of others results in ACODs not developing a sense of themselves. It is a setup for codependency. ACODs spend more time externally focused than internally aware. They can reach their twenties and not realize they are separate human beings with their own identities."

An overly responsible nature can be closely linked with a

need for control. It's a natural reaction for children who grow up in a family marred by turmoil to grasp at anything they can to control their environment. This tendency may manifest itself in adult intimate relationships in unhealthy ways. Many daughters of divorce crave constancy and security because they feel they couldn't control the reality of their parents' divorce. Really, what they achieve is only an illusion of control, because they are never truly able to control others. Theresa reflects on an interesting trend she has noticed in her romantic relationships as she says, "I always tend to go for guys who don't make a lot of money. I think it's because I like to be in control of money. I like to know that in some way, a guy needs me or might depend on me." Although Theresa is by no means wealthy, she is still a competent professional who makes a decent salary. Her choice of partners who lack career ambition reflects her need for others to depend on her, and for her to rely solely on herself for financial security.

It is important to note that Theresa's need for control is subtle. She doesn't barge around her home and workplace telling people what to do. Instead, if she wants something to get done, she only trusts herself to do it and leaves little room for partners to come through for her. She feels this way because she believes all she has is herself. As a product of divorce, she is convinced relationships don't last, so why bother relying on anyone else to come through?

Since adult children of divorce wish to avoid their parents' fate, they mistakenly believe there is something they can do to make their partners stay with them. Fassel writes that adult children of divorce "control in order not to feel their own feelings. Their efforts to control keep them busy with the illusion that they can make a difference. But the evidence of all ACOD stories is just the opposite. The more they control, the less they get what they want.

Their adult relationships and situations frustrate them as much as did their family of origin. Ultimately, they are thrown back on themselves and their own pain." By focusing on others, a woman with a need for control is distracted from focusing on her own issues. Only when she addresses her need for control can she get to its root.

Unhealthy self-reliance can also develop when children are no longer the center of the family. Divorce, in the eyes of children, is a selfish decision. It is based solely on the wishes of the adults, with little or any input from them. Author Elizabeth Marquardt, in her book *Between Two Worlds*, indicates that an important shift occurs when children no longer feel in control of their families. She writes that when divorce occurs, children feel forced to bridge their parents' disparate lives. They become "little adults" burdened by anxiety and sadness. Marquardt posits that children who experience the breakup of their homes often feel like they lost their childhoods. The carefree nature of childhood frequently disappears. Marquardt writes, "Almost everyone we surveyed from intact families agrees, 'My childhood was filled with playing,' but just three-quarters of children of divorce say the same thing (and only 43 percent of us strongly agree that our childhood was filled with playing, compared to 70 percent of those from intact families)." And so it is clear that self-reliance can be a direct result of feeling burdened and anxious about the breakup of a family unit.

* * *

Catherine, a happily married lawyer, provides a good example of a daughter of divorce who became overly responsible for herself and others while still grappling with the challenges of adolescence.

Though she was only eleven when her parents divorced, she can still remember today the intense pain and loneliness she felt both before and after her parents divorced. Her father was an alcoholic, and an adulterer to boot, who didn't provide for Catherine and her siblings financially or emotionally when he left. Here is how Catherine put it: "I felt abandoned when my father was home, invisible, but even more so when he left. My mother worked two full-time jobs most of my childhood, so it was up to me to help out with chores and care for my siblings." Catherine recalls that due to her family's financial hardships, she started working and contributing to her family's expenses at the age of fourteen. Robbed of her innocence, she felt like she missed out on the pleasures of childhood. Because her mother was so preoccupied with providing for her family, she felt even further neglected.

A competent-opportunist, Catherine was an excellent student who had the good fortune of beauty and an outgoing, charming personality. Devoting herself to her siblings left little time for social activities, but she was skilled in all academic subjects and had a close-knit group of friends. Catherine was able to secure a full academic scholarship to a private college, where she pursued her dream of obtaining a degree in political science, which allowed her to attend law school and eventually become a successful attorney in a large law firm.

As an adolescent, Catherine helped raise her two younger siblings and even worked two summer jobs to help her mother pay the bills. She says softly, "Being the oldest at age eleven, I was responsible for my two younger siblings. Sometimes we would go visit my mother at the pharmacy, her second job, where she worked nights and weekends." Fortunately, Catherine experienced a close bond with her younger sister Emma, which has remained strong to this day. Hetherington explains that a close bond between female siblings after parental divorce can enhance their ability to cope with marital transitions. Catherine's nurturing relationship with Emma served as a protective factor—safeguarding her from the adverse consequences of family conflict and disharmony.

Catherine does acknowledge that her childhood wasn't completely bereft of happiness. She describes family parties full of music and dance, as well as trips to the beach in the summer time. "It was during these times I was able to be a kid and forget my worries, if only for a while," she says. Catherine refers to her mother as a role model: "Though not pleasant at times, my mother was teaching me lessons that were invaluable for me to reference and carry over to my adult life. One lesson learned was the importance of a strong work ethic and being able to depend on myself. My mother also instilled what it means to be considerate, respectful, and mindful of others as well as to myself." Catherine recognizes that were it not for her mother's nurturing, independent, and hardworking spirit, she may have turned out a very different person.

Because of her competent-opportunist personality style, Catherine used the challenges of growing up in a divorced family to become more successful. Keep in mind that competent-opportunist women all possess the unique ability to utilize their great social skills to access resources from higher status people—such as peers, teachers, and others in power. Often competent-opportunist women have mothers who encourage their autonomy and independence.

However, the downside of extreme self-reliance is that it can prevent you from achieving a balanced relationship that affords you the love, support, and intimacy you deserve. Often, it will make you feel overburdened by all you have to do and resentful of your partner, who you may feel isn't pulling his or her weight, when in reality you haven't allowed your partner to (or he or she may not even know you need help). Asking for support and sharing your vulnerabilities is key to sustaining long-lasting love!

LIVING IN TWO WORLDS

Some daughters of divorce became self-reliant and mature early because they were skilled at moving between their parents' two worlds. Madeline, in her midtwenties, experienced her parents' divorce when she was nine years old. Neither one of her parents remarried. Today a successful businesswoman, she is still able to recall the difficulties of moving between her mother and father. She shared her time with both of her parents weekly—literally moving back and forth every few days. "As an adult, I understand where my parents were coming from, but as a child it was hard moving around so much," she explains. Madeline goes on to say that by living in two houses thirty minutes apart, it was hard to develop her friendships, because her dad worked a lot and she couldn't have friends over. As a result, she missed out on birthday parties, sleepovers, and many other kernels of childhood.

Madeline successfully navigated the stresses of living in two homes throughout most of her childhood. Like other competent-opportunist women, Madeline was encouraged by her mother to be independent. She has a close bond with both of her parents and is self-assured, creative, and intelligent. Madeline exudes confidence. Madeline acts as if she can do anything. Rather than allowing her parents' divorce to defeat her, she sees the world as a place without limits. Her parents' divorce has deepened her drive to seek a successful career and personal life. Growing up in a divorced home has made her clear about what she wants in life. But one drawback of her situation is that she often feels burdened by visiting both of her parents' homes as an adult, when she comes home to visit from a nearby state where she resides. However, Madeline admits that she has difficulty communicating with her boyfriend, Ryan, because she hasn't lived with two parents for most of her childhood.

AVOIDING CONFLICT

A hallmark of women who grew up in divorced homes is that they fear conflict. Although conflict doesn't necessarily need to be feared, many children who experience parental divorce witnessed dysfunctional conflict. For the most part, if their parents had been able to resolve differences, they would still be married. Although daughters of divorce have experienced different levels and severity of conflict, its unpredictability has forever imprinted their hearts. Children trust their parents will take care of them. A parent's inability to resolve conflict, whether violent or subtle, is scary to children. It makes them feel that only they can take care of themselves. When Madeline reflects on the breakup of her last long-term relationship, she says, "We had communication issues. That's always true for me. I'm a natural-born pleaser and I go out of my way for others. That comes naturally and I'm happy doing it, and if something starts to bother me, I'll wait. Then more things happen and one day it piles up and I just totally explode." This is common for many daughters of divorce. Failing to speak up when something bothers her, Madeline seeks to avoid conflict. However, when frustrations reach the boiling point, she has only herself to blame. She acknowledges that she never sought to address the issue when it first occurred.

Divided loyalties are very common among children from disrupted homes. Madeline is adept at bridging the gap between her mother and father. As a child, she was asked to play the messenger between her parents, and when a conflict arose, she was in a position where she felt she had to take sides. As a young adult, she has a realistic perspective on her divorce experience as a child and she understands that her parents didn't intentionally try to put her in the middle. Unfortunately, loyalty conflicts are a frequent experience for many daughters of divorce who seek acceptance and want to please both of their parents.

Madeline says of her parents today: "My parents are both my best friends in the whole world. The only part that is hard for me is when I want to share a special day with them together (birthdays, holiday, etc.)." It was harder for Madeline when she was a child. As an adult, she is closer to her parents than ever. In fact, both parents were able to come together at the same dinner party for her twenty-fifth birthday. Now, she routinely invites them to her birthday celebrations and other events, even though she still anticipates that it might be tense.

To mitigate this, Madeline informs both of her parents before an event that she's not responsible for entertaining them and expects them to be cordial with one another. So far, setting limits and coaching her parents beforehand has proved to be a successful strategy. Madeline's looking forward to many more years of sharing special occasions with both of her parents and other family members.

SELF-PROTECTION

To avoid getting close to others or losing out on love, Rachel uses her self-reliance as a protection and armor. An engaging brunette in her late twenties, she provides an example of a woman who learned to be self-reliant due the turmoil she experienced after her parents' divorce. Her mother and stepfather uprooted Rachel and her sister from their small town on the East Coast to Las Vegas, where their stepfather pursued an illegal business venture. Crime, infidelity, and drug and alcohol abuse broke apart Rachel's family and robbed her of a father figure. Their family returned to the East Coast and Rachel says, "I became very insecure, felt unworthy compared to others, and sought comfort in anyone that showed the slightest interest in being a friend. I chose friends who I thought were on 'my level.' I was afraid to let others know about my past and my home life." Eventually Rachel's life became so unmanageable that she dropped out of school.

Rachel's resilience shone through, and she went back to school and earned her GED. She is currently taking college classes and works for a Fortune 500 company. She is also engaged to a wonderful man who makes her feel loved and secure. But Rachel's still waiting for the other shoe to drop. "I still feel like I have to take care of me. I feel like I never want to depend on anyone because that's what my mom did, and look what happened to her." When Rachel's fiancé proposed to her after three years of dating, she felt bewildered and embarrassed. Marriage, and the thought of wholly relying on another person in a permanent partnership, was completely foreign to her. Recently, Rachel and her fiancé opened a joint checking account, an idea she found terrifying and that still causes her great discomfort.

Money plays a critical role in self-reliance. Based on her research, author Deidre Laiken has found that many daughters of divorce learn that money is freedom. In Rachel's case, her mother relied on two men who abandoned her emotionally and financially, leaving her vulnerable and imprisoned in a cycle of unhappiness. Divorce nearly always leaves women and children with a weakened financial standing. Often daughters growing up with financial instability promise themselves that they'll make it on their own. Like Rachel, they create their own security. She strives to never go through as an adult what she endured as a child.

Many daughters of divorce feel that having their own money allows them to separate themselves from relationships that aren't working. If they are financially autonomous, they can leave their partners at any time. Laiken indicates the need for economic security is cultivated in women growing up in divorced homes. She writes, "I was still at war, still putting away stores for the long winter, building my defenses in preparation for imminent collapse. I still didn't know that security was a result of mutual trust and that families don't always mean war and that love doesn't always have to result in pain and loss." The very idea that security is borne out of mutual trust is a concept entirely foreign to women from disrupted homes. For the most part, creating security has been their responsibility alone.

According to Laiken, money serves merely as "a metaphor for examining the price, value, and cost of something far more important than material objects." Money is simply the mechanism Rachel uses to ensure her sense of safety and well-being, because she knows she can't trust others to provide that for her. And if she stops to acknowledge for just a moment how sad it is that she doesn't believe the people who love her will take care of her, the true nature of self-reliance comes to light. It's not about money, security, or independence at all. It's that she simply doesn't have faith in love.

SELF-SABOTAGE

Rachel reflects the feelings of many women just like her: "I'm engaged but I still don't see it really happening..." While she loves her fiancé with all her heart, fear plagues her. She questions herself and her relationship all the time, wondering if it will work out. Rachel wonders if this is a defect within herself. Is she subconsciously sabotaging her relationship, waiting for the moment when it will all be over? When that moment comes, she is convinced she can take care of herself. She has been arming and protecting herself for so long in preparation for what her heart feels is the inevitable.

This is the tragedy of the double-edged sword of reliance. On the surface, it's wonderful to be independent, self-sufficient, and resilient. But when you believe you must do everything for yourself, it's hard to let your partner in. It's hard to give him or her room to come through for you. But if you are ever to enjoy the full nature of intimacy, you must. In small doses, self-reliance is positive. But when it pervades your approach to the world, it can deprive you of true love and intimacy. To avoid this fate you must rein in your self-reliance and practice being more vulnerable with your partner.

GROWING UP TOO FAST

Not all women are as lucky as Catherine, Madeline, and Rachel. Melissa was eight years old when her parents divorced. The experience left her feeling vulnerable and abandoned. "I always blamed my father for not spending more time with us," she says.

"I learned to fend for myself. I was always finding excuses for them both to give me attention. I started lying a lot, hoping I would get attention. I stopped listening to the rules of either house," she says. "I'd get off the bus by myself, make my own snacks and stuff like that. My dad didn't cook dinner, he'd get takeout." Melissa says her parents were so distracted by their own lives that she felt very alone. "So I learned to take care of myself. If I had a problem, I'd go to my brother. Even as I grew older, neither one of my parents were emotionally there for me. They both tell me they love me, don't get me wrong, but they don't show it." Sadly, divorce left Melissa without crucial support systems in her life.

Self-reliant to an extreme, Melissa moved out of both parents' households at the age of fifteen and moved in with her friend's parents. "I had a lot of anger and resentment toward them," she says of her parents. "When I started dating, I realized that you can't force yourself to stay. I go back and forth with whether or not it was better or worse for them to divorce to this day." Now a college student in her early twenties, Melissa recognizes that her parents' divorce made her a stronger person. But she also regrettably acknowledges that it has left her with heightened levels of vulnerability, depression, and anxiety.

Many daughters of divorce have trouble setting limits in their personal lives and seek approval from others. "I constantly beat myself up and blame myself," says Melissa. "I'm too busy thinking about everyone else to think about myself." She says ruefully, "Every time I think about myself I piss everyone off—so I go back to the way I was and lose myself. I get a little depressed or a bit down and it's a vicious cycle. I'm a people pleaser and a caregiver." Melissa's need for approval is insatiable. No one can make anyone happy all the time. Feeling helpless, she knows she can only rely on herself to meet her needs.

Communication has been a big issue for Melissa, as it is for many daughters of divorce. "I feel as if I don't communicate with my partner the way I wish I could. This stems from the lack of emotional support I received growing up. I have trouble expressing how I feel and what I want. When I do express things, they always come out the wrong way," Melissa says. "I'm concerned I will never be able to communicate or be myself enough for anyone to truly be happy with me," she says sadly. Her comments reflect her desire to receive validation from her partner, instead of first cultivating it from within. Competent-at-a-cost, Melissa often feels powerless to navigate her way through intimate relationships. She is far away from implementing Step 6 in her life because of her fear of being vulnerable and risking rejection by her partners.

SELF-RELIANCE VS. INTIMACY

As we have discussed, extreme self-reliance and intimacy are fundamentally at odds with one another. In divorced households, children usually don't learn how to be truly vulnerable, close, and trusting of others. Some of the women we met with were independent mostly because the only person they felt they could rely on was themselves. They taught themselves to become self-reliant because they are perpetually scared of loss. Wallerstein explains this is because instances of divorce don't present us with one great loss, but many successive losses, which play themselves out over and over again. Wallerstein writes, "Children of divorce are held back from adulthood because the vision of it is so frightening. From the outset, they are more anxious and uncomfortable with the opposite sex, and it's harder for them to build a relationship and gradually give it time to develop. Feeling vulnerable and bewildered, and terribly alone, driven by biology and social pressures, these young men and women throw themselves into a shadow play of the real thing involving sex without love, passion without commitment, togetherness without a future."

As a daughter of divorce, intimacy may be like a puzzle to you. You may scramble to fit all the pieces together. Sometimes, you might force pieces into places they don't belong. Melissa wasn't able to completely solve the puzzle; she was left scratching her head and unsure of how to proceed. She went to extremes because she lacked directions for how to establish a close connection with a romantic partner. You might pick someone who is unsuitable for you without knowing why. Or you might push away a person who is right for you. There are no rules for intimacy. As a result, you are forced to make it up as you go along.

INTERDEPENDENCE IS NOT A BAD THING!

Dependence is often seen as a dirty word in our culture. It conjures up images of weakness and insecurity. If a woman depends too much on others, she may be afraid of losing herself. But certain levels of dependence in intimate relationships can be helpful and sustaining. Intimacy serves to help illuminate parts of oneself never truly realized. Healthy partnerships bring out the best in people, because when they feel safe and loved, they are free to grow and explore who they are as human beings. Instead of depending on a partner, women should instead seek interdependence. As a daughter of divorce you must believe that you don't have to go through life alone.

> If you have an issue with being overly self-reliant, you must remember that allowing yourself to depend on others can actually help you to develop your autonomy and strength as a woman. Over time, as you reveal vulnerability with your partner, you may realize there isn't anything to be afraid of. Letting go of control, fear, and other intense emotions helps to make relationships more solid. As you grow secure in the idea that others love you and won't let you go, you learn that independence and love don't need to exist on separate planes. When you depend on others, you are at your strongest.

Judith Siegel, in *What Children Learn from Their Parents' Marriage*, underscores the importance of interdependence, and asserts that it is what makes the difference between happy and unhappy partnerships. Society prizes self-sufficiency, but if a woman takes it to an extreme, it deprives her of love and nurturance. Even if it's uncomfortable, a daughter of divorce must allow her partner to come through for her. She may be on the alert, always preparing for the imminent collapse of an important security blanket—such as a relationship or job. Even though it's hard, she must learn to let go and realize it's OK to show weakness and allow others to nurture her. Siegel notes that mutual respect, maintaining trust in word and deed, and reciprocity help sustain interdependence.

REINING IN SELF-RELIANCE

Nearly every woman interviewed for this book stated that as a result of her parents' divorce, she became more independent and self-reliant. Many women from disrupted homes take pride in being able to take care of themselves no matter what challenges come their way. While self-sufficiency and autonomy are certainly positive traits, and help people deal with adversity, they can also deprive individuals of true intimacy. Many adult daughters of divorce take self-reliance to the extreme and feel unable to rely on their partners. They fear people they love will leave them.

Let's take a closer look at Rachel. Because her mother was overly dependent on men, Rachel set out to be her opposite. She saw in her mother a type of emotional dependence that she sought to avoid at all costs. Since her mother fell apart after both of her divorces, Rachel wouldn't let men penetrate her protective shield. She avoided commitment by picking men who were wrong for her and changing relationships often. Rachel ran scared when potential partners got too close until she met Nick, who was able to break through her armor of self-reliance.

Often daughters of divorce strive to avoid making the same mistakes as their parents did—particularly their mothers—so like Rachel they disidentify with them. After all, it's only natural that she would want to create her own sense of security since she experienced so much upheaval as a child. However, not all daughters of divorce disidentify with their mothers. Another scenario related to self-reliance might be a tendency to identify with one's mother and repeat her patterns. A woman might depend excessively on a partner to meet her emotional needs and to give her approval. This could cause her to dive headlong into relationships and fall in love quickly. This pattern makes sense since girls tend to spend more time with their mothers than fathers after a divorce. In any case, self-reliance is truly a double-edged sword and can cause women to lose out on love. Some women from divided homes believe they must do everything for themselves. Consequently, they are reluctant to reveal their vulnerabilities and ask for what they need. Rachel's story provides a good example of this pattern:

I was so afraid to let Nick know how I grew up in the beginning of our relationship. I didn't want to let him know I grew up in Las Vegas, that my father wasn't around, or that I didn't graduate high school. I thought these things would make me a less attractive partner. Eventually I did let Nick in and told him everything. His response wasn't what I expected. I expected him to be judgmental or dismissive. He was so moved and shocked by my story. He said it showed him how strong and amazing I truly am. It was like a weight was lifted from my shoulders! From then on, I wasn't afraid to tell him anything. It made our relationship stronger, and I was so relieved to know that I could confide in him with anything that I needed to say.

Rachel developed the quality of self-reliance as a result of her mother's shortcomings. She describes her mother as affectionate and loving but dependent on others—as someone whose self-worth was tied into who would come to her rescue. Her story highlights the importance of examining your family background and gaining insight. Rachel survived a childhood filled with turmoil due to her father deserting her family when she was young and her stepfather subjecting them to infidelity, emotional abuse, and financial ruin. She says, "Life was extremely up and down when I was a child. My mother told us everything at a young age as if we were her friends or maybe even her therapists. We struggled to survive, and I'm surprised we did. Life was always filled with worry over where we were going to live, is Mom drunk, etc. She did show us extreme affection and love though, and I believe that is how I survived. When she was sober, life was OK."

Rachel is a competent-opportunist who has built a successful career and has a wide circle of friends. On the other hand, she has difficulty showing weakness to Nick and is fearful of depending on him. However, she is becoming more conscious of her need to balance closeness and separateness—realizing that her tendency to be self-reliant impedes her ability to achieve emotional closeness with Nick. Willard Harley Jr., PhD, a marriage counselor and author, defines interdependent behavior as activities of a spouse that are conceived and executed with the interests of both spouses in mind. Rachel is coming to terms with how her feelings about her mother's dysfunctional marriages influenced her attitudes and beliefs about relationships. Through this awareness, she is on the verge of embracing Step 6.

For Rachel, dependency in relationships is a key issue. On the surface, she is a beautiful brunette with a lot going for her. But on the inside, she fears being abandoned by her fiancé and worries about exposing herself. Because she disidentified with her mother from a young age, she struggles to maintain autonomy for fear that she'll get swallowed up and then left by a romantic partner. After all, her dependent mother taught her that it's not acceptable to need someone. Rachel learned at an early age that if you do show weakness, you'll be left—just like her father and stepfather deserted her mother.

Certain levels of dependence in intimate relationships can be beneficial and promote emotional closeness. Healthy partnerships foster mutual understanding and allow us to feel safe and secure. Siegel writes, "In marriages where partners don't offer mutual support, partners have become disappointed in each other and have come to believe that they must look out for themselves first." Siegel explains that mutual dependence is a trademark of a healthy relationship. She believes that reciprocity—being able to give and take support—is an essential ingredient in a successful marriage. Further, she advises that teaching children the value of interdependence is one of the most important lessons they can learn.

Rachel is coming to terms with the fact that letting go of fear and other intense emotions will make her relationship with Nick more solid. She's learning that it's a good thing to show weakness and to let Nick nurture her. As you might recall, money often plays a critical role in self-reliance. Having her own money helped Rachel to separate herself from becoming intimate with Nick until she examined her attitudes and beliefs. Rachel beams with pride as she explains her decision to let Nick cosign a loan with her:

It wasn't easy in the beginning of our relationship to let Nick in emotionally, but even harder was letting him in financially. I was afraid to ask for help from anyone that I was in a relationship with. I also felt like asking for financial help made me look weak, small, and less independent. I am definitely a giver more than a receiver. I was the first to offer to add him to such things as my cell phone plan or my insurance plan. So when Nick cosigned a $27,000 loan so I could purchase my brand-new

Altima Hybrid last year, it was hard for me to accept. At first the car didn't feel like it was mine, even though I was making the payments.

HOW TO ACHIEVE INTIMACY AND INTERDEPENDENCE

Rachel has learned that developing interdependence in a relationship is key to overcoming unhealthy self-reliance. While all relationships present us with risks, there are risks worth taking. You must surrender your shield and let others in. The following steps will guide you on your journey to achieving Step 6.

ACTION STEPS

* **Determine if your self-reliance is extreme or moderate.** If it's extreme, pinpoint the source of it and examine your thoughts, attitudes, and beliefs.
* **Visualize yourself in an honest and open intimate relationship** and work toward allowing yourself to be more vulnerable with your partner and others. Start with small things—such as sharing your feelings or concerns about day-to-day situations or events. As you feel more comfortable being open with your partner, take a risk and begin to disclose your innermost thoughts, feelings, and wishes about more important issues.
* **Challenge your beliefs and self-defeating thoughts about accepting nurturing from your partner.** What stops you from asking for the support you need?
* **Set a goal to be more vulnerable and accepting of**

support and nurturing from your partner. Practice being open about your thoughts, feelings, and wishes in small steps. Resist the urge to be too self-reliant around hot-button issues such as money, work, or family matters—like how you celebrate holidays.

❋ **Put together a vision board or write down what you want your relationship to look like.** Include words, images, and affirmations that reflect the type of partnerships that feel comfortable and safe for you. Make a point to reflect upon this image or written passage at least twice a day and revise it periodically.

❋ **Keep a journal or talk to a therapist or close friend about your progress.** You can be close to others without losing parts of yourself. The payoff from sharing your vulnerabilities is a deeper level of love, trust, and intimacy.

❋ **Remind yourself daily that it's healthy to accept help from others** and a sign of strength rather than weakness. Affirmations such as "It's a good thing to ask for help when I need it" can help you achieve your goal.

❋ **Develop a policy of joint agreement with your partner if you are in a relationship.** This term, coined by Harley, describes an agreement couples adopt to resist making important decisions without an enthusiastic agreement between partners.

Reining in self-reliance will help you build a trusting relationship. When you first discover that your independent nature sometimes prevents you from true intimacy, you may be unsure about how to change this pattern. It is often hard to decipher whether self-reliance is positive or negative. Becoming more conscious of your partner's needs and the value of mutual under-standing is critical to developing lasting love. Taking ownership of your own unhealthy patterns that prevent you from true intimacy is crucial. You must let others in and embrace the idea that you don't have to go through life alone. Healthy partnerships are within your reach if you let go of fear and believe you are worthy of love and all of the gifts it has to offer.

A Word From Terry: A Mother's Perspective

Of all of the chapters that we researched for *Daughters of Divorce*, the findings from this chapter were the most surprising to me. As a young woman growing up in a divided home, I remember prizing my self-reliance and wearing it like a badge. From my perspec-tive, being independent and not relying on others were positive qualities. After all, I observed both my mother and grandmother survive as single parents largely due to their ability to take care of themselves and support themselves financially. However, Rachel's story helped me to see that being self-reliant can rob a woman of intimacy and that I have a lot to learn about interdependence.

As a result of this recent insight, I'm more keenly aware of how my extreme self-reliance may not have been the best example for Tracy when it comes to intimate relationships. Asking my part-ner for support has never come easily. For example, my children have witnessed me unloading a dozen bags of groceries from my car rather than asking for help. Armed with self-awareness about my unhealthy pattern of self-reliance in relationships, I'm striving to examine my beliefs daily and to realize that allowing others to come through for me is a sign of strength rather than weakness.

A Word From Tracy: A Daughter's Perspective

Many daughters of divorce fall into one of two categories. They are either fiercely independent or become enmeshed with their partners and constantly look to them for approval. Our society prizes independence and tends to encourage it in girls as they grow up. Certainly, there isn't anything wrong with working hard and becoming self-sufficient. But at its root, self-reliance is about fear. Many women tend to overcompensate for what their surrounding environments lack. They did it as children trying to deal with chaotic households, and they do it as adults when they don't want to rely on a partner for fear of being left.

I inherited self-reliance from my mother and grandmother, who were, at various times in their lives, single and working two jobs while raising children. My grandmother was unique in that she was born to a teenage mother and grew up poor, but put herself through college and earned two master's degrees, becoming a successful nurse and educator. She was also a shrewd businesswoman who developed wealth in the California real estate market. Despite these achievements, she never found a man she could truly share her life with. Although I've inherited many of her self-reliant characteristics, I know she wouldn't want me to miss out on all the joys of intimacy. It motivates me to do my best to strike a balance in my own life.

9

Step Seven:

Making Smart Decisions about Love and Marriage

"You focus on your children and one day you wake up
and you're not committed. You've fallen out of love;
especially with your busy lives and three kids. I want
my marriage to succeed with my whole heart."

—Maura, age 37

In our research, we discovered that many daughters of divorce can't picture their wedding day. The concept of a wedding, or even a successful marriage, seems alien to them, since they didn't have a model for a happy marriage. For a lot of them, this is a source of sadness. Our society tends to view marriage as the ultimate sign of satisfaction and fulfillment in a woman's life. To have a successful marriage and family is proof to the outside world that a woman has "got it together." She has created some semblance of stability and healthiness in her personal life, so she must be OK. Women, and especially daughters of divorce, can put undue pressure on themselves to find the right partner, marry, and develop a happy home life. But if they possess this goal, it can present many problems. Most women from disrupted homes don't have a healthy template to follow when it comes to nurturing and sustaining a committed relationship, making it difficult for them to know where to start. Perhaps the first step for daughters of divorce is to reevaluate their view of relationships and adjust their expectations.

Even in the twenty-first century, when ideas about the nature of modern families have changed, many notions about marriage remain the same. Women raised in divorced homes can be especially hard on themselves when it comes to making their relationships work. They tend to feel if their relationships end, there is something wrong with them. The reality is that with time people grow and change. This doesn't mean love has failed. Simply because love doesn't last forever doesn't mean there was something wrong with it. Relationships, whether they last three months or three decades, can provide their participants with the love, understanding, and intimacy they need at the time. Often, the courage to end a relationship that is no longer meeting both partners' needs shows the greatest strength.

While commitment can make us feel safe and secure, it's crucial to determine what we want from a relationship before we make a commitment. For instance, some women, like Elizabeth, desire children and believe in being married beforehand. She also values mutual trust and companionship even though she didn't observe her parents get along or spend much time together. Maura craves financial security and chose a partner partially based on his income, career, and earning potential. On the other hand, a woman who hasn't taken the time to evaluate what she wants from a relation ship may find herself confused or chronically unhappy.

Certainly, children raised in divorced homes learned the hard way that marriage isn't a sure thing. It's also likely that most daughters of divorce desire commitment and the security a stable, long-term relationship can bring. But many are delaying commitment in hopes that they will be luckier in love than their parents were. This is all the more reason to examine some of the cultural trends that impact one's decision to take a risk on love and perhaps marriage.

It's no surprise that the marriage rate has been declining in recent years, since the United States has the highest divorce in the Western world. Currently, over 40 percent of first-time marriages end in divorce. According to a recent report from the National Marriage Project, marriage has shifted from being the cornerstone to the capstone of adult life. In fact, young adults are now delaying marriage until they feel more financially and psychologically independent. From 1960 to 2007 the percentage of American women who were married fell from 66 to 51 percent, and the percentage of men who were married fell from 69 to 55 percent. The good news is that studies show the longer you wait to get married, the more successful your marriage will be.

However, it's not likely that you'll wait to get married to live together since the rate of cohabitation has risen dramatically in the United States in recent years. Today, about 60 percent of all couples live together before marriage. From 1960 to 2007 couples living together without being married increased fourteen-fold—from 439,000 to more than 6.4 million. What remains unclear is whether cohabitation leads to divorce.

Consequently, it makes sense to examine the literature on marriage, cohabitation, and divorce proneness in an effort to lessen your chances of divorce. As a daughter of divorce, you have a much better chance at relationship stability if you explore ways to avoid marrying the wrong person and understand how to achieve the factors that can contribute to a successful marriage. If you are married, read on because we will soon offer tips on making love and marriage last!

A CLOSER LOOK AT DIVORCE PRONENESS

As we've seen throughout this book, there are certain factors that have been proven to put daughters of divorce at greater risk for getting divorced themselves, not the least of which is experiencing parental divorce. Unfortunately, you can't turn back the clock and change the fate your parents handed you, but there are other factors you do have control over. In his essential work, *The Marriage-Go-Round*, Andrew Cherlin explains that individuals who have achieved more in their education and careers are less likely to experience divorce. The economic stresses that often plague individuals of low education tend to put them at greater risk for breaking up. Marrying one's socioeconomic equal is also seen as a protective factor when trying to avoid divorce.

Adults who grew up in disrupted homes tend to have more permissive attitudes about divorce. In *Alone Together*, Paul Amato discovered that women from divorced homes are more likely than their male counterparts to initiate and file for divorce. This phenomenon can be attributed to women who "hedge their bets against failure by withholding full commitment to the marriage," as sociologists Norval Glenn and Kathryn Kramer found. Many women go into marriage with a lingering thought in the back of their heads that tells them it won't work out. When the marriage fails, these skeptical women aren't surprised. What they feared all along has come to fruition.

Tara Parker-Pope's analysis of marriage, *For Better: The Science of a Good Marriage* notes that marrying young is one of the greatest risk factors for divorce. She encourages people to wait until at least twenty-five to marry and notes that divorce rates are lower for those who marry after the age of thirty. She also indicates that cohabiting before marriage puts one at a greater risk for breaking up. This may be especially true for partners who have different expectations about what living together will mean. She notes, "According to the U.S. Census, 6.4 million heterosexual couples were cohabitating in 2007, compared to fewer than 1 million thirty years ago. Studies show that infidelity rates are highest among couples who cohabit before marriage."

With cohabitation gaining momentum, marriage seems to have become less of a necessity. Living together without the commitment of marriage has become increasingly accepted, but it's important to examine potential risks. Cherlin's study indicates that among couples who start a cohabiting relationship, over half are broken up within five years. The implications for children born to cohabiting couples carry great weight. By the age of fifteen, about 75 percent of said children no longer live with both parents, and the legacy of a disrupted home is passed on.

DOES LIVING TOGETHER BEFORE MARRIAGE PREDICT DIVORCE?

It is often said that living together before marriage puts couples at greater risk for divorce. But it turns out the findings are mixed. Researcher Arielle Kuperberg from the University of North Carolina at Greensboro discovered that couples who live together before marriage tend to be younger, and since marrying at a young age increases the likelihood of divorce, it appeared in previous research that cohabitation did as well.

On the other hand, researchers Galena K. Rhoades, PhD, Scott M. Stanley, PhD, and Howard J. Markman, PhD, demonstrated the "cohabitation effect"—showing that couples who cohabit before marriage are less satisfied with their marriages and more likely to divorce than couples who waited until they were engaged to move in together. According to Meg Jay, author of *The Defining Decade*, the "cohabitation effect" is not fully explained by demographics such as politics, education, or religion. Jay writes, "Research suggests that at least some of the effect may lie in cohabitation itself." She posits that one of the main factors putting cohabiting couples at risk for breakup is "sliding not deciding." This means that a couple gradually decides to move in together mostly out of convenience and passes over discussing expectations about their commitment to one another. A recent RAND report also highlights the risks of cohabiting without a commitment. Regardless of whether cohabitation can be an accurate indicator of divorce, one thing is clear: for a long-lasting relationship, it's crucial that you and your partner are on the same page in terms of your commitment to each other.

It's incredibly important that you enter into intimate partnerships with clarity and realistic expectations about love and commitment if you want to lessen your chance of divorce. If you are in a committed relationship, make sure that you are on the same page in terms of your goals and aspirations. And if you are single, there are many things you can do to prepare for a strong future.

SEVEN BENEFITS TO BEING SINGLE AT SOME POINT (OR SEVEN REASONS NOT TO RUSH INTO MARRIAGE)

Often single women may be especially reluctant to acknowledge the challenges of being alone for fear of being seen as desperate or needy. A groundbreaking study by Stephanie S. Spielman, a professor of psychology at the University of Toronto, demonstrates that fear of being single is a meaningful predictor of settling for less in relationships and staying with a partner who is wrong for you. The first step in facing your fear of being alone is shrugging off any stigma attached to being single.

> Many of the stereotypes we have about single women are misleading. Perhaps we need new norms for understanding single women in our culture because in times past they were seen as lonely spinsters, quietly languishing in their studio apartments. Being single can actually allow you time to prepare for a bright future and healthy relationships.

Here are seven good reasons to remain single, or if you're in a relationship, *not* to rush to the altar:

1. **You worry that the clock is ticking.** Often women over thirty start to panic because they get concerned they'll be too old to have children. This mind-set can make you feel desperate and marry someone who is wrong for you.

2. **You feel anxious or panicked when your partner doesn't call you** when he or she said they would or when you aren't with him or her. These are signs of emotional

dependence, not love, and could drive your partner away in the long term if you don't deal with them now.

3. **You are in a relationship that brings you down or often dissatisfies you.** Ask yourself: Does my significant other inspire me to do my best? Perhaps your partner is overly critical or too focused on his or her needs to be supportive of you.

4. **You feel you have to change yourself**—your values, goals, or dreams—for your partner to accept you. Since your partner is unwilling to compromise, you morph into someone else to accommodate his or her needs and subsequently lose vital parts of your identity.

5. **You want to take your time to pick a partner who shares similar values and interests**—this will enhance your chances of staying together.

6. **You have a healthy respect for commitment** and just haven't met someone you want to make a permanent commitment with. Avoiding marriage before your late twenties and dating a partner for at least two years has been proven to reduce your risk of divorce.

7. **You're content being single and don't have a compelling reason to tie the knot.**

Growing up, you probably weren't given good examples of being alone. Everything you see in the media promotes how to find the right partner and make it work. There's nothing wrong with seeking love, because it's beautiful and can bring about some of the most treasured moments in our lives. But very few people know how to be alone and do it well. They aren't happy to be alone and often rush into marriage. They fear it and seek love wherever they go. Too often the pleasure they find with falling in love is the sweet release of no longer being by themselves in the world. But many fail to give enough consideration to what it takes to make a marriage work and have unrealistic expectations— setting the stage for marital discontent.

"BROKENHEARTED INDEPENDENCE"

All too frequently, daughters of divorce find themselves in self-destructive relationships. Crushed by their parents' divorce, they see love as the salve for their wounds—even if the relationship is bad for them or doesn't meet their needs. "The feelings of love are stronger than reason," writes Sara Shandler, author of *Ophelia Speaks*. "We hear the warnings of our parents, our friends, even our own minds, but our emotions will rarely be restricted. We lose ourselves in love. We love with abandon, and then, love abandons us." By enduring the heartache of bad relationships, women emerge with what Shandler calls broken-hearted independence. But daughters of divorce can move forward stronger and more realistic about love and its requirements. Although deeply affected by relationships gone wrong, they can learn from them.

It is important for you, as a woman from a disrupted home, to keep your partnerships in perspective. The truth is that all relationships end, either through breakup or death. Many daughters of divorce find themselves preoccupied by the fear of a relationship ending. But it is crucial to remember everyone has the same fate. Accepting that all relationships end can, in a strange way, free you. It helps you to live in the moment. It helps you to remember it is the joy experienced in the relationship, regardless of its length, that is the most important thing. Many people remain married for decades, build careers, buy homes, and bear children—but aren't happy. Relationship failure? If there is any, maybe it is that.

> Marriage need not be the institution that defines you as a woman. That being said, many women still seek lasting commitment in the form of marriage. This is a healthy desire if you bring healthy expectations to it. For instance, there is no such thing as a soul mate or perfect partner. Marriage can give the closest semblance of permanence you can find, and often as an adult child of divorce, this is something you crave because you never experienced it in childhood.

Twenty-four-year-old Diana is a perfect example of a woman who yearns for commitment but doesn't have faith that relationships will work out. "I'm very pessimistic," Diana says candidly. "I'm always looking for the worst in men, and they have to prove me wrong." Diana is currently in a relationship with a wonderful young man who treats her well. But fear plagues her. "I've wanted to walk away many times, wanted to run, because maybe deep down I know it's real. But I'm not used to real—it's never been real…it's like a self-fulfilling prophecy. I'll create the demise of the relationship because I don't trust him," she says. What Diana so desperately wants—love, commitment, and the comfort of a permanent relationship—is what she most fears. If she were to lose her boyfriend, she would reenact the pain of her divorce experience. This is an outcome she'll stop at nothing to avoid.

GET READY FOR LOVE AND COMMITMENT!

By acting from a place of mistrust and apprehension, Diana is most certainly creating her future, or what she calls a "self-fulfilling prophecy." There are no guarantees in any relationship. Some work out and some don't. But approaching relationships with fear, sadness, or doubt almost guarantees a negative outcome.

Psychologist Nathaniel Branden has written extensively about fear in love relationships. When you feel unlovable, your relationship becomes what Branden refers to as a ticking time bomb, destined for failure. "It isn't the fear of loss that destroys us," he writes. "It is denying the fear. If we own it, if we express it, we discover that gradually it disappears. And when it is still present, it doesn't manipulate us into behaving in ways that sabotage love." This point can't be emphasized enough. The best partner is one you can be completely vulnerable with, one who reacts to your fears from a place of understanding and love. When you recognize your fears and accept them, they can be diffused.

Many daughters of divorce, like Kayla, have a fear of commitment. Ironically, they can't see a relationship working out, but they still desperately want one. Competent-and-caring, Kayla is a compassionate woman in her late twenties who is trying to heal from a father-daughter wound. Although she says she doesn't believe in love, Kayla wants a partner who will be a true match for her, and she thinks she has found one in her fiancé, Tom. "Trust and communication are major difficulties for me. It takes a lot to gain my trust—if it's broken it might not be earned back." Her desire for a foolproof relationship is unrealistic and will only cause her to feel dissatisfied, because such relationships aren't achievable. Even individuals who come from intact homes are faced with this reality—relationships, even marriages, provide no guarantees.

But if lasting, healthy, and fulfilling love is something you want, how do you attain it? To be ready for love, you must believe in your worthiness and be autonomous. You don't look for a partner to heal your wounds. This is work you have done yourself. Your self-esteem isn't in a state of constant change. Although you are one with your partner, you are also content in your aloneness. You understand that being alone is normal and healthy, and while you enjoy the companionship and intimacy your partner provides, you don't need him or her out of any sense of dependency.

EMOTIONAL INTIMACY ISN'T DEPENDENCY

Earlier, we touched on the point that emotional intimacy is not necessarily dependency, but we want to reiterate it now with an illustration of this small but crucial distinction. Newlywed Elizabeth provides a great example of how working through the pain of the divorce experience has allowed her to enjoy a happy relationship. She's fortunate enough to have known her husband, Zane, since childhood, and they dated for five years before they married. When they tied the knot, she wanted to make sure she knew the man she was committing her life to. Elizabeth is very realistic about who her husband is. This is one of the hallmarks of mature love. In relationships that don't last, women often feel wounded when their partner turns out to be someone they didn't expect. While one can never know everything about a person, time helps to reveal an individual's basic character. In fact, people tell you who they are very early on in a relationship if you have the courage to truly listen.

Although Elizabeth feels happy and secure in her relationship, it hasn't always been this way. "I used to get very jealous," she says bluntly. "I've gotten to the point where I know he loves me and I'm very confident that he loves me and only me. No matter what happens, he's going to come home to me. He's earned my trust. I might not have said that three years ago, but he definitely has proven himself." There are times when Elizabeth still feels vulnerable or sad. After all, every relationship has its challenges. But she is able to make clear to Zane what she wants. "He wants to know what I want," she explains. "Guys don't know. I've learned to be more specific with him." If they have a disagreement, Elizabeth is very clear about what it will take to resolve the situation. She gives an example of Mother's Day, when Zane hadn't put much thought into showing how much he valued her as a mother. He ran to a gas station at the last minute to pick something up. It wasn't that Zane didn't appreciate what a great mother Elizabeth is; he just hadn't thought to prepare. But after Elizabeth explained what an important day it was for her, Zane understood that being a devoted mother has special significance for her. Now Elizabeth feels honored on Mother's Day. She's taught her husband how she wants to be treated, and he's happy to comply.

One of the most striking qualities of Elizabeth's husband is his devotion. Zane doesn't come from a divorced family. "He doesn't have it in his head that people will get a divorce," says Elizabeth. "He won't leave. I've actually kicked him out and he'll sleep in the car in the front of the house." She laughs and makes light of her relationship, remembering a conversation with Zane's mother where she said, "He won't leave. I don't have to worry about your son leaving, because he won't leave, I've tried." And she laughs as she remembers telling Zane, "I'll never let you go, all the hard work that I've put into you." While it's heartening to hear Elizabeth make light of the struggles she has endured, it reinforces the notion that in order for their relationships to work, women need to believe they are worth being treated well. Elizabeth is very explicit about her needs. Only by showing her vulnerabilities and communicating with her husband can these needs be met. She has achieved Step 7 by developing a healthy respect for commitment.

While it is clear that you need to develop trust, vulnerability, and communication in order to sustain a healthy relationship, there is another component that is often overlooked—admiration. Branden reflects that mutual admiration is the most important foundation of a relationship. "To ask 'Do I admire my partner?' is to risk discovering that I may be bound to him or her more through dependency than admiration, more through immaturity or fear or 'convenience' than genuine esteem," he writes. Your partner may treat you well, but how do you see him as a human being? Your boyfriend or husband may cook you dinner or massage your feet at the end of a long day, but how is he outside the context of your relationship? Branden reflects that when trying to endure the storms of life, admiration helps sustain a relationship. Furthermore, if both you and your partner have high levels of self-esteem, admiration tends to be at the core of your relationship.

ADMIRATION AND MUTUAL RESPECT

Jenna, a nursing student, is engaged to Trevor. While Jenna doesn't put him on a pedestal, she maintains a strong level of admiration for him. She admires him not just for the way he makes her feel, but for who he is. This is a hallmark of mature love, something not simply arrived on by chance, but actively cultivated. "To people on the outside they may see him as this overly playful individual, but through my eyes I see a beautiful spirit. Something this world could use more of," she says warmly. "Something an individual like myself—controlling, worrisome, and high-strung—needs in her life." She goes on to say that she sees qualities in Trevor that will make him a good husband. She says sincerely: "I have never been with someone so honest and pure-hearted in my life before. Trevor putting his trust in me has allowed me to readily and wholeheartedly put my trust in him." Jenna openly admits how lucky she feels to have a partner who is honest, trustworthy, empathetic, and dedicated to the success of their relationship. This took her some time to find.

The challenge, then, is to fall in love with the right person. And this is no easy task. When you fall in love, this feeling tells you nothing about whether the person you are falling in love with is good for you. The experience of being in love can delude you, making you miss important aspects of your relationship that point toward its eventual demise. The husband-and-wife team Les and Leslie Parrott advocate a new kind of love, which they call "smart love." You may understand the components of a healthy relationship, but how do you forge one for yourself? Smart love is the answer.

MAKING SMART DECISIONS ABOUT LOVE

Perhaps the single most important action you can take as a daughter of divorce is making clear to your partner what is acceptable and what is unacceptable to you in your relationship. These nonnegotiable expectations are often referred to as "deal breakers." Many self-help dating books, so proliferous in pop culture, advocate holding strong to your deal breakers. And this is good advice. You tell your partner how you wish to be treated, and if he or she falls short of that, you must let him or her know. Smart love doesn't shy away from conflict. As the Parrotts advocate, smart love maintains standards in a relationship. Whatever your bottom line, you must be explicit with your partner about what it is, and you must be willing to enforce it.

The Parrotts go further to explain that smart love is realistic about the demands of a relationship. It "has faith in the ebb and flow of love, knowing that it is fluid and free. Smart love works day to day at being in love. It doesn't sit back and get sucked under by the happily-ever-after myth. Smart love practices loving ways of being," they write. The kind of love that lasts is more than a feeling. It requires decision and action, especially when infatuation wears off. Romantic love can sometimes be artificial. Women fall in love because of the way their partners make them feel. Smart love is the daily act of choosing to be devoted to a partner, even when those superficial feelings fade. Most importantly, smart love is never at a cost to oneself.

Making decisions in relationships can be hard for daughters of divorce. As we have mentioned previously, daughters of divorce are more likely to undergo a divorce themselves as adults. In fact, when the wife alone comes from a divided home, she is 59 percent more likely to divorce than her female counterparts who lived with both parents. Even more alarming, if both partners experienced parental divorce, their marriage is three times more likely to end in divorce when compared to couples who grew up in intact homes. At the root of marital instability is the belief that divorce is a viable option. Hetherington's study found that 70 percent of young people from divorced families versus 40 percent of young people from non-divorced homes viewed divorce as an acceptable alternative to an unhappy marriage, even if children are involved.

EMBRACING STEP SEVEN

These research findings are startling and can't be ignored. But awareness and willingness to work on the issues that create the seeds of divorce can help you to avoid this fate. Thirty-seven-year-old

Maura provides a great example of a woman who has embraced Step 7. She experienced divorce as a child and came out the other side as an adult, capable of maintaining a healthy and cohesive marriage. Maura says she didn't want to endure a divorce of her own, so she found herself very cautious in relationships, but this caution didn't prevent her from finding happiness.

Maura dated her husband, Curt, for five years before they married, and they waited another five years to have children. Taking her time has proven to be successful for Maura. "I really try to talk about things before I get upset about them. I want to have a relationship with Curt where he can talk to me about things that he's upset about and he can trust that I won't get upset," she says thoughtfully. In her relationship with her husband, Maura is competent-caring, as she tries to remove judgments and clear the air. They are both committed to their marriage and their children. Maura does acknowledge, however, that lacking healthy role models as a child has made marriage more difficult for her. At times she grapples with how to resolve the day-to-day conflicts inherent in married life.

Curt is also a child of divorce. When both partners grow up in divorced families, marriage, or any committed relationship, can be more challenging. Psychologist Mary Hirschfeld reflects that adult children of divorce (who she refers to as ACDs) tend to see marriage as a risk and approach it warily. Furthermore, when both partners come from divorced families, they may find it especially difficult to resolve conflict or bring realistic expectations to their own marriage. Hirschfeld emphasizes, "Most ACDs not only want to be married, but also want to have the perfect marriage that eluded their parents. Often they set marital standards so high that they alienate all potential mates. Marital partners aren't failure proof, nor, unfortunately, do they come with satisfaction guaranteed or your money back. ACDs fervently wish they did." Marriage brings with it inevitable complications, and because adult children of divorce never saw their own parents successfully work through conflict, they have little idea of how to negotiate marital issues in their own lives.

CREATING A HEALTHY RESPECT FOR COMMITMENT

Feelings of shame, anxiety, and fear often plague adult children of divorce. Authors Beverly and Tom Rodgers, adult children of divorce married to one another, posit that such feelings can lead women to take too much responsibility in their relationships, putting them at risk for codependency. Conversely, it can make them take too little responsibility, and they become disengaged. In the initial stages of a relationship, these qualities may not be apparent, but they inevitably surface. The Rodgerses indicate the first step to healing is to become aware of past wounds. They write, "As we started feeling the pain of our parents' divorces, we discovered something surprising. We learned that pain could be positive. It can even be a wise teacher that illuminates the soul. We learned that pain wasn't the real problem. It was our inability to deal with pain that was causing us trouble." Confronting fears and communicating with their partners will help women overcome the odds that they'll experience relationship dysfunction.

Hirschfeld makes an important point, which is that most adult children of divorce aren't confident in their ability to make a marriage work. You may recognize that you made a bad choice in your partner but still look to him to provide you with marital satisfaction. The key to making your relationship work is to believe you have all the tools you need to create and nurture a lasting committed relationship. Hirschfeld suggests the following elements will help create marital success for adult children of divorce.

* Possessing a high level of mutual trust
* Speaking out when you have something on your mind
* Being sensitive to each other's needs
* Encouraging growth in each other
* Having a giving attitude
* Being able to balance intimacy and autonomy
* Having an unfaltering intention to stay married
* Nurturing a capacity for forgiveness

Uncertainty and anxiety in intimate relationships create a recipe for disaster for daughters of divorce. When doubt, ambiguity, or insecurity invade your relationship, you may seek to control your partner or you may act from a place of weakness or mistrust. At the core of your fear is likely the belief that your partner has or will stop loving you. Of course, intimacy is wrought with risks, but communicating with your partner is the greatest and best risk you can take. You must understand that your partner cannot heal the wounds from your past. This is work that you must do on your own. But together, you can establish an incredibly supportive trust and bond, which will help you create a beautiful future together. As we've said before, you *aren't* doomed to repeat the mistakes of your parents. You have the ability to make different choices.

Maura has made it a point to make different decisions than her parents. She is at peace with the reasons for the demise of her parents' marriage, which occurred when she was three years old. But since their marriage wasn't a model for her to follow, she has had to chart her own path. Maura brushes her thick hair away from her brow and says, "I have a circle of friends with happy marriages and they have been a good influence on me. If they are successful and you see what they are doing right, you can apply it to your own life." Surrounding herself with healthy role models, even though they aren't her own parents, has been helpful.

Although Maura and Curt have worked hard to make their marriage a priority, Maura still admits to some doubts. "Sometimes I worry this might change," she confesses. "You focus on your children and one day you wake up and you're not committed. You've fallen out of love; especially with your busy lives and three kids. I want my marriage to succeed with my whole heart." Maura recognizes her fears but doesn't let them rule her life. She and her husband are still working on their marriage, and overall, they are happy. Demonstrating a healthy respect for marriage, Maura doesn't let any self-defeating messages about the future of her marriage get in the way of embracing the principles of Step 7.

In *Overcoming Your Parents' Divorce*, author and therapist Elisabeth Joy LaMotte, an adult daughter of divorce herself, recognizes that she went through a great deal of pain as a young woman enduring relationships that weren't right for her. But they also provided her with a richer sense of what love is. She writes, "I am convinced that if my parents had continued forward in a false and unworkable life, I would have been much more likely to marry younger and more easily, as they did. However, I probably would have chosen a relationship that sparkled on the surface, like my parents' marriage, but would never bring true intimacy and lasting happiness. Without their divorce, I can easily picture myself making unconscious decisions reflecting how their anguish remained alive, yet unacknowledged; how our lives seemed picture perfect from the outside, while masking torment from within." LaMotte's musings show that growing up with divorce gives you unique strengths. It forces you to be honest, strong, and unequivocal in your beliefs about love.

When you have experienced parental divorce as a child, it is crucial to admit that your attitudes toward marriage are forever altered. Theresa reflected in her interview that she is in awe of friends who come from intact homes and talk casually about marrying their boyfriends, with unwavering faith that their relationships will work out. They are excited to plan who will be in their bridal parties and what kind of house they'll move into after they get married. Theresa has never entertained these thoughts. The idea that she'd even get to a place where marriage was a possibility is a struggle enough for her, let alone the idea that such a union would work out. But she is also encouraged by the fact that her vision of love is honest, and she maintains a deeper understanding of its requirements. With passion in her voice, she says, "Marriage matters so much to me. My parents decided to end a marriage that wasn't working for them. As an adult, I can respect the strength that took. It motivates me to live my life with intention every day. My partnership with my boyfriend is a choice, every day. All of it matters, so much." Theresa's thoughts reflect a respect for marriage, but also a sober understanding of its fragility.

In Nena O'Neill's *The Marriage Premise*, the profound value of marriage is emphasized—even though matrimony is beset with its own problems, obstacles, and goals. But each participant enters marriage for the same reason: they want something more. In the twenty-first century, different lifestyles are becoming more commonplace and accepted. Many couples are opting to live together before they marry. Others choose to have serial relationships, never permanently settling down with one person.

Some choose not to marry at all. But still there remains the largest proportion of Americans who decide to marry. Despite the fact that barely half of the U.S. adult population are currently married, 72 percent have been married at least once. And so marriage endures for most as the preferred institution in which to create a family and express enduring love.

MARRIAGE AND WELL-BEING

While marriage isn't necessarily desirable for everyone, it does bring many undeniable benefits to its participants. Researcher David Myers indicates that "the success or failure of one's marriage is one of the most important predictors of personal well-being. Married people drink and smoke less, live longer, earn more (a phenomenon attributed partly to healthy, successful people marrying more and partly to the motivations and social support that marriage offers)." Depression rates for those who are unmarried are significantly higher than those who are married. Such research is well substantiated and widely acknowledged. Tara Parker-Pope writes, "Studies consistently show that marriage is good for us, resulting in more sex, better sleep, and better mental and physical health." While just about anyone who has ever been married can testify to its challenges, there is incontrovertible evidence that it brings with it great rewards. It is important to note, however, it is only the functional and satisfying marriage that will bring out the best in its participants. Understandably, the unhealthy marriage will work against one's well-being.

The task, then, is to determine what elements are required for a healthy relationship to flourish. Of course, there is no exact science to this. Reflecting on the success of her marriage, Elizabeth says of her husband, "He comes home after work, he wants to be home, he helps around the house and with the kids, he loves me and the children and tells us all the time he would do anything for us." Elizabeth acknowledges the challenges that come with maintaining a relationship and raising children. "We remember to respect each other and always have a united front… We love well, each other and our kids, we communicate well, and understand and respect each other without limits." More than anything, the unfaltering intention to stay married has kept Elizabeth and Zane together. It is something they work on together every day, and never lose sight of.

Experience has shown you that marriage isn't always forever, but divorce is. As a woman from a divided home, it is likely that you tend to approach marriage with a mix of reverence and trepidation. The journey to finding a healthy committed relationship is a long one for many daughters of divorce. But when you come to a place of healing, the sense of satisfaction is that much sweeter. Marisa reflects on the obstacles she has overcome growing up in a divorced home, and how she struggled through her own first marriage, which ended in divorce. Unflinchingly, she says, "What I've come to learn is that pain was put on me by another person, and it wasn't mine to own… I finally realized that I didn't have to attach myself to it and there is so much freedom in that." Now in a loving second marriage that has lasted twenty-one years, Marisa is proud to call herself a survivor. "My husband, Dan, believes in me and validates me as a woman." Love and marriage are weighty undertakings laden with great risks, but also great rewards. Although love may scare you and present you with the possibility of great pain, you must believe that you are worthy of taking part in a healthy relationship. Happiness and commitment are available to you, if you are willing to do the work to find them. The cornerstone of completing Step 7 is gaining insight about the choices you make when it comes to love, and developing a healthy respect for commitment.

ON A JOURNEY TO FIND LOVE, COMMITMENT, AND POSSIBLY MARRIAGE

Elizabeth provides an example of a woman who endured the hardship of her parents' divorce and has made a "good enough" adjustment to adulthood. Her life was transformed when her father moved to another state when she was nine years old. After her father left, Elizabeth rarely saw him because he avoided conflict with his former wife. To make matters worse, she had a stormy relationship with her mother, who was preoccupied with surviving life as a single parent and had a series of boyfriends. Resilient from a young age, Elizabeth joined the military at age eighteen as a way to forge an identity of her own. She describes the four years that she was enlisted as a time when she became more self-aware and began to visualize the type of relationship she wanted. Fortunately, a year after she returned to her hometown, she was able to reestablish a connection with her high school sweetheart, Zane, whom she married shortly after our first interview. Elizabeth takes pride in the fact that she went into their marriage with her eyes wide open. She spent several years in therapy healing from her parents' divorce and visualizing the type of relationship she wanted before accepting Zane's proposal of marriage.

However, things don't always go smoothly for Elizabeth and Zane. At times, they disagree about how to raise their children or financial issues. During these times, Elizabeth fears that something bad may happen, but she can't picture her life without Zane. She says, "I do have fears, but mostly I remind myself that he is my soul mate, my other half. I remind myself that he is honest and he loves me—he loves our family. He is my best friend and I remind myself that I don't worry about my friends leaving. Also, I think if someday we part ways it will be horrible, if it happens. But why waste our time together—our happiness—worrying about something in the future that may or may not happen. I make sure that I tell him every day that I love him. I make sure to be interested in things he cares about, because I love his happiness as much as mine."

STEPS TO OVERCOMING FEAR OF RELATIONSHIP FAILURE

The first step in overcoming your fears of failure in intimate relationships is to examine your thoughts, beliefs, and expectations. You learned in chapter 7 that women with trust issues doubt that a lasting partnership or marriage is possible. Finding a partner to build love, trust, and intimacy with is a primary issue for adult children of divorce. Perhaps one or more of the following beliefs have crossed your mind:

* ※ I believe that most relationships are doomed to fail.
* ※ Marriages and relationships may work for a while, but they always end badly.
* ※ I believe that if I get close to someone, he or she will eventually leave me.
* ※ I believe that I need to protect myself in a relationship by not relying on my partner too much.
* ※ I believe that avoiding conflict is the best way to keep a relationship strong.
* ※ Conflict and anger are signs that a relationship is failing.
* ※ I believe that if my partner loves me, he has to prove it.

❊ No matter what I do, I believe that my marriage will end in divorce because my parents' did.

❊ There is something wrong with me, and I don't have what it takes to make a relationship last.

Once you examine your thoughts, beliefs, and attitudes about love and commitment, you are ready to take a closer look at intimacy. In general, love means wishing the best for other people. Like Elizabeth, most women know instinctively that loving someone means you want them to be happy and you have their best interests in mind. Love also means that while women may have moments of frustration, impatience, and anger toward their loved ones, they do their best to overcome them. For daughters of divorce, this can be a tricky issue since many have been caught in the approval trap. They may have a tendency to be caretakers, causing them to avoid conflict at all costs.

Smart women know that all relationships have ups and downs and that conflict goes with the territory. Yet as an adult child of divorce you may avoid conflict because it may have signified the end of your parents' marriage. Marriage counselor Michele Weiner Davis explains that avoiding conflict backfires in marriage. She posits that bottling up negative thoughts and feelings doesn't give your partner a chance to change his or her behavior. On the other hand, she cautions that one of the secrets of a good marriage is learning to choose battles wisely and to distinguish between petty issues and important ones. Elizabeth's Mother's Day story provides a good example of a hot-button issue that needed to be resolved. You might recall that she felt it was important to inform Zane about her hurt feelings regarding the gift he purchased at a gas station—at the last minute. It wasn't the cost of the gift that bothered Elizabeth, but Zane's lack of planning something meaningful to express his appreciation of her on Mother's Day. As Elizabeth suspected, he didn't realize the magnitude of her hurt feelings until she disclosed them. Since then, Zane has faithfully purchased a special Mother's Day gift or cooked her favorite meal every year, and Elizabeth feels valued and loved by him.

STEPS TO RESOLVING CONFLICTS

The following steps to resolving conflicts and improving communication with intimate partners will help you to incorporate Step 7 into your life:

* **Take a risk and deal with hurt feelings honestly—especially if it is an important issue.**
* **Focus on the feelings behind your anger, not just why you are angry.** Be mindful of enduring vulnerabilities—such as loss and betrayal from the past—that may cause you to become irrational or overreact to something your partner says or does.
* **Use "I" statements rather than "you" statements that tend to come across as blameful.** For example, "I" statements such as "I felt hurt when you forgot to call when you were running late" can enhance communication. This will get you a better result than saying "You are always late." People weaken their communication by using "you" statements since they're a way of avoiding responsibility and depersonalizing a message.
* **Stay on the topic.** Try hard not to bring up past grievances that are water under the bridge or throw in the kitchen sink in a tirade of "you do everything wrong." That won't help resolve the issue at hand. Nor will rehashing all your

previous frustrations make you feel better or heal your hurt or anger. Doing this will only wind up hurting your partner and make him or her feel resentful toward you as well—or worse, it will push your partner away.

* **Don't make threats.** Avoid saying things you might regret the next day. It is never worth hurting your partner in the heat of the moment, no matter how angry or hurt you are.

* **Avoid saying "never" or "always."** Overgeneralizations are usually a red flag that you are being reactive about something, and they don't reflect what is going on in the present. They can also sound very accusing of your partner, which will make your partner shut down rather than communicate so you can get to a resolution.

* **Take a short break if you feel "flooded"**—a term coined by renowned marriage expert John Gottman, PhD, that means you're emotionally overwhelmed and can't think clearly or participate in a meaningful way. This can help you calm down and regain perspective.

* **Approach conflict with a problem-solving attitude.** Resolving conflicts in a healthy way isn't about proving a point. Conflict can be viewed as a normal aspect of intimate partnerships. Relationship issues can only be resolved through deepening your communication with your partner and shifting to a more positive approach.

WHAT ARE THE INGREDIENTS OF A LONG-LASTING RELATIONSHIP?

After years of research, Gottman has revealed seven principles that will prevent a marriage from breaking up. In *The Seven Principles for*

Making a Marriage Work, he highlights four communication issues that can change the dynamic of a marriage in a negative way. If you and your partner can avoid these or keep them to a minimum, you're guaranteed to build a solid foundation for a great relationship. Keep in mind that one of Gottman's guiding principles for a successful marriage is the five-to-one ratio—meaning for every negative interaction in a relationship, you need five positive interactions.

GOTTMAN'S FOUR COUNTERPRODUCTIVE COMMUNICATION STYLES

In Gottman's acclaimed book, *Why Marriages Succeed or Fail*, he uses a metaphor of the Four Horseman of the Apocalypse (depicting the end of times in the New Testament) to elaborate on his theory of couples' communication. This metaphor can be used to describe the following communication styles to depict the end of a relationship. To make them clearer to you, we've given illustrations or examples of these four styles. Gottman posits that it's not conflict that is problematic or destructive to a relationship but how you deal with problems that arise.

♦ **Criticism:** According to Gottman, criticizing your partner is different than offering a critique or voicing a complaint. The latter two are about specific issues, whereas the former is an attack on the character of a person. For instance, a complaint is: "I was worried when you were late. We agreed that you'd call when you were running late." In comparison, a criticism might be: "You never think about me, you're so selfish!"

- **Contempt:** When you communicate in this manner, you are being disrespectful—using sarcasm, ridicule, mimicking, icy tone of voice, or name-calling. The goal is to make the person feel despised or worthless, which almost always backfires or makes the situation worse.

- **Defensiveness:** We all get defensive at times—especially when a relationship is on the rocks or we feel we're being treated unfairly. However, defensiveness is a way of tuning out your partner, blaming him or her, and not taking responsibility for your own actions.

- **Stonewalling:** Perhaps the most damaging to your relationship, this is when one partner shuts down or withdraws from the interaction. Unfortunately, this can become a habit, and issues that get swept under the rug are never resolved—leaving the partner who wants to engage feeling hurt and resentful.

Love also means risking occasionally getting your feelings hurt; it's a price you occasionally have to pay for intimacy because you both are being open with each other about everything. In all intimate relationships there exist conflicting needs for closeness and space, according to Gay Hendricks, PhD, author of *Conscious Loving*. When issues come up with either of those needs, it is essential that you discuss the issues with your partner and find creative ways to meet both of your needs. Allowing yourself to be vulnerable and take risks is hard work, but the payoff is tremendous, as you'll see below from

Gottman's Four Principles for a Successful Marriage. To make things easier for you, we've highlighted and adapted four of Gottman's seven principles—the ones we find the most crucial to promoting a happy marriage!

GOTTMAN'S FOUR PRINCIPLES FOR A SUCCESSFUL MARRIAGE

♦ **Nurture your fondness and admiration:** Remind yourself of your partner's positive qualities—even as you grapple with his flaws—and express your positive feelings out loud several times each day.

♦ **Let your partner influence you:** Search for common ground rather than insisting on getting your way when you have a disagreement. Listen to his point of view and avoid the blame game.

♦ **Overcome gridlock:** Often perpetual conflicts go unresolved when we get stuck in negative patterns of relating such as the distance-pursuer pattern—a tug-of-war where one person actively tries to change the other person, and the other resists it.

♦ **Create shared meaning:** Gottman found that couples who have an intentional sense of shared purpose, meaning, values, and customs for family life—such as rituals for holidays—are generally happier.

STEPS TO ACHIEVING LOVE AND COMMITMENT

The task, then, is to learn from your parents' failed relationships and your own, and to create new ones that are healthy and lasting.

With courage and determination, you can restore your faith in love and achieve Step 7.

By practicing the action steps below, along with everything else you've learned in Step 7, you will gain a better sense of whether you have a healthy respect for commitment. You'll be able to fine-tune your expectations about the kind of partner who's a good match for you and to proceed to the next chapter of your life. If you are single, there are many things you can do to prepare for a strong future. If you are currently in a committed relationship, you can take steps to improve your level of love, trust, and intimacy.

ACTION STEPS

* **Identify specific ways you might be avoiding commitment** such as rejecting partners who might be a good match for you, not discussing the future, or not setting a date for a wedding if you are engaged.

* **Gain awareness about how your own history—dating back to childhood—impacts your feelings about love and commitment.** For instance, if you are a people pleaser, you might be drawn to partners whom you attempt to fix or repair.

* **Examine your choice in partners and confront qualities they have in common.** Becoming more aware of self-defeating patterns and not repeating them is the goal here.

* **Take responsibility for your part in relationship dynamics.** For instance, if you've experienced a distance-pursuer pattern, work on changing it.

* **Evaluate the impact your relationship patterns have**

had on your self-esteem and life choices. Make a list of six qualities in a partner that are a priority to you.

※ **Set a goal to become more deeply invested in a romantic relationship** (with a current or new partner) that possesses several of the qualities you find desirable in a partner. There is no such thing as a soul mate, and it is self-defeating to wait for one to appear.

※ **Make sure to have a discussion about expectations for the future with your partner**—especially if you plan to move in together or get married. This may sound obvious, but it's not necessarily a comfortable conversation and so couples tend to avoid it.

※ **Don't rush into making a commitment or living with a partner.** Avoid making a commitment to someone whom you've dated for less than two years; make sure you're at least in your late twenties; know your partner well; and share similar backgrounds, values, and interests.

※ **Attempt to pick a partner with whom you have chemistry and compatibility** since both are essential to a long-lasting healthy intimate relationship. Keep in mind that chemistry refers to both physical and intellectual attraction. On the other hand, compatibility is about sharing common values and goals, having fun together, and liking each other.

※ **Take on the attitude that your marriage or committed relationship is worth saving**. Since daughters of divorce are more likely to consider divorce as an option, try to stay married or in a committed relationship for at least ten years (unless it is abusive). Some marriages improve over time. If you have chosen to cohabit, openly discuss options that work well for both you and your partner.

❋ Don't be afraid to take risks to create a relationship that allows you to open yourself up to real love and intimacy. We support you on your journey!

As a daughter of divorce, you can learn much about love from making a commitment to love consciously and fully—to not be restrained by the legacy of your parents' divorce. This means committing yourself to being vulnerable and intimate with your partner and revealing your authentic self. Once you decide to take this path, and take responsibility for the quality of your relationships, the future is yours to create.

A Word From Terry: A Mother's Perspective

Looking for security, I married young and didn't realize how clueless I was about all of the challenges that come with commitment. After sixteen years of marriage, I divorced. Like many daughters of divorce, I brought unrealistic expectations to my first marriage. The problem was that I didn't grow up with an example of a healthy relationship. Lacking in self-confidence and fiercely independent, my idealized standards set me up to fail. I'm so pleased that Tracy seems to have a healthy respect for commitment and more realistic expectations about marriage than I had at her age.

• • • • • • • • • •

A Word From Tracy: A Daughter's Perspective

When I think of commitment, I think of fear. I fear that even if I do everything right, including picking a partner well-suited to me, taking my time in a relationship, and balancing intimacy and autonomy, I will still fail to keep a happy and cohesive relationship. Writing this chapter has helped me to realize that relationships can't be defined simply as successes and failures. Whether your relationship is three months old or thirty years old, it's important to remember that if it ends, it isn't the end of you. Your losses will make your life richer, and you will be a better woman for it.

10

Breaking the Legacy of Divorce

"We are strong and determined people because of our experiences, making us who we are now. Our mom instilled important values, to depend on ourselves and no one else, and that we can get through anything. Your absence from our lives made us more determined to stand up for ourselves and to work on those things that we need and want."

—*sisters Catherine and Emma, ages 39 and 36*

Believe it or not, divorce runs in families. This has proven to be true for the women we interviewed, and it's been true in our own lives. So the question then becomes—how can you break the legacy of divorce in your life? If you've been divorced, you surely don't want to endure another. And if you grew up in a divorced home, you surely don't want the same fate for your child. As we discussed earlier, studies show that adult children of divorce have double the risk of divorce compared to counterparts from intact homes. The truth is that it's hard to get out from under the shadow of divorce when at times we feel wired to re-create the past.

Wallerstein writes, "Ultimately your goal is to close the door on your parents' divorce, to separate the now from the then. By giving up wanting what you didn't have, you can set yourself free." Although Wallerstein devoted much of her prolific career to preventing divorce, she also believed that a divorce undertaken thoughtfully and realistically could teach children how to confront serious life problems with compassion. We know divorce has been our greatest teacher. It has taught us about what's really important in life, and it's made us more careful when it comes to making a commitment in our relationships and in all other aspects of our lives. When you grow up in a divorced home, you view love through a different lens as an adult. When you have a marriage of your own, you may desperately fear it ending. But as a daughter of divorce, with courage and persistence, you can learn to develop a relationship based on love, trust, and unfaltering commitment.

The breakup of a family may signify the loss of childhood for girls. These same girls may grow into womanhood and become particularly vulnerable to fears and anxieties about the future—just as they are forming their own romantic relationships. When they fall in love, it reopens the wounds that were created in childhood. As we've seen, many daughters of divorce have trouble with trust and intimacy and fear that no matter what they do, they'll be left. Consequently, they tend to pick partners who are all wrong for them and lack confidence in their ability to make love last.

But it doesn't have to be that way. Catherine's story provides an example of how the legacy of divorce can be changed in families, against all odds. Most people with Catherine's childhood would have crumbled; instead, as an adult, she has learned to thrive. As we discussed earlier, thirty-nine-year-old Catherine has been happily married to Ethan for close to a decade. She radiates the confidence you would expect from a successful professional. We chose to feature Catherine in several chapters because she is a resilient woman who hasn't allowed herself to become a victim. Today, she believes her early experiences, whether positive or negative, have profoundly shaped her outlook.

After a few years of counseling, Catherine came to terms with the qualities she needed to find in a partner in order for her to feel secure and rebuild trust in relationships. After dating several unsuitable partners, she met her husband, Ethan, in her late twenties. They took three years to get to know each other before deciding to get married. Last year, Catherine gave birth to their second child, a baby girl, and she is determined to work on her marriage. She says, "My marriage is the exact opposite of my parents'. My husband is a stable person, hardworking, loving, responsible, and dependable. He is thoughtful, considerate, and took our vows seriously—he is a real man!"

The most admirable quality about Catherine is that she refuses to let her parents' divorce and her father's abandonment define her. Instead, these events have given her strength and insight. They have proven to be motivating factors to make her relationship with her husband work. Her divorce experience as a child made her understand what it is that she really needs—someone who will be there for her, no matter what. And after taking time to get to know Ethan, she found it. Catherine could have chosen to blame her father, to let his alcoholism, infidelity, and the resulting financial hardships impact the rest of her life. There's no doubt these things brought her pain. But the difference is that she made a deliberate decision to accept the bad things that happened, and not let them hold her back from the best life has to offer.

BREAKING THE CYCLE OF DIVORCE

So how can a daughter of divorce break the cycle of destructive relationships and divorce? Self-awareness and a willingness to work on self-defeating relationship patterns is an important first step. You can learn to recognize destructive dynamics that exist in intimate relationships and take steps to change them. Breaking patterns can be as basic as reversing roles with your partner and making a decision not to get stuck in the same old disagreements. For instance, Catherine and Ethan decided he would be the one to prepare dinner since he gets home first, and she would clean up so they would both have time to relax with their two children in the evening. Since Catherine is self-reliant to a fault, she never asked Ethan to cook previously and would feel resentful because she took on too much responsibility and didn't have time for herself or her family. Small changes can go a long way to add to feelings of happiness and equality in a relationship.

The good news is that, as you've seen throughout this book, you have the opportunity to learn from your parents' mistakes (and your own) and to create a healthy, long-lasting relationship. In fact, there may be a silver lining to experiencing parental divorce. In *Overcoming Your Parents' Divorce*, Elisabeth Joy LaMotte writes: "Children of divorce are more likely to enter young adulthood with their eyes wide open, and such awareness holds the potential for great relationship success." How you use that awareness and whether you let it help you move forward will make the difference in your ability to create great relationships.

If you are a daughter of divorce, it is important to explore reasons why intimate relationships can present challenges so that you can overcome them. Kayla is a college student and single mom in her late twenties who was raised by her mother and grandmother. She was one year old when her father left—announcing that he was moving in with his girlfriend. Kayla was too young to remember the incident or his engagement to her stepmother less than a year later. But she does know that she felt a sense of emptiness because she longed for more contact with her father and only visited him occasionally due to conflicts between her parents.

Although Kayla didn't attribute her difficulties in romantic relationships to the absence of her father until recently, she entered young adulthood with a pervasive sense of doubt related to her ability to sustain an intimate relationship. Due to her father leaving suddenly when she was an infant, Kayla had an unsurprising inherent mistrust of men and a simultaneous longing for their attention and recognition. "Throughout my teens," she tells me, "I had a very low self-image, and if I ever did date, I'd hang on and throw hysterical fits if they even hinted at leaving." She reflects: "My fiancé, Tom, is teaching me what's normal in a relationship. When we first got together I'd get mad easily, but I've learned I don't have to get mad to show love. I used to believe that if I could hurt you first, you're not going to hurt me. Tom is showing me that love doesn't have to be paired with pain."

When we sat down for coffee at the cyber café at the college where Kayla attends nursing classes, she explains, "After I had Shelby last year, I realized that things could be different between her and my father so I decided to give it a try. In fact, he's watching her right now while I'm in school, and I'm living vicariously through her." When I asked Kayla what the main reason was for her willingness to work on her relationship with her father even though she felt hurt and rejected by him in the past, she said:

"I'm looking to give Shelby a different kind of life than I had growing up. What's helping me is that my dad's trying to be a good grandpa."

Kayla's story is a reminder of a lesson that we learned throughout the writing of this book: even the most troubled, baggage-laden relationship isn't entirely without hope. Though growing up in a divorced home presented them with challenges, most of the women in our study found something of value in their relationships with their parents and reasons to forgive them. These women taught us that forgiveness is an essential aspect of forging healthy relationships with others.

FINDING LOVE WE CAN BE SURE OF

Every person harbors a desire to love and be loved, but the problem for many daughters of divorce is that they fear they won't be loved and cared for, and that their partner won't have their best interests at heart. Healthy partnerships are within reach if you let go of fear and believe you are worthy of love and all of the gifts it has to offer.

It may be obvious at this point that the best relationships are ones born out of trust and vulnerability. And we can't stress this enough. In positive relationships, each partner approaches one another as an equal. The relationship doesn't drain its participants; instead it nourishes. Differences between partners are complementary, not conflicting. These differences are advantageous; they don't create a hindrance to the relationship but instead contribute to its growth. In a healthy relationship, partners draw out untapped possibilities in one another. A successful romantic relationship is where you feel at your best.

Like all challenges in life, greater awareness and willingness to work on an issue can bring about change. And the fact of the matter is that you can create more trusting relationships if you give yourself permission to be vulnerable and take risks. We are living proof that it is possible to restore your faith in love, and that every person, regardless of what they have been through, is worthy of finding love they can be sure of.

As a daughter of divorce, intimate relationships and marriage may present many challenges for you, but you must also recognize that you are armed with your own strengths to face these and embrace them. It's likely that you don't take commitment for granted. Your relationships are sacred to you, in ways that those who come from intact homes can't understand. You probably find it's easy to second-guess yourself, and you may be convinced that your life would have been better if you had grown up with a happier home life. But the experience of growing up in a divorced family can provide you with a deeper well of emotion to pull from and a greater appreciation for the sacredness of commitment and marriage.

Personal growth means shaping and reshaping your thoughts, attitudes, and beliefs, like those mentioned above. It can be hard to "unlearn" these deep-rooted ideas from the legacy of your parents' divorce. But real growth and happiness occur when you face your disappointments and losses and work through them. No matter how old you are, it's never too late to fully embrace the Seven Steps to a Successful Relationship we presented here and to restore your faith in yourself and in love. Faith means having a hopeful attitude toward life—one that will help you get out of those stuck places and move into profound healing. Only then can you build relationships based on love, trust, and intimacy. You are worthy of love and, more importantly, you are capable of it. Now go get it!

A Word From Terry: A Mother's Perspective

Most of the women we interviewed for our book weren't like Catherine or Kayla. This isn't a statement intended to put down the courageous women who were willing to share their stories with us. But the truth about most of the women we spoke with is that pain marked their romantic experiences. The majority of them hadn't quite shaken off the ghosts from their pasts. They were trying furiously to restore their faith in love. But many of them truly didn't trust the men they were in relationships with. Deep down, they believed that ultimately they would be abandoned. In the long run, they didn't trust their own judgment and believed they didn't have what it took to choose the best partner.

Intimacy can be an important source of comfort and provide predictability in an uncertain world. The truth is that all relationships end: through breakup, death, or divorce. Why waste time being preoccupied with fear of your relationship ending? It is possible to be vulnerable with others without losing parts of yourself. By doing this, you'll be able to restore your faith in love, trust, and intimacy.

A Word From Tracy: A Daughter's Perspective

If you believe that your relationship will inevitably end, you can't be blamed for how you feel. If you had no example of a love that was real, how can you understand something you've never had? Every person in this world deserves love they can be sure of. Most likely, the pain you carry around has been with you quite a while. Don't let it prevent you from experiencing this truth: committing your life to another person is the greatest risk you can take. When you learn to trust yourself, and when you find that you can rely on your partner for love and intimacy, the world becomes yours for the taking. We wish you the best of luck on your journey and hope you find happiness, wherever life takes you.

Acknowledgments

There are many people whose assistance and support have made this book possible. First, we would like to thank all of the participants in our daughters of divorce study. Your voices form the heart of this book, and are testimonies to both your strength and hope for a bright future. Also, we are grateful to all of the staff and Terry's colleagues at Bristol Community College where our study took place.

Daughters of Divorce would never have existed without the unwavering support of our agent, Jaqueline Flynn of Joelle Delbourgo Associates. Jacquie's late afternoon chats always managed to keep Terry's stress level down by offering reassurance and empathy!

Thanks to Joelle Delbourgo, who took on two unknown authors and gave us the opportunity to pursue our dream. We appreciate your faith in us and kind notes of encouragement.

And thanks to Stephanie Bowen, our amazing editor at Sourcebooks, who cheerfully pushed us to revise the manuscript to its current state. Thanks, Stephanie, for your insightful and wise comments! In addition, Shana Drehs at Sourcebooks is a considerate and hardworking editor who came on board during the final editing stages and supported us throughout this process.

Thanks to the late Dr. Judith Wallerstein, distinguished therapist, author, and researcher, who inspired the idea for the book. In the summer of 2009, Terry inhaled every page of *The Unexpected Legacy of Divorce: The 25-Year Landmark Study* and sat down with Tracy over a cup of tea to map out her vision for the book. Terry cherishes the email that Dr. Wallerstein sent to encourage her research.

And thanks to Terry's colleague and mentor Roger Clark, PhD, professor of sociology at Rhode Island College, who sparked her passion for research and helped her believe in her ability to write this book.

Thanks to Jim Emond, Karl Schnapp, Jack Conway, and the late Sandra Boone, who gave Terry countless hours of support while researching daughters of divorce at Bristol Community College.

Terry wants to thank Sue Rousseau, reference librarian, for her kindness, interest, and technical support. And thanks to all of the librarians at the Portsmouth Public Library who supported Terry while she spent countless hours preparing the manuscript and copying it.

We are grateful to our dear friends Barbara Lamagna, Betsy Dees, Janet Oakley, Kathy Leisge, Barbara Coppola, and Dale Rheault, who listened patiently to our stories, hopes, and dreams for *Daughters of Divorce*.

Most importantly, our family means the most to us. Thanks to Craig, Terry's husband, and her children Catherine and Sean (Tracy's siblings) for their love and encouragement. And Terry's parents Herbert and Leslie (Tracy's grandparents).

Resources for Readers

RECOMMENDATIONS FOR FURTHER READING

While conducting research for *Daughters of Divorce*, we spent countless hours at the library, bookstores, and on the Internet trying to increase our awareness of issues facing daughters of divorce. We have composed a list of nonfiction books on the topic, as well as many relevant websites. Finally, we've presented other resources you might find helpful such as suggested resources for finding a therapist.

GENERAL NONFICTION WORKS ON DAUGHTERS OF DIVORCE AND RELATED TOPICS

Ahrons, Constance. *We're Still Family: What Grown Children Have to Say about Their Parents' Divorce*. New York: Harper Collins, 2004.

Amato, Paul R., and Alan Booth. *A Generation at Risk: Growing Up in an Era of Family Upheaval*. Cambridge, MA: Harvard University Press, 2000.

Amato, Paul R., Alan Booth, David R. Johnson, and Stacy J. Rogers. *Alone Together: How Marriage in America is Changing*. Cambridge, MA: Harvard University Press, 2007.

Anderson, Susan. *The Journey from Abandonment to Healing.* New York: Berkley Books, 2000.

Barash, Susan Shapiro. *Women of Divorce: Mothers, Daughters, Stepmothers—The New Triangle.* Far Hills, NJ: New Horizon Press, 2003.

Beattie, Melody. *Beyond Codependency: And Getting Better All the Time.* New York: Harper Collins, 1991.

Bloomfield, Harold H., and Leonard Felder. *Making Peace With Your Parents.* New York: Ballantine Books, 1983.

Branden, Nathaniel. *The Psychology of Romantic Love.* New York: Jeremy P. Tarcher, 1980.

———. *The Psychology of Self-Esteem.* New York: Bantam Books, 1971.

Brown, Brené. *Daring Greatly: How the Courage to Be Vulnerable Transforms the Way We Live, Love, Parent, and Lead.* New York: Gotham Books, 2012.

———. *The Gifts of Imperfection.* Center City, MN: Hazelton, 2010.

Coleman, Joshua. *When Parents Hurt: Compassionate Strategies When You and Your Grown Child Don't Get Along.* New York: Collins Living, 2008.

Davis, Michele Weiner. *The Divorce Remedy: The Proven 7-Step Program for Saving Your Marriage.* New York: Simon & Schuster, 2001.

Gilligan, Carol. *In a Different Voice: Psychological Theory and Women's Development.* Cambridge, MA: Harvard University Press, 1982.

Gottman, John M., and Nan Silver. *The Seven Principles for Making Marriage Work: A Practical Guide from the Country's Foremost Relationship Expert.* New York: Three Rivers Press, 1999.

Gottman, John M., and Joan DeClaire. *The Relationship Cure: A 5 Step Guide to Strengthening Your Marriage, Family, and Friendships.* New York: Three Rivers Press, 2001.

Hetherington, E. Mavis, and John Kelly. *For Better or For Worse: Divorce Reconsidered.* New York: W.W. Norton & Co., 2002.

Hirschfeld, Mary. *The Adult Children of Divorce Workbook: A Compassionate Program for Healing from Your Parents' Divorce.* Los Angeles: Jeremy P. Tarcher, 1992.

Laiken, Deidre S. *Daughters of Divorce: The Effects of Parental Divorce on Women's Lives.* New York: William Morrow and Co., 1981.

LaMotte, Elisabeth Joy. *Overcoming Your Parents' Divorce: 5 Steps to a Happy Relationship.* Far Hills, NJ: New Horizon Press, 2008.

Luskin, Fred. *Forgive For Good: A Proven Prescription for Health and Happiness.* New York: Harper Collins, 2002.

Marquardt, Elizabeth. *Between Two Worlds: The Inner Lives of Children of Divorce.* New York: Three Rivers Press, 2005.

Meeker, Meg. *Strong Fathers, Strong Daughters: 10 Secrets Every Father Should Know.* New York: Ballantine Books, 2007.

Milford, Anne, and Jennifer Gauvain. *How Not to Marry the Wrong Guy: Is He "the One" or Should You Run? A Guide to Living Happily Ever After.* New York: Broadway Books, 2010.

Nielsen, Linda. *Between Fathers and Daughters: Enriching and Rebuilding Your Adult Relationship.* Nashville, TN: Cumberland House, 2008.

Paul, Pamela. *The Starter Marriage and the Future of Matrimony.* New York: Random House, 2003.

Pipher, Mary. *Reviving Ophelia: Saving the Lives of Adolescent Girls.* New York: Penguin, 1994.

Richo, David. *Daring to Trust: Opening Ourselves to Real Love and Intimacy.* Boston: Shambhala, 2010.

Rodgers, Beverly, and Tom Rodgers. *Adult Children of Divorced Parents: Making Your Marriage Work.* San Jose, CA: Resource Pub., 2002.

Rosenthal, Sarah Simms. *The Unavailable Father: Seven Ways Women Can Understand, Heal, and Cope with a Broken Father-Daughter Relationship.* San Francisco: Jossey Bass, 2010.

Shandler, Sara. *Ophelia Speaks: Adolescent Girls Write about Their Search for Self.* New York: Harper Perennial, 1999.

Staal, Stephanie. *The Love They Lost: Living with the Legacy of Our Parents' Divorce.* New York: Delacorte Press, 2000.

Subotnik, R. S., and Gloria G. Harris. *Surviving Infidelity: Making Decisions, Recovering from the Pain.* Avon, MA: Adams Media, 2005.

Wall, Cynthia. *The Courage to Trust: A Guide to Building Deep and Lasting Relationships.* Oakland, CA: New Harbinger Publications, 2004.

Wallerstein, Judith, Julia M. Lewis, and Sandra Blakeslee. *The Unexpected Legacy of Divorce: The 25-Year Landmark Study.* New York: Hyperion, 2000.

Weber, Jill P. *Having Sex, Wanting Intimacy: Why Women Settle for One-Sided Relationships.* New York: Rowman & Littlefield Publishers, Inc., 2013.

Zimmerman, Jeffrey, and Elizabeth S. Thayer. *Adult Children of Divorce: How to Overcome the Legacy of Your Parents' Breakup and Enjoy Love, Trust, and Intimacy.* Oakland, CA: New Harbinger Publications, 2003.

INFORMATIONAL WEBSITES ON DIVORCE, DAUGHTERS OF DIVORCE, RELATIONSHIPS, AND MARRIAGE

www.movingpastdivorce.com. Weekly blogs, resources, and support geared for helping people embrace love, trust, and intimacy. Excerpts from our book are featured on this website.

www.huffingtonpost.com/divorce. Daily blogs on topics related to relationships and divorce. This website has high quality content by experts in the field of divorce.

www.sincemydivorce.com. This website is geared for divorced adults and offers weekly blogs and resources.

www.divorcedmoms.com. This website offers a wide variety of articles and resources for divorced adults.

www.lifescript.com. This is a women's informational website that provides easy access to hundreds of articles on women's psychosocial health issues.

www.coldfeetpress.com. This website offers information and resources about relationship issues. Anne Milford and Jennifer Gauvain offer tips from their book *How Not to Marry the Wrong Guy*.

http.smartmarriages.com. This website for the Coalition for Marriage, Family, and Couples Education is full of helpful resources—and it's not limited to married people. The recommended resources are relevant for couples at any stage—dating, engaged, newlywed, or cohabiting.

SUGGESTED RESOURCES FOR FINDING A THERAPIST

Making your own recovery a priority is essential to healing from your parents' divorce. It requires making a commitment of time and sometimes finances. There are good psychotherapists everywhere, and most insurance companies will provide their clients with a list that includes their specialty areas. We recommend that you look for a therapist who specializes in divorce and/or women's issues. Most agencies accept health insurance or flexible fees, but they do require a weekly or biweekly commitment. Support groups are usually of minimal cost and meet weekly for several months. The following websites can help you locate a certified therapist in your area. You can also contact your insurance company or your state licensing board for mental health providers.

http.find-a-therapist.com. The largest online database of therapy providers.

www.goodtherapy.org. Resources for individual, couples, marriage, family, or group therapy.

www.networktherapy.com. This provider directory features a searchable database of psychologists, psychiatrists, social workers, counselors, and treatment centers and support for people with mental health concerns.

www.therapistlocator.net. A public service of the American Association of Marriage and Family Therapy (AAMFT).

www.psychologytoday.com. Click on "Find a Therapist."

Notes

INTRODUCTION

xix *security they didn't receive as a child:* Stephanie Staal, *The Love They Lost: Living with the Legacy of Our Parents' Divorce* (New York: Delacorte Press, 2000), 186.

xxi *close bond with her father:* Meg Meeker, *Strong Fathers, Strong Daughters: 10 Secrets Every Father Should Know* (New York: Ballantine Books, 2006), 23–24.

xxi *adult children of divorce in 1995 and 1996:* Terry Clifford and Roger Clark, "Family Climate, Family Structure and Self-Esteem in College Females: The Physical vs. Psychological Wholeness Divorce Debate Revisited," *Journal of Divorce and Remarriage* 23, no. 3–4 (1995): 97–112; Roger Clark and Terry Clifford, "Towards a Resources and Stressors Model: The Psychological Adjustment of Adult Children of Divorce," *Journal of Divorce and Remarriage* 25, no. 3–4 (1996): 105–36.

xxii *counterparts from intact homes:* Paul R. Amato and Danelle D. DeBoer, "The Transmission of Marital Instability Across Generations: Relationship Skills or Commitment to Marriage?" *Journal of Marriage and Family* 63, no. 4 (November 2001): 1038–51.

xxiii   *lowered feelings of closeness with their fathers:* Paul R. Amato and Alan Booth, *A Generation at Risk: Growing Up in an Era of Family Upheaval* (Cambridge, MA: Harvard University Press, 2000), 21–22.

xxiii   *benefits of shared custody:* Linda Nielsen, *Between Fathers and Daughters: Enriching and Rebuilding Your Adult Relationship* (Nashville, TN: Cumberland House, 2008), 158.

xxiv   *passed down in families:* E. Mavis Hetherington and John Kelly, *For Better or For Worse: Divorce Reconsidered* (New York: W.W. Norton & Co., 2002), 1–16; Amato and DeBoer, "The Transmission of Marital Stability Across Generations," 1038–51; Judith Wallerstein, Julia M. Lewis, and Sandra Blakeslee, *The Unexpected Legacy of Divorce: The 25-Year Landmark Study* (New York: Hyperion, 2000), 294–316.

xxiv   *Wallerstein studied women separately from men:* Judith Wallerstein and Shauna B. Cobrin, "Daughters of Divorce: Report from a Ten-Year Follow-Up," *American Journal of Orthopsychiatry* 59, no. 4 (October 1989): 593–604.

xxiv   *the powerful effects of parental divorce:* Ibid.

xxiv   *following in their parents' footsteps:* Wallerstein, Lewis, and Blakeslee, prologue to *The Unexpected Legacy of Divorce*.

xxv   *altered relationship with their fathers:* Hetherington and Kelly, *For Better or For Worse*, 232–48.

xxv   *we sought to examine the impact of parental divorce on women specifically:* Ibid., 1–16; Wallerstein, Lewis, and Blakeslee, prologue to *The Unexpected Legacy of Divorce*.

xxvi   *parental divorce prior to the age of eighteen:* Amato and Booth, *A Generation at Risk*, 10.

xxvi   *original research study in 1995:* Clifford and Clark, "Family
        Climate, Family Structure and Self-Esteem," 97–112.

xxvi   *Wallerstein's groundbreaking findings:* Judith S. Wallerstein,
        "The Long-Term Effects of Divorce on Children: A
        Review," *Journal of the American Academy of Child and
        Adolescent Psychiatry* 30, no. 3 (May 1991): 349–60.

xxvi   *variables such as abuse were controlled:* Clifford and Clark,
        "Family Climate, Family Structure and Self-Esteem," 97–
        112.

xxvi   *model for children of divorce:* Paul R. Amato, "Children's
        Adjustment to Divorce: Theories, Hypothesis, and
        Empirical Support," *Journal of Marriage and the Family* no.
        55 (1993): 23–28.

xxvii   *sustain healthy interpersonal relationships:* Clark and Clifford,
        "Towards a Resources and Stressors Model," 105–36.

xxvii   *marry companions from similar backgrounds:* Nicolas H.
        Wolfinger, "Family Structure Homogamy: The Effects
        of Parental Divorce on Partner Selection and Marital
        Stability," *Social Science Research* 32, no. 1 (March 2003):
        80–97.

xxviii *from an intact home:* Tara Parker-Pope, *For Better: The
        Science of a Good Marriage* (New York: Dutton, 2010), 269.

xxviii *increased risk for divorce:* Amato and DeBoer, "The
        Transmission of Marital Instability Across Generations,"
        1038–51; Hetherington and Kelly, *For Better or For Worse,*
        240–50.

xxviii *root of marital instability:* Hetherington and Kelly, *For Better
        or For Worse,* 240–50.

xxviii *endured multiple parental divorces:* Amato and Booth, *A
        Generation at Risk,* 10–11.

xxviii   *learn how to resolve conflicts in adult relationships:* Paul R. Amato, "Parental Divorce and Adult Well-Being: A Meta-Analysis," *Journal of Marriage and Family* 53, no. 1 (February 1991): 43–58.

xxix   *or sons of divorce:* Susan E. Jacquet and Catherine A. Surra, "Parental Divorce and Premarital Couples: Commitment and Other Relationship Characteristics," *Journal of Marriage and Family* 63, no. 3 (August 2001): 627–38.

xxix   *a proposal to wed:* Sarah W. Whitton et al., "Effects of Parental Divorce on Marital Commitment and Confidence," *Journal of Family Psychology* 22, no. 5 (October 2008): 789–93.

xxix   *40 percent of first marriages end in divorce:* Heritage Foundation, *2014 Index of Cultural Opportunity* (Washington, DC: Heritage Foundation, 2014), 20, http://index.heritage .org/culture/overview-of-2014-index/.

xxx   *are living with a partner:* D'Vera Cohn et al., *Barely Half of U.S. Adults Are Married—A Record Low* (Washington, DC: Pew Research Center, December 14, 2011), 1–8, www.pewsocailtrends.org/2011/12/14/barely-half-of-u -s-adults-are-married-a-record-low/.

xxx   *down 5 percent from 2009 to 2010:* Ibid.

xxx   *per one thousand unmarried women:* Heritage Foundation, *2014 Index of Cultural Opportunity,* 1–5.

xxx   *will marry at some point in their lives:* Wendy Wang and Kim Parker, *Record Share of Americans Have Never Married* (Washington, DC: Pew Research Center, 2014), 1–6.

xxx   *will marry by the age of thirty-five:* Ibid.

xxx   *said they would like to marry someday:* Ibid.

xxxi   *"more of their psychological and social needs than ever before".*

Stephanie Coontz, *Marriage, A History* (London: Penguin Books, 2005), 23.

xxxi   *two-thirds of divorces in the United States:* Margaret F. Brinig and Douglas W. Allen, "'These Boots Are Made For Walking': Why Most Divorce Filers are Women," *American Law and Economics Review* 2, no. 1 (2000): 126–69.

xxxi   *less than 1 percent in 1920:* Julissa Cruz, *Marriage: More Than a Century of Change*, FP-13-13 (Bowling Green, OH: National Center for Family & Marriage Research, 2013), 1–2, http://ncfmr.bgsu.edu/pdf/family profiles /file131529.pdf.

xxxi   *successful marriage as a victory:* Meg Jay, introduction to *The Defining Decade* (New York: Twelve, 2012).

xxxi   *"all know someone who has":* Ibid., 72.

xxxii   *her landmark study was undeniable:* Wallerstein, Lewis, and Blakeslee, prologue to *The Unexpected Legacy of Divorce*.

CHAPTER 1

1   *marriage is disposable or impermanent:* Pamela Paul, *The Starter Marriage and the Future of Matrimony* (New York: Random House, 2003), 28–30.

2   *"long-term relationships are just not worth it":* Jeffrey Zimmerman and Elizabeth S. Thayer, *Adult Children of Divorce: How to Overcome the Legacy of Your Parents' Breakup and Enjoy Love, Trust, and Intimacy* (Oakland, CA: New Harbinger Publications, 2003), 141.

3   *"approval trap":* Harold H. Bloomfield and Leonard Felder, *Making Peace with Your Parents* (New York: Ballantine Books, 1983), 80.

7   *"unworthy of acceptance and belonging"*: Brené Brown, *Daring Greatly: How the Courage to Be Vulnerable Transforms the Way We Live, Love, Parent, and Lead* (London: Gotham Books, 2012), 69.

7   *seek connectedness through that:* Carol Gilligan, *In a Different Voice: Psychological Theory and Women's Development* (Cambridge, MA: Harvard University Press, 1982), 121–27.

8   *"sleeper effect"*: Wallerstein, Lewis, and Blakeslee, preface to *The Unexpected Legacy of Divorce*; Wallerstein, "The Long-Term Effects of Divorce on Children," 349–60.

10   *"what as girls they have experienced and known"*: Lyn Mikel Brown and Carol Gilligan, *Meeting at the Crossroads: Women's Psychology and Girls' Development* (Cambridge, MA: Harvard University Press, 1992), 2.

11   *in all of the men they meet:* Deidre S. Laiken, *Daughters of Divorce: The Effects of Parental Divorce on Women's Lives* (New York: William Morrow and Co., 1981), 127.

12   *"by an active, engaged father"*: Hetherington and Kelly, *For Better or For Worse*, 231–32.

13   *"fantasy fathers"*: Suzanne Fields, *Like Father Like Daughter: How Father Shapes the Woman His Daughter Becomes* (New York: Little & Brown, 1983), 258–260.

14   *dress rehearsal for love and marriage:* Ibid., 152.

15   *"prisoners of our past"*: Martin E. P. Seligman, *What You Can Change and What You Can't: The Complete Guide to Self-Improvement* (New York: Fawcett Columbine, 1993), 237.

17   *uncertainty, risk, and emotional exposure:* Brown, *Daring Greatly*, 34.

20   *competent-opportunist, and "good enough":* Hetherington and Kelly, *For Better or For Worse*, 149–59.

20   *for nearly three decades:* Ibid.

20   *their parents' emotional caretakers:* Ibid.

21   *"competent-caring":* Ibid.

23   *and psychological functioning:* Ibid.

24   *healthy families come in all types:* Constance Ahrons, *We're Still Family: What Grown Children Have to Say about Their Parents' Divorce* (New York: Harper Collins, 2004), 11.

CHAPTER 2

43   *"we're damn good at shame":* Brown, *Daring Greatly*, 61.

CHAPTER 3

48   *"forgiveness allows us to repair our ability to love":* Mary Hirschfeld, *The Adult Children of Divorce Workbook: A Compassionate Program for Healing from Your Parents' Divorce* (Los Angeles: Jeremy P. Tarcher, Inc., 1992), 2.

53   *Elisabeth Joy LaMotte's survey:* Elisabeth Joy LaMotte, *Overcoming Your Parents' Divorce: 5 Steps to a Happy Relationship* (Far Hills, NJ: New Horizons Press, 2008), 17–23.

54   *"actual strengths and weaknesses":* Zimmerman and Thayer, *Adult Children of Divorce*, 101.

57   *improve and reach your personal goals:* Carol Dweck, *Mindset: The New Psychology of Success* (New York: Random House, 2006), 1–14.

CHAPTER 4

63   *feeling frustrated and skeptical:* Judith Wallerstein and Sandra Blakeslee, *Second Chances: Men, Women, and Children a Decade After Divorce* (New York: Ticknor & Fields, 1989), 4.

63   *"sleeper effect" described in Wallerstein's book:* Wallerstein, Lewis, and Blakeslee, preface to *The Unexpected Legacy of Divorce.*

64   *"'What must I do to please others?'":* Mary Pipher, *Reviving Ophelia: Saving the Lives of Adolescent Girls* (New York: Penguin, 1994), 22.

64   *because of their socialization:* Gilligan, *In a Different Voice,* 121–27.

66   *"memory storage about the experience":* Louann Brizendine, *The Female Brain* (New York: Broadway Books, 2006), 128.

66   *family disharmony or breakup:* Ibid.

66   *"implications for the rest of their lives":* Pipher, *Reviving Ophelia,* 72.

69   *Freud's theory of repetition compulsion:* Calvin S. Hall, *A Primer of Freudian Psychology* (New York: Penguin Books, 1999), 85–96.

70   *"long-term implications for their lives":* Wallerstein and Blakeslee, *Second Changes,* 61.

73   *"as they walk out on our lives":* Laiken, *Daughters of Divorce,* 53.

76   *"their sense of themselves and their character":* Brown and Gilligan, *Meeting at the Crossroads,* 2.

79   *study conducted by Candan Duran-Aydintug:* Candan Duran-Aydintug, "Adult Children of Divorce Revisited: When They Speak Up," *Journal of Divorce and Remarriage* 27, no. 1–2 (1997): 71–83.

82   *"grievance stories":* Fred Luskin, *Forgive for Good: A Proven Prescription for Health and Happiness* (New York: Harper Collins, 2002), 3–45.

82   *shift to an impersonal perspective:* Ibid., 19.

83   *"experiences that you have in the present":* Ibid., 111.

83   *Luskin's model:* Ibid., 211.

CHAPTER 5

88   *"motivations that shaped him and his actions":* Peggy Drexler, *Daughters, Fathers, and the Changing American Family: Our Fathers, Ourselves* (New York: Rodale, 2011), 197.

88   *"in terms of love relationships":* Jasmin Lee Cori, *The Emotionally Absent Mother: A Guide to Self-Healing and Getting the Love You Missed* (New York: The Experiment, 2010), 152

90   *"and a wound may occur":* Linda Schierse Leonard, *The Wounded Woman: Healing the Father-Daughter Relationship* (Boston: Shambhala, 1998), 10.

90   *"daddy game":* Laiken, *Daughters of Divorce*, 127.

90   *after a family dissolves than girls do:* Nielsen, *Between Fathers and Daughters*, 157–92.

91   *"an ongoing relationship with his children":* Joshua Coleman, *When Parents Hurt: Compassionate Strategies When You and Your Grown Child Don't Get Along* (New York: Collins Living, 2008), 153.

91   *"most vulnerable to disruption with a divorce":* Ibid., 152.

96   *becoming "pursuers" in their own intimate relationships:* Hetherington and Kelly, *For Better or For Worse*, 25–28.

97   *"her positive self-concept":* Sarah Simms Rosenthal, introduction to *The Unavailable Father: Seven Ways*

Women Can Understand, Heal, and Cope with a Broken Father-Daughter Relationship (San Francisco: Jossey-Bass, 2010), xviii.

99   *"broke through the silences":* Victoria Secunda, *Women and Their Fathers: The Sexual and Romantic Impact of the First Man in Your Life* (New York: Delta, 1993), 202–3.

100   *"you fear being left on your own":* H. Norman Wright, *Healing for the Father Wound* (Minneapolis, MN: Bethany House, 2005), 84.

100   *"protection and closeness they've felt with their families in childhood":* Pipher, *Reviving Ophelia*, 64–66, 131–45.

101   *"shies away from intimacy":* Elyce Wakerman, *Father Loss: Daughters Discuss the Man That Got Away* (New York: Henry Holt and Co., 1984), 110.

102   *"anyone's pain or joy but their own":* Secunda, *Women and Their Fathers*, 206.

103   *"The absence of a father is worth grieving":* Monique Robinson, *Longing for Daddy* (Colorado Springs, CO: Water Brook Press, 2004), 36, 41.

105   *"buffer them from adversity":* Hetherington and Kelly, *For Better or For Worse*, 180–201.

105   *"and sometimes continued for decades":* Ibid., 181–201.

107   *"in a daughter's life is great":* Susan Shapiro Barash, *Women of Divorce: Mothers, Daughters, Stepmothers—The New Triangle* (Far Hills, NJ: New Horizon Press, 2003), 5.

108   *"a close relationship with their stepmothers":* Coleman, *When Parents Hurt*, 154–55.

109   *"two or sometimes three families":* Wallerstein, Lewis, and Blakeslee, *The Unexpected Legacy of Divorce*, 236–53.

110   *"a successful life and marriage":* Kevin Leman, *What a*

Difference a Daddy Makes (Nashville: Thomas Nelson, 2000), 8.

110 *a crucial role in their daughters' lives:* Paul Mandelstein, *Always Dad: Being a Great Father During and After Divorce* (Berkeley, CA: Nolo, 2006), 6.

111 *fiery foes after a divorce:* Ahrons, *We're Still Family*, 160–90.

111 *"the adult children's sense of family":* Ibid., 179.

112 *"Daddy's Little Girl":* Leman, *What a Difference a Daddy Makes*, 5.

113 *equal access to both parents:* Joan B. Kelly and Robert E. Emery, "Children's Adjustment Following Divorce: Risk and Resilience Perspectives," *Family Relations* 52, no. 4 (October 2003): 352–62.

113 *on a weekly and regular basis:* Richard A. Warshack, "Social Science and Parenting Plans for Young Children: A Consensus Report," *Psychology, Public Policy, and Law* 20, no. 1 (2014): 40–67.

116 *"it may control our lives":* Melody Beattie, *Beyond Codependency: And Getting Better All the Time* (New York: Harper Collins, 1989), 80.

118 *guidelines for healing were adapted from:* Wright, *Healing for the Father Wound*, 122–38; Robin Casarjian, *Forgiveness: A Bold Choice for a Peaceful Heart* (New York: Bantam, 1992), 71–94.

CHAPTER 6

126 *"instances of feedback from others":* Nathaniel Branden, *The Psychology of Romantic Love* (New York: Jeremy P. Tarcher, 1980), 63.

127 *"fulfilling relationships will follow":* Jill P. Weber, *Having Sex, Wanting Intimacy: Why Women Settle for One-Sided*

Relationships (United Kingdom: Rowman & Littlefield Publishers, 2013), 25–44.

127   *"as being worthy of happiness":* Nathaniel Branden, *The Psychology of Self-Esteem* (New York: Bantam Books, 1969), 109–39.

128   *with parental separation:* I. Culpin et al., "Father Absence and Depressive Symptoms in Adolescence: Findings from a UK Cohort," *Psychological Medicine* 43, no. 12 (December 2013): 1.

129   *risks for low self-esteem:* Clark and Clifford, "Towards a Resources and Stressors Model," 105–36.

129   *"Only then can he help her":* Meeker, *Strong Fathers, Strong Daughters*, 42.

131   *social connections to give them a sense of self-worth:* Gilligan, *In a Different Voice*, 121–27.

133   *weather adversity and maintain a healthy sense of well-being:* Hetherington and Kelly, *For Better or For Worse*, 134.

133   *"too good for her own good":* Claudia Bepko and Jo-Ann Krestan, *Too Good for Her Own Good: Searching for Self and Intimacy in Relationships* (New York: Harper Perennial, 1991), 7.

133   *"nurturing other family members":* Harriet Lerner, *Life Preservers* (New York: Harper Collins, 1996), 4.

134   *disharmony in the family:* Hetherington and Kelly, *For Better or For Worse*, 159.

135   *essential to the human experience:* Brown, *Daring Greatly*, 10–11.

135   *"love, belonging, or connection":* Ibid., 68–69.

138   *and those who don't:* Branden, *The Psychology of Romantic Love*, 73.

138   *"not to create it in those who lack it":* Ibid., 72.

142   *"discouragement was a backdrop, fear an undercurrent":* Gay Hendricks, *The Learning to Love Yourself Workbook* (New York: Simon & Schuster, 1990), 15.

143   *"we have accepted without any critical investigation?":* Virginia Satir, *Your Many Faces: The First Step to Being Loved* (New York: Celestial Arts, 2009), 80.

143   *"reconstructed, bypassed, and built anew":* Ibid., 79.

144   *"the self says, 'I am a mistake'":* Marilyn J. Mason, *Making Our Lives Our Own: A Women's Guide to the Six Challenges of Personal Change* (New York: Harper Collins, 1991), 69.

145   *during early to middle adulthood:* Seligman, *What You Can Change,* 225–43.

146   *"proficiency in dealing with it":* Branden, *The Psychology of Self-Esteem,* 121.

CHAPTER 7

165   *feel like you are something wrong:* Mason, *Making Our Lives Our Own,* 69.

167   *"develop resilience to shame":* Brown, *Daring Greatly,* 61.

168   *highlights the following experiences:* Ronald Potter-Efron and Patricia Potter-Efron, *Letting Go of Shame: Understanding How Shame Affects Your Life* (New York: Hazelden Books, Harper Collins Pub., 1989), 76.

175   *may cause you to overreact:* Martin E. P. Seligman, *Authentic Happiness: Using the New Positive Psychology to Realize Your Potential for Lasting Fulfillment* (New York: Free Press, 2002), 204.

CHAPTER 8

180   *"that's an intense form of vulnerability"*: Brown, *Daring Greatly*, 34.

181   *"who have earned the right to hear them"*: Ibid., 45

183   *"with their own identities"*: Diane Fassel, *Growing Up Divorced: A Road to Healing for Adult Children of Divorce* (New York: Random House Value Publishing, 1993), 72.

185   *"and their own pain"*: Ibid., 76.

185   *"those from intact families"*: Elizabeth Marquardt, *Between Two Worlds: The Inner Lives of Children of Divorce* (New York: Three Rivers Press, 2006), 54.

187   *ability to cope with marital transitions:* Hetherington and Kelly, *For Better or For Worse*, 150–53.

191   *learn that money is freedom:* Laiken, *Daughters of Divorce*, 38.

192   *"result in pain and loss"*: Ibid., 36.

192   *"far more important than material objects"*: Ibid., 42.

196   *"passion without commitment, togetherness without a future"*: Wallerstein, Lewis, and Blakeslee, *The Unexpected Legacy of Divorce*, 38, 236–53.

197   *happy and unhappy partnerships:* Judith Siegel, *What Children Learn from Their Parents' Marriage* (New York: Quill, 2000), 44–66.

200   *with the interests of both spouses in mind:* Willard J. Harley Jr., *Love Busters: Protecting Your Marriage from Habits That Destroy Romantic Love* (Grand Rapids, MI: Revell, 1992), 158.

201   *"they must look out for themselves first"*: Siegel, *What Children Learn*, 64.

203   *an enthusiastic agreement between partners:* Harley, *Love Busters*, 164–65.

CHAPTER 9

208   *over 40 percent of first-time marriages end in divorce:* Heritage Foundation, *2014 Index of Cultural Opportunity,* 1–5.

208   *recent report from the National Marriage Project:* Kay Hymowitz et al., *Knot Yet: The Benefits and Costs of Delayed Marriage in America* (National Marriage Project at the University of Virginia, National Campaign to Prevent Teen and Unplanned Pregnancy, and The Relate Institute, 2013), 1–10, http://twentysomethingmarriage.org/summary/.

208   *fell from 69 to 55 percent:* Ibid.

208   *60 percent of all couples live together before marriage:* W. Bradford Wilcox, "The Evolution of Divorce," *National Affairs,* no. 1 (Fall 2009): 1–7.

208   *from 439,000 to more than 6.4 million:* Ibid., 3.

209   *less likely to experience divorce:* Andrew Cherlin, *The Marriage-Go-Round: The State of Marriage and Family in America* (New York: Alfred A. Knopf, 2009), 168, 179–92.

209   *to initiate and file for divorce:* Paul Amato, Alan Booth, David R. Johnson, and Stacy J. Rogers, *Alone Together: How Marriage in America is Changing* (Cambridge, MA: Harvard University Press, 2007), 86.

209   *it won't work out:* Norval D. Glenn and Kathryn B. Kramer, "The Marriages and Divorces of the Children of Divorce," *Journal of Marriage and the Family* 49, no. 4 (November 1987): 811–25.

210   *"couples who cohabit before marriage":* Parker-Pope, *For Better,* 268.

210   *the legacy of a disrupted home is passed on:* Cherlin, *The Marriage-Go-Round,* 168, 179–92.

210   *that cohabitation did as well:* Council on Contemporary Families, "Cohabitation No Longer Predicts Divorce— And Possibly Never Did: New Research by Senior CCF Scholar Arielle Kuperberg," press release, March 10, 2014, https://contemporaryfamilies.org/cohabitation-divorce -press-release/.

211   *to move in together:* Galena K. Rhoades, Scott M. Stanley, and Howard J. Markman, "Working with Cohabitation in Relationship Education and Therapy," *Journal of Couple & Relationship Therapy* 8, no. 2 (April 2009): 1–12.

211   *"sliding not deciding":* Jay, *The Defining Decade*, 91–92.

211   *cohabiting without a commitment:* Michael Pollard and Kathleen Mullan Harris, "Cohabitation and Marriage Intensity: Consolidation, Intimacy, and Commitment" (RAND Working Paper 1001, RAND Labor & Population, 2013), 1–22, www.rand.org/content /dam/rand/pubs/working_papers/WR1000/WR1001 /RAND_WR1001.pdf.

212   *a partner who is wrong for you:* Stephanie S. Spielman, "Settling for Less out of Fear of Being Single," *Journal of Personality and Social Psychology* 105, no. 6 (December 2013): 1049–73.

214   *"and then, love abandons us":* Sara Shandler, *Ophelia Speaks: Adolescent Girls Write about Their Search for Self* (New York: Harper Perennial, 1999), 207.

216   *"behaving in ways that sabotage love":* Branden, *The Psychology of Romantic Love*, 112.

219   *foundation of a relationship:* Ibid., 164.

219   *admiration helps sustain a relationship:* Ibid., 157.

220   *smart love maintains standards in a relationship:* Les Parrott

and Leslie Parrott, *Relationships: How to Make Bad Relationships Better and Good Relationships Great* (Grand Rapids: Zondervan, 1998), 111.

221   *"practices loving ways of being":* Ibid., 119.

221   *who lived with both parents:* Parker-Pope, *For Better*, 269.

221   *even if children are involved:* Hetherington and Kelly, *For Better or For Worse*, 243.

222   *approach it warily:* Hirschfeld, *The Adult Children of Divorce Workbook*, 158.

223   *"ACDs fervently wish they did":* Ibid.

223   *pain that was causing us trouble:* Beverly Rodgers and Tom Rodgers, *Adult Children of Divorced Parents: Making Your Marriage Work* (San Jose, CA: Resource Publications, 2002), 38.

223   *their ability to make a marriage work:* Hirschfeld, *The Adult Children of Divorce Workbook*, 196.

224   *marital success for adult children of divorce:* Ibid.

225   *"while masking torment from within":* LaMotte, *Overcoming Your Parents' Divorce*, 10.

226   *they want something more:* Nena O'Neill, *The Marriage Premise* (New York: Bantam Books, 1977), 183–84.

227   *72 percent have been married at least once:* D'Vera et al., *Barely Half of U.S. Adults Are Married—A Record Low*, 1.

227   *"motivations and social support that marriage offers":* David Myers, *The American Paradox: Spiritual Hunger in an Age of Plenty* (New Haven, CN: Yale University Press, 2000), 42–43.

227   *better mental and physical health:* Parker-Pope, *For Better*, 118.

231   *to change his or her behavior:* Michele Weiner Davis, *The*

Divorce Remedy: The Proven 7-Step Program for Saving Your Marriage (New York: Simon & Schuster, 2001), 51.

233   *if you feel "flooded":* John M. Gottman and Nan Silver, *The Seven Principles for Making Marriage Work: A Practical Guide from the Country's Foremost Relationship Expert* (New York: Three Rivers Press, 1999), 34–35.

234   *the dynamic of a marriage in a negative way:* Ibid., 2–24.

234   *five positive interactions:* John M. Gottman and Joan DeClaire, *The Relationship Cure: A 5 Step Guide to Strengthening Your Marriage, Family, and Friendships* (New York: Three Rivers, 2001), 65–68.

234   *theory of couples' communication:* John M. Gottman and Nan Silver, *Why Marriages Succeed or Fail* (New York: Simon and Schuster, 1994), 68–103.

235   *conflicting needs for closeness and space:* Gay Hendricks and Kathlyn Hendricks, *Conscious Loving: The Journey to Co-commitment* (New York, Bantam Books, 1990), 5.

236   *Gottman's Four Principles for a Successful Marriage:* Gottman and Silver, *The Seven Principles for Making Marriage Work*, 47–243.

238   *dated for less than two years:* Parker-Pope, *For Better*, 251–70.

CHAPTER 10

242   *"you can set yourself free":* Wallerstein, Lewis, and Blakeslee, *The Unexpected Legacy of Divorce*, 306.

244   *"potential for great relationship success":* LaMotte, *Overcoming Your Parents' Divorce*, 4.

Index

Chemistry, 44–45, 238

Childhood, loss of, 185, 186

Codependency, 89, 183, 223

Cohabitation before marriage, xxix–xxx, 208, 210–211

Commitment

authors' perspectives on, 239–240

vs. being single, 212–214, 238

cultural trends in, xxix–xxx, 1, 208, 210–211

fear of, 18–19, 106–107, 160–161, 216, 239–240

having healthy respect for, 43–46, 223–230

steps to achieving, 236–239

Communication, 44–45, 177, 189, 195, 220

building self-esteem, 140–141, 143

hot-button issues, 175–176, 231–232

improving, 231–235

revealing vulnerability, 115–116, 199, 202–203, 218–219

Compassion. *See* Empathy; Forgiveness; Loving yourself

Compatibility, 44–45, 238

Competent-at-a-cost personality style, 20–21

Competent-caring personality style, 21–22

Competent fathers, 93, 109–112

Competent-opportunist personality style, 22–23

Conflict with partner, 175–176, 189–190, 231–233, 236, 244

See also Communication; Parental conflict

Control of partner, need for, 115, 156, 184–185

Coparenting, 23–25, 91–92, 110–114, 128–129

D

"Daddy game," 90

"Daddy issues," 123–124

I

Infidelity, 9–10, 14–15, 74–75, 155–158, 171–173, 210

Insecurity. *See* Self-esteem issues

Interdependence, 196–197, 200–201

Interview questions, 49–53

Intimacy. *See* Romantic relationships; Trust issues; Vulnerability

J

Joint agreements, 203

Journal keeping, 49, 56, 147, 148, 203

L

Loving yourself, 33, 131, 139–142, 170

Loyalty conflicts, xviii, 7, 104, 105–109, 190

M

Marriage

    cultural trends in, xxix–xxx, 1, 208, 210–211

    rates of, xxx, 208

    reasons not to rush into, 212–214, 238

    steps for success, 230–239

    women's expectations about, xix, xxx–xxxi, 206–207, 215,
        222–223, 239

    See also Commitment; Remarried fathers; Romantic relationships

Memories, emotional, 65–66

Mind-set, 57, 80–84, 147–149, 163–164, 175, 230–231

Money issues, 107–109, 122–123, 184, 191–192, 201–202

Mother, role in father-daughter relationship, 90–91, 123

Mother-daughter relationship, xviii

T

V

About the Authors

Terry Gaspard, MSW, LICSW, is a licensed therapist with over thirty years of clinical experience specializing in divorce, children, and families, as well as a nonfiction writer and college instructor. She is a sought-after speaker who frequently offers commentary on divorce and her research on daughters of divorce. Two of Terry's research studies on adult children of divorce have been published in the *Journal of Divorce and Remarriage*. Terry is a regular contributor to Huffington Post Divorce, divorcedmoms.com, and yourtango.com.

PHOTO BY MELISSA QUINTAL

Tracy Clifford is a writer and conducted the in-depth study of daughters of divorce with her mother, Terry Gaspard. Terry and Tracy are co-owners of movingpastdivorce.com.